PETROGRAD 1917

PETROGRAD 1917

Witnesses to the Russian Revolution

JOHN PINFOLD

Bodleian Library
UNIVERSITY OF OXFORD

First published in 2017 by the Bodleian Library
Broad Street, Oxford OX1 3BG

www.bodleianshop.co.uk

ISBN 978 1 85124 460 7

Extracts from Florence Farmborough, Nurse at the Russian Front: A Diary, 1914–1918,
Constable, London, 1974, are reprinted by kind permission of Little, Brown.

Extracts from the papers of Charles Sydney Gibbes are reprinted by
kind permission of Charles Gibbes Paveliev and Andrew Gibbes.

Extracts from Edward T. Heald, Witness to Revolution: Letters from Russia,
1916–1919, Kent State University Press, Kent OH, 1972, copyright © 1972
by The Kent State University Press. Reprinted with permission.

Extracts from the papers of Arthur Henderson are reprinted
by kind permission of the Labour Party.

Extracts from the papers of Arthur Marshall are copyright © the Estate of Arthur
Calder-Marshall. Reproduced with the kind permission of Johnson & Alcock Ltd.

Extract from Siberian Garrison by Rodion Markovits, translated by George Halasz,
copyright 1929 by Genius Kiadás, Budapest, translation copyright © 1929
by Horace Liveright, Inc., copyright renewed 1956 by Liveright Publishing
Corporation, used by permission of Liveright Publishing Corporation.

Extracts from the diaries of Sir Hugh Cholmondeley Thornton
(MS. Milner dep. 23/1) are reproduced by kind permission
of the Warden and Scholars of New College, Oxford.

Every effort has been made to trace copyright holders and to
obtain permission for the use of copyright material; any errors or
omissions will be incorporated in future editions of this book.

The publisher would like to thank Kaylee Kain and Naomi Polonsky
for their help with this book.

Cover design by Dot Little at the Bodleian Library

Designed and typeset in 11½ on 14 Monotype Joanna
by illuminati, Grosmont
Printed and bound in Great Britain by TJ International Ltd, Padstow, Cornwall
on 80 gsm Premium Munken Cream

British Library Catalogue in Publishing Data
A CIP record of this publication is available from the British Library

Contents

Timeline

1914

March   Strikes and riots break out at the Putilov steel factory and are violently crushed by the imperial militia.

1 August   Germany declares war on Russia after Russia refuses to stop its mobilization of troops against Austria-Hungary.

4 August   Britain declares war on Germany; outbreak of First World War.

August/September   Russian Empire suffers major defeats at Tannenberg and the Masurian Lakes.

1915

September   Nicholas II replaces Grand Duke Nicholas as supreme commander of the Russian Army after the loss of Warsaw. Mikhail Rodzianko, president of the Duma, advises him against personally leading his troops at the front.

1916

30 December   Grand Duke Dmitri and Prince Felix Yusupov assassinate Rasputin.

1917

8 March   Start of the 'February Revolution'.

11 March   The Petrograd Soviet of Workers' and Soldiers' Deputies is established. Kamenev and Stalin return from exile in Siberia and commit the Bolshevik Party to partial support for the Provisional Government.

13 March   The Provisional Government composed of the Kadet coalition led by Prince George Lvov is established. Alexander Kerensky is appointed Minister of Justice.

15 March   Abdication of Nicholas II.

16 April   Lenin returns to Petrograd after almost sixteen years

	in exile in Switzerland and calls for the overthrow of the Provisional Government by the Soviets.
4 May	Kerensky becomes Minister of War following the resignations of Pavel Milyukov and Alexander Guchkov. Trotsky returns to Petrograd from exile.
16 June–7 July	The 'First All-Russia Conference of the Councils of Workers' and Soldiers' Delegates' takes place.
1 July	Kerensky orders several new offensives along the Eastern Front in an attempt to boost morale in the army.
1–23 July	The 'Galician Offensive' led by General Lavr Kornilov ends in a humiliating retreat for the Russian Army.
16–20 July	Soldiers and industrial workers mount spontaneous armed demonstrations against the Russian Provisional Government in a Bolshevik-inspired uprising. The 'July Days' riots are brutally suppressed, Trotsky is arrested and Lenin is forced into hiding.
July	Prince Lvov's Kadet coalition is replaced by Kerensky's Socialist coalition.
1 August	Kornilov appointed Commander in Chief of the Russian Army by Kerensky after commanding the only successful front in the disastrous Russian offensive of June 1917.
August	Kornilov leads troops into Petrograd to settle unrest. Kerensky alleges that this is a *coup d'état* and orders Kornilov's arrest. Trotsky is released from prison.
3 September	German troops enter Riga threatening the security of Petrograd.
October	Lenin returns to Petrograd and calls for the Central Committee to agree to the overthrow of the Provisional Government.
24 October	Military units, backed by armed bands of workers, known as Red Guards, take control of major strategic points, causing Kerensky to flee.
25 October	Lenin proclaims to the Petrograd Soviet that the Provisional Government has been overthrown.
7 November	Soviet Federative Socialist Republic (SFSR) is established with Lenin as its leader. Trotsky is appointed People's Commissar for Foreign Affairs.
8 November	Lenin declares peace with Germany.

15 December	A ceasefire between SFSR and the Central Powers is declared.

1918

18–19 January	Bolsheviks fail to gain a majority in the elections to the Constituent Assembly. It is subsequently dissolved by order of the Congress of Soviets.
3 March	Signing of the Brest-Litovsk peace treaty with the Central Powers.
17 July	Assassination of the Tsar and his family.
11 November	First World War ends.
November	Civil war breaks out between the Bolshevik-led Red Army and the counter-revolutionary White Army.

Introduction

The Revolution and the coming to power of the Communist Party in Russia in 1917 are among the most dramatic and significant events in modern history. The story has been told many times[1] and it has been analysed from many different angles. It is not the purpose of this book to present any new interpretation of the tumultuous events of 1917, but rather to give the impression of what it was like for foreigners who were in Russia at the time to live through the Revolution, using for the most part their own words as written down either immediately after the events they describe or very shortly afterwards.

There were many foreigners in Russia in 1917, not just officials such as diplomats or military attachés, but also journalists, businessmen, governesses, nurses, jockeys and (often overlooked) prisoners of war. Some were members of the establishment, with close links to members of the tsarist government; others were of working-class origin. All were aware that they were living through momentous events, even if their level of understanding of what they were witnessing varied considerably, and many of them recorded their experiences in letters and diaries, newspaper interviews and articles, and, in due course, memoirs of what they had seen. The most well known of these is John Reed's classic *Ten Days That Shook the World*, first published in New York in 1919 and still in print today, but there were many others, and this book offers a selection of eyewitness accounts of some of the key events of 1917 as viewed by people who were present at the events they describe. Some of those whose writings have been used are relatively well known, whilst others have been largely forgotten, but taken as a whole they provide a compelling picture of what it was like to live through the dramatic events of 1917, without the benefit of knowing, as we do today, the eventual outcome. It may be true, as A.J.P. Taylor wrote in his introduction to John Reed's book, that 'Foreign observers stood outside the events' and were 'writing about strange events in a strange country', but this does not negate their value as witnesses of what they saw. A hundred years on, their testimony provides a valuable window into the excitement, the exhilaration, the apprehension, and sometimes the fear felt by those caught up in events whose full significance was only gradually to become apparent.

Although the majority of the witnesses whose writings have been selected for inclusion in this book were English, the writings of Americans, Australians, French and a solitary Hungarian have also been included.

AUTHOR'S NOTE

The accounts quoted in this book use a variety of transliterated spellings for Russian names, places and common phrases. These have been reproduced as they appear in the original sources, with the result that some frequently occurring names appear with several different spellings (e.g. Protopopoff, Protopopov). These variants have been listed in the index to avoid confusion.

Otherwise, the text broadly follows the Library of Congress system of transliteration, except where common usage differs; for example, Nevsky Prospekt, Trotsky, Kerensky. Some first names have been anglicized for ease of reading.

Dates, where available, are given throughout the book according to the Gregorian calendar ('New Style'), which in 1917 was thirteen days ahead of the Julian calendar ('Old Style'). The latter was used in Russia up until 14 February 1918. In sources where the calendar style is unclear, dates have been retained as they appear in the original document.

A map of Petrograd appears on Plate 14.

The key witnesses

MERIEL BUCHANAN (1886–1959) was the daughter of the British ambassador to Russia from 1910 to 1918, Sir George Buchanan. During the war she worked as a nurse at the Anglo-Russian Hospital in Petrograd. She had begun her literary career with two novels published before the war, but after her return from Russia in 1918 she wrote a number of books about the last years of Imperial Russia and the Revolution, including Petrograd: The City of Trouble, 1914–1918 (1918), Recollections of Imperial Courts (1923) and The Dissolution of an Empire (1932). Later in life she gave an account of her father's mission to Russia in Ambassador's Daughter (1958). In 1925 she married Major Harold Knowling of the Welsh Guards. Her journal for 1910–14 and her photograph album for 1910–18 are held by the University of Nottingham Library.

BERNARD ('BROWNIE') CARSLAKE (1886–1941) was an Australian jockey, born in Melbourne, who came to ride in England in 1906. When war broke out in 1914 he was riding in Vienna and was interned there (although still able to ride). In 1916 he escaped to then neutral Romania, disguised as a railway engine fireman, and from there went to Russia where he became champion jockey, riding for the oil tycoon Leon Mantashev. After fleeing Russia in 1917 he resumed his riding career in England. Among other big race victories he won the Thousand Guineas twice (1918 and 1922), the Two Thousand Guineas (1920), the Oaks (1934) and the St Leger three times (1919, 1924, 1938); of the Classics only the Derby eluded him. He collapsed in the weighing room at Alexandra Palace in 1940 and died the following year. There was an autobiography advertised shortly before he died, but this was never published.

EDWIN CHARLES FAIRCHILD (b. 1874) was a leading member of the British Socialist Party, serving on the executive committee in 1916/17

Meriel Buchanan

Bernard 'Brownie' Carslake

and becoming acting secretary of the party in 1918. A tailor by trade, he was a conscientious objector during the First World War and worked for a time on a market garden near Glastonbury. In later life he worked for the Co-operative Permanent Building Society and wrote a number of books on housing policy. His date of death is not known but he was still active in the 1940s, writing on the need to plan for housing after the Second World War.

FLORENCE FARMBOROUGH (1887–1978) was born in Buckinghamshire. She went to Russia to work as a governess for a family in Kiev in 1908. In 1910 she moved to Moscow to teach English to the daughters of Dr Usov, a famous heart surgeon. When the First World War broke out she volunteered for Red Cross work and served as a nurse at the front from 1915 to 1917. She returned to Moscow at the time of the October Revolution, and left Russia for England via the Trans-Siberian Railway in 1918. She was elected a fellow of the Royal Geographical Society, and in 1926 was appointed as a university lecturer in English at Valencia. Strongly anti-communist as a result of her experiences in Russia, she sided with the Nationalists during the Spanish Civil War, working as a radio newsreader. She served with the Women's Voluntary Service during the Battle of Britain, and was later involved in the rehabilitation of Spanish-speaking Gibraltarians who had been evacuated to Britain. She published sections of her World War I diaries as *Nurse at the Russian Front* in 1974, and this was followed in 1979 by a collection of her Russian photographs in *Russian Album, 1908–1918*. Her original diaries are now held by the Imperial War Museum.

CHARLES SYDNEY GIBBES (1876–1963) was born in Rotherham and was educated at the University of Cambridge. He went to Russia as a teacher of English in 1901 and became vice-president of the St Petersburg Guild of English Teachers. From 1908 to 1918 he was English tutor to the daughters of Nicholas and Alexandra, and from 1913 also to the Tsarevich. He voluntarily accompanied the imperial family into exile in Siberia up until the time of their incarceration in the 'House of Special Purpose' in Ekaterinburg. He later assisted the Sokolov inquiry into the fate of the imperial family and identified some of the remains that were found. During 1919–20 he served on the staff of the British High Commissioner for Siberia, and from 1920 to 1932 was employed by the Chinese Maritime Customs at Harbin in Manchuria. In 1934 he entered the Orthodox faith, subsequently becoming a monk and

(*above*) Florence Farmborough   (*below*) Charles Sydney Gibbes

priest under the name of Father Nicholas. In 1938 he was created Archimandrite (Mitred Abbot), working with Orthodox communities in London and, from 1940, Oxford, where he established the Orthodox chapel and community centre in Marston Street (St Nicholas House). He died in 1963 and is buried in Headington Cemetery.

J.S. GOODE (dates unknown) was Lecturer in Russian at the University of Melbourne, and was for a time a lecturer at a military college in Petrograd.

BERT HALL (1885–1948) was an American airman who during the First World War volunteered for service with the French Flying Corps, joining the famed Lafayette Escadrille. However, he was also something of a con man, and it is unclear how much combat experience he actually had. He was in Petrograd during the Revolution, but later returned to America via Siberia. In 1918 he made an adventure film, *A Romance of the Air*, in which he played himself, which received the somewhat barbed comment from *Moving Picture World* that 'Lt. Hall rings true, but his story does not'. Extracts from his diary from when he was in Russia during the Revolution appear in his book *One Man's War*, published in 1929.

EDWARD T. HEALD (1885–1967) was born in Hood River Valley, Oregon, and graduated from Oberlin College in 1907. After a short time working in business in Peoria, Illinois, he joined the YMCA, becoming student secretary at Colorado College. He subsequently served in Manhattan, Kansas and Toledo, Ohio, before moving to Davenport, Iowa. It was from there that he was sent in 1916 by the YMCA to work with their prisoner-of-war relief programme in Petrograd. He moved to Kiev in September 1917, and subsequently to Siberia, leaving Russia for Japan via Manchuria in May 1919. Returning to the USA he continued to work for the YMCA, mostly in Canton, Ohio, until he retired. He then devoted himself to local history, planning and subsequently running the Stark County Historical Center and writing a six-volume county history. At the time of his death he was engaged in compiling a pictorial history of President William McKinley. An edited version of his diaries and letters relating to his time in Russia were published as *Witness to Revolution* in 1972.

ARTHUR HENDERSON (1863–1935) was an iron moulder and Labour politician, who was first elected to Parliament in 1903. He was leader

Edward Heald and his wife Emily in Vladivostock, 1918

of the Labour Party 1908–10, and became the first Labour politician to be a member of the Cabinet when he joined Asquith's coalition government as President of the Board of Education in 1915. After Lloyd George replaced Asquith as Prime Minister he served in the War Cabinet as Minister without Portfolio. He resigned from the government in August 1917 in a dispute over plans to call an international conference on the future direction of the war. He lost his seat in 1918 but returned to Parliament in a by-election. He later served as Home Secretary in the Labour government of 1924, and Foreign Secretary in

1929–31. When Ramsay Macdonald formed the National Government, Henderson refused to join him and became Leader of the Opposition, 1931–32. He chaired the Geneva Disarmament Conference and in 1934 was awarded the Nobel Peace Prize. His papers are held by the People's History Museum, Manchester.

JANET JEFFERY (dates unknown) was a governess who at the time the Revolution broke out was working for Princess Vera Mestchersky in Tsarskoye Selo. The family moved to Moscow in the summer of 1917, and subsequently to the Crimea, where 'everyone was on strike', and Novorossiysk, which they were forced to leave by Red sailors, before reaching Kislovodsk in the Caucasus in 1918. After her return to England she gave several newspaper interviews about her experiences in Russia and wrote an article, '"In the Name of the Soviet": A Personal Narrative of an English Girl's Experiences in Bolshevik Russia', which was published in *The Sphere* in 1920.

STINTON JONES (1884–1979) was a consulting engineer who first went to Russia in 1905 on behalf of Westinghouse, and stayed there for twelve years on what he described as 'some special business', forming his own company, Merrett & Jones, which had its offices on the Nevsky Prospect. Jones returned to Britain on 6 April 1917, becoming the first Englishman to arrive from Petrograd and describe the February Revolution as an eyewitness. He recounted his experience in numerous newspaper articles, and his book *Russia in Revolution* was published later the same year. He later emigrated to South Africa, and in the 1970s wrote an unpublished memoir, 'The Czar Looked Over My Shoulder', which is now held by the Brotherton Library of the University of Leeds.

H.V. KEELING (dates unknown) was a member of the Litho Artists' and Engravers' Society and served as vice-president of its London Branch. He was sent to Petrograd by his employer in 1914 to set up a patent photolitho process. For a time he was chief photographer to the Committee of Public Education. He escaped from Russia in 1919. His *Bolshevism: Mr. Keeling's Five Years in Russia* was published in 1919.

MAJOR-GENERAL SIR ALFRED KNOX (1870–1964) was born in Ulster and educated at St Columba's College, Dublin, and the Royal Military College, Sandhurst. He was ADC to the Viceroy of India 1899–1900,

Arthur Henderson

and subsequently fought on the North-West Frontier 1901–02, when he was mentioned in despatches. He was the British Military Attaché in St Petersburg 1911–18, and Chief of the Military Mission to Siberia 1918–20. On his return to England he published his *With the Russian Army, 1914–1917* in 1921; this is based to a large extent on his diaries. He was elected as the Conservative Member of Parliament for Wycombe in 1924, holding the seat until 1945.

RODION MARKOVITS (1888–1948) was of Hungarian Jewish extraction and was born in Kisgérce, Transylvania (now Gherţa Mică, Romania). He studied law at the Eötvös Loránd University, Budapest, but mainly concentrated on his career as a writer with left-wing journals such as *Népszava*. He was mobilized into the Austro-Hungarian army soon after the outbreak of the First World War, and was captured by the Russians during their summer offensive in 1916. After the Revolution he spent the next seven years in Siberia and the Russian Far East, fighting for a time with the Red Guards, before returning to Transylvania, now part of Romania, and resuming his writing career. His documentary novel *Siberian Garrison* – a work he described as 'collective reportage' – was published in Hungarian in 1927 and in English in 1929. In 1931 he moved to Timişoara, where he became editor of the Hungarian-language *Temesvári Hírlap*. In 1944 he became active in the Hungarian People's Union, associated with the Romanian Communist Party. It was announced in 2011 that his home in Gherţa Mică was to become a museum.

ARTHUR MARSHALL (1875–1958) was educated at St Paul's School and the Regent Street Polytechnic, where he studied electrical engineering. In 1905 he set up his own consulting electrical engineering business, and in 1913, when in Vladivostock, he discussed the possibility of opening up Siberia for British electrical products. He subsequently formed the co-operative selling organization known as the British Engineering Company of Siberia (BECOS), with himself as managing director. The outbreak of the First World War changed the commercial activities of the company so that it became concerned chiefly with the export of British war materials to Russia and the building of cars and trucks in that country, under licence from Crossley Brothers. After the Revolution the factory was expropriated, together with all the firm's assets in Russia, and Marshall returned to England in 1918 having lost a fortune. However, he continued to believe in the possibility of doing trade with the Bolsheviks, and was a founder member of

Janet Jeffery

the Russo-British Chamber of Commerce, of which he was chairman for many years. Between the wars he negotiated the Lena Goldfields settlement, although later the Soviet government suspended payments on the agreement. At the time of his death he was described as 'an energetic, determined and colourful personality' who was 'an incurable optimist', all qualities which are abundantly clear from his letters from Russia to his wife during the Revolution; these are now held by the Bodleian Library (MS. Eng c. 2722).

Tom Quelch at the Baku Conference (*front row standing, second from left*)

DORA B. MONTEFIORE (1851–1933) was both a militant suffragette, jailed for her part in a demonstration in the Lobby of the House of Commons in 1906, and a radical socialist who was a member of the Social Democratic Federation and, from 1911, the British Socialist Party, before being elected to the provisional executive committee of the Communist Party at its founding conference in 1920. She represented the Australian Communist Party at the 5th Congress of the Comintern in Moscow in 1924. She was a prolific author, writing for such journals and newspapers as *The Social Democrat, New Age, Justice, The Daily Herald, The Call* and *The Communist*. Her autobiography *From a Victorian to a Modern* was published in 1925.

JOHN WILLIAM ('JACK') PINCOTT (dates unknown) was an Australian who came from Burnley, Victoria. In 1914, when war was declared, he was working in Paris as the agent of a British trading company. He immediately enlisted in the British forces and joined the Armoured Cars Division of the Royal Naval Flying Corps, attaining the rank of Petty Officer. A detachment of 500 men and 50 cars from this Corps, under the command of Oliver Locker-Lampson, was sent to Russia in 1915 to strengthen the Russian forces, and Pincott saw service in the Caucasus and Turkish Armenia before being transferred to the South-Western Front against the Romanians. For his gallantry during the retreat in Galicia, Pincott was awarded the DSM, having earlier been awarded the Russian Order of St George. He returned to Australia after the war, but then fell on hard times. In 1920 he was arrested in Melbourne on charges of 'having insufficient lawful means of support' and having been involved in a jewellery robbery, but was not convicted, his war record counting in his favour. At the time he was working as an advertising agent for a journal called The Circle, but nothing more is known of his later life.

MORGAN PHILIPS PRICE (1885–1973) was born in Gloucester, the son of William Edwin Price, the Member of Parliament for Tewkesbury. His father died when he was just one year old, leaving him an estate of 2,000 acres. He was educated at Harrow and Trinity College, Cambridge. Before the First World War he was a Liberal and was the prospective parliamentary candidate for Gloucester from 1911 to 1914. However, he was opposed to the war in 1914, and was subsequently recruited by the Manchester Guardian to become its correspondent on the Eastern Front and later in Petrograd. After the First World War Price joined the Labour Party and was its candidate for Gloucester in the general elections of 1922, 1923 and 1924, losing on each occasion. He was subsequently elected Member of Parliament for Whitehaven (1929–31), the Forest of Dean (1935–50) and West Gloucestershire (1950–59). He published My Reminiscences of the Russian Revolution in 1921, and his memoir, My Three Revolutions, in 1969.

TOM QUELCH (1886–1954) was the son of the more well-known early socialist Harry Quelch (1858–1913), and was a member of the British Socialist Party. He was one of the thirteen convenors of the convention held in Leeds on 3 June 1917 to hail the Russian Revolution, and was appointed a member of the Central Committee of the Council of Soldiers' and Workers' Delegates at the same event. He attended both the 2nd Congress of the Comintern and the Congress of the Peoples of the East held at Baku in 1920.

JEAN SCHOPFER (1868–1931) was born in Switzerland to a French Protestant family who had been living in exile for two hundred years. He was educated at the Sorbonne and the École du Louvre and found fame as a tennis player, winning the French Championships in 1892 when he defeated Francis Fassit; the following year he again reached the final but lost to Laurent Riboulet. He began his writing career in 1899 and wrote many novels, plays and travel books; his best-known book was *Ariane, jeune fille de russe* (1920), which Billy Wilder adapted for his 1957 film *Love in the Afternoon*. His *Through the Russian Revolution: Notes of an Eye-witness, from 12th March–30th May*, based on his diary, was published in 1917. He used the pseudonym Claude Anet.

GERARD SHELLEY (1891–1980) was born in Sidcup and educated at the University of Heidelberg and the Major Seminary and Collège Saint-Sulpice in Paris. In 1907 he was attending an Italian college near Lake Garda when he was induced to travel to Russia by the Countess Bobrinsky. He learnt Russian at Kharkhov University and during the early part of the First World War worked as a translator for prisoners of war. After the October Revolution he was arrested by the Bolsheviks several times as a counter-revolutionary and eventually escaped to Finland disguised as a woman. He published two books about his experiences in Russia, *The Speckled Domes* and *The Blue Steppes* (both 1925), as well as numerous translations of Russian poetry. He later became a priest and joined the Oblates of St Joseph. In 1950 he was ordained a bishop in the Old Roman Catholic Church in Great Britain, and two years later became the Primate of the ORCCGB and Archbishop of Caer-Glow (Gloucester). Owing to differences with Rome, he was excommunicated from the Roman Catholic Church in 1965.

EDWARD STEBBING (1872–1960), forester, was educated at St Paul's School and the Royal Indian Engineering College, Cooper's Hill, winning the Prize in Forest Entomology in 1892. He joined the Indian Forest Service in 1893 and was Forest Entomologist to the Government of India 1901–02 and 1904–06, and Forest Zoologist to the Government of India and Member of the Imperial Forest Research Institute 1906–09. He was lecturer in Forestry at the University of Edinburgh from 1910, and professor from 1920 to 1952. In 1918 he was sent to Archangel by the British government on a mission to assess the potential of northern Russia as a source of timber for the Allied war effort. Shortly after his return he published the journal of his time

Gerard Shelley

in Russia as *From Czar to Bolshevik*. In later life he was one of the first people to warn of the dangers of desertification.

ALBERT ('BERTIE') STOPFORD (1860–1939) was an antiques and art dealer who specialized in Fabergé and Cartier. His father, the Rev. Frederick Manners Stopford, was Chaplain Royal to Queen Victoria,

Edward VII and George V, royal connections that Bertie Stopford used, along with others, to further his career. In his early life he had worked for Lloyds, and he had links to Admiralty intelligence, being used by them on a secret mission to the Balkans in 1912. During the war he became involved with the Anglo-Russian Hospital in Petrograd, and his close links with both the British Embassy and the Russian court enabled him to become the unofficial 'eyes and ears for the Allied authorities'. He was responsible for smuggling many of the Romanov jewels out of Russia, including the Vladimir Tiara now owned by Queen Elizabeth II. After his return to England in 1918 he was convicted of 'acts of gross indecency with a male person' and sentenced to twelve months' hard labour in Wormwood Scrubs. His diaries of the Revolution were published anonymously after his release in 1919. He subsequently lived abroad, mainly in France and Italy, and died in straitened circumstances in Paris, where he was buried in a common grave in the Bagneux Cemetery. He is the subject of a biography, *Hidden Treasures of the Romanovs: Saving the Royal Jewels*, by William Clarke (published 2009).

ALEX M. THOMPSON (1861–1948) was born in Karlsruhe of English parents and was brought up partly in Paris, where as a young boy he witnessed the Commune of 1871. After moving to England he started work as a journalist, and was co-founder with Robert Blatchford of *The Clarion*, which in the years leading up to the First World War was the most popular socialist newspaper in Britain, becoming also the sponsor of a whole series of clubs (cycling, rambling, handicraft, choirs and others) which became a vehicle for promoting socialism throughout the country. However, *The Clarion* supported the war in 1914, and lost a large number of its readers as a result. Thompson also wrote for other newspapers and journals including the *Manchester Guardian*, *Daily Mail* and *News Chronicle*. He also had a second career as a librettist of musical comedies; among other projects he collaborated with Lionel Monckton on the hit musical *The Arcadians*, and adapted Leo Fall's operetta *Der Liebe Augustin* for the English stage as *Princess Caprice*. His autobiography, *Here I Lie: The Memorial of an Old Journalist*, was published in 1937.

SIR HUGH CHOLMONDELEY THORNTON (1881–1962) was the son of a clergyman. He was educated at Kelly College, Tavistock, and Christ Church, Oxford. He worked for Conservative Central Office 1907–14.

Hugh Walpole

He was commissioned into the Middlesex Regiment in 1914 and the following year transferred to the Duke of Cornwall's Light Infantry and promoted to major. In 1916 he became private secretary to Lord Milner in the British War Cabinet, serving Milner when he was both Secretary of State for War and Colonial Secretary. After the war he served as a Crown Agent for the Colonies and retired as Senior Crown Agent in 1943. His wartime diaries form part of the Milner deposit held by the Bodleian Library.

SIR HUGH WALPOLE (1884–1941) was born in New Zealand, but was sent to England in 1893 for his education at a series of schools in Marlow, Canterbury and Durham (where his father became principal of Bede College), before studying history at Emmanuel College, Cambridge. He published his first novel, The Wooden Horse, in 1909, thereafter becoming a prolific writer, producing on average a book a year until his death. Walpole's poor eyesight precluded him from serving in the armed forces during the First World War, but he volunteered to work for the 'Sanitar' (a wing of the Red Cross) on the Eastern Front. Whilst there he single-handedly rescued a wounded Russian soldier, for which he was awarded the Cross of St George. In 1916 he moved to Petrograd to work for the Anglo-Russian Propaganda Bureau, along with Arthur Ransome of the Manchester Guardian and Harold Williams of the News Chronicle. He later used his experiences in Petrograd during the February Revolution to write The Secret City, which was published in 1919 and won the inaugural James Tait Black Memorial Prize for Fiction. Some of the scenes in this draw directly on his diary entries for the period. Selections from the diaries are included in Duff Hart-Davis's biography, published in 1952; the originals are at the Harry Ransom Center in Texas.

JULIUS WEST (1891–1918) was born in St Petersburg, the son of Semon Rappoport, a Russian Jewish émigré who lived in London. He was educated at Haberdashers' Aske's School. At some point he converted to Christianity and changed his name to West. After working for a time as a library assistant for the University of London, he became a clerk in the Board of Trade before working for the Fabian Society and the New Statesman. Turned down for a commission in 1914 (supposedly because he was registered as a Russian national), he joined an ambulance corps, before going to Russia to report for The Clarion. He died in the flu epidemic of 1918.

HARRY YOUNG (1901–1995) was born in London and brought up on the Holloway Road. As a teenager he joined the British Socialist Party and the Herald League, both of which were absorbed into the Communist Party in 1920. He became the first national organizer of the Young Communist League, and from 1920 to 1929 lived in Moscow where he worked for the Young Communist International (a part of the Comintern). Disillusioned with Stalinism, he returned to England, where he worked successively as a cab driver, as an ambulance driver (during the Blitz) and for many years as a science teacher. He never lost his faith in Marxism and socialism and well into his nineties could be found at Speakers' Corner on Sundays. In later life he gave many talks and interviews on his time in the Soviet Union.

His autobiography remains unpublished; the draft is held by Brunel University Library as part of its Archive of Working Class Writing. He was one of the last surviving witnesses of the heroic early period of Soviet history, and the only one known personally by the compiler of the present volume, who was privileged to have him as a friend.

In some cases it has proved impossible to establish the true identity of the writer, the CORPORAL MILLER whose account of conditions in Petrograd immediately prior to the Bolshevik Revolution reached the British Cabinet table being perhaps the most notable, and a number of anonymous accounts have also been included.

It should also be noted that the great majority of the witnesses, whilst generally sympathetic to the aims and objectives of the February Revolution, were hostile to the Bolsheviks. To provide an element of balance and to place some of the events described into context, extracts from some of the contemporary writings of Leon Trotsky, Maxim Litvinov and Georgy Chicherin have also been included where appropriate.

Harry Young

Eyewitness accounts

Prologue

PETROGRAD IN 1914: A WORKMAN'S VIEW

In February 1914 Henry Keeling, a British lithographer and print worker, who was vice-president of the London Branch of the Litho Artists' and Engravers' Society, was sent by his firm to help set up a patent photolitho process in St Petersburg. He was also a committed trade unionist and hoped to use his time in Russia to explain to his fellow workers how British trade unions were organized, something which, as he himself said, 'was by no means a safe thing to do' under the tsarist regime. These were his first impressions of the city at that time and of the lives led by its working-class population:

> When in February, 1914, I left England and crossed the frontier out of Germany into Russia my heart sank. The contrast between the spick and span German towns and villages and the rude and rough appearance of the Russian countryside made one feel like leaving a house to live in a barn. To myself, a stranger who had never been further away from home than a day trip to Boulogne, it appeared most inhospitable and forbidding, and for many weeks after my arrival in Petrograd I found myself continually sighing for the familiar sights of London. Before the edict which forbade the sale of vodka there was a frightful amount of drunkenness in Russian towns. In my time I have seen plenty of drunkenness in England, especially on Saturday nights in mining and manufacturing districts, but never have I seen such horrible degradation as was to be met with at every turn in some parts of Petrograd. Never shall I forget the disgust and astonishment with which, on the first occasion, I observed half a dozen men sit down in a gateway opposite the

Petrograd in 1914

window of the factory where I worked, and in less than ten minutes become helplessly drunk upon the contents of several bottles of vodka, which could be bought at that time at a very trifling cost. Afterwards I became quite used to such sights. In some of the lower parts of the city I was told there were murders almost every night as the direct result of the consumption of this raw, ardent spirit.

Before the Revolution the life of the ordinary workman in Petrograd, although restricted in many important directions, was not without its compensations. He generally worked rather longer hours than we do in England, and there was no Saturday half holiday, except in a few British factories, a thing which I missed at first very much. Work was also carried on in some places on Sunday mornings. On the other hand, there were the Church holidays, over fifty in the year, on which no work was done, whilst the workmen received full pay, and double pay if for some cause or other their services were required. It was also the custom, at least in the printing trade, to allow each workman to take a week or a fortnight's leave upon full pay each year and as far as possible the men were allowed to arrange the days to suit their own convenience.

In the summer it was quite the thing for large numbers of the workmen to send their families into the country – many of them going back to their own native villages and helping in the harvesting, etc.

24

In the towns there were the summer gardens with variety performances and open air cafes. The Narodny Dom (People's Palace) in Petrograd was very popular; I have spent many a pleasant evening there. In 1914 there were theatres, kinemas, circuses, and small variety shows open everywhere. There were tea-houses in every street, generally provided with an automatic organ, usually of Italian make. Some of the latest ones played remarkably well. These places were patronised by workmen who in England would be called the artisan class, and if it had not been for the terrible weakness of many of the workmen for vodka, which unfortunately could be bought so cheaply at that time, I am inclined to think that, except in the matter of political freedom, the Russian workmen were in many respects better off than many of the same class in England. They were not kept so closely at their work in the factories as most of our workmen are, but were able to stop and have a drink of tea almost whenever they liked. I visited many factories on different occasions and found the workmen making themselves very comfortable. Like everyone else, they craved for what was denied to them – free speech. I have often seen small groups of political prisoners being deported to, I suppose, Siberia. Their crime was rarely more than a trumpery political offence, yet in other directions liberty almost amounted to licence. As long as one did not bother with politics it was possible to do many things which are more or less forbidden in England. I cannot imagine any place being more 'gay' than most of the large towns in Russia.[2]

'Troubled by war'

NICHOLAS AND ALEXANDRA

Nicholas II was born in 1868 and succeeded his father, Alexander III, in 1894. Unprepared to ascend to the throne at such a young age, and inexperienced in government, he was determined to retain the autocracy of his father, but lacked any clear political programme of his own. Neither he nor Alexandra was popular among either the other members of the royal family or the intelligentsia, and the lack of support from these key groups was to prove fatal in 1917.

As a consequence of the 1905 Revolution, the Tsar had been forced to accept the establishment of a parliament, or Duma, but this had little real power, as the Tsar continued to appoint the government ministers, who were responsible solely to him. This led to feelings of frustration on the part of the members of the Duma, whilst the Tsar felt resentful at their very existence.

The Tsar's inability or unwillingness to court popularity among those sectors of society which should have been natural supporters of the monarchy was exacerbated by the fact that during the years before the First World War, and especially after the birth of the Tsarevich in 1904, the imperial family lived in almost total seclusion at Tsarskoe Selo, where few foreigners, even those who were members of the Diplomatic Corps, ever got to meet or even see them. H.J. Bruce, for example, who was Head of Chancery at the British Embassy (and married to the famous ballet dancer Karsavina), wrote in his memoirs:

> Except for the Blessing of the Waters at Epiphany, the Emperor, so far as we knew, never came to Petersburg. The Empress I never set eyes on. The only time we met the Emperor at close quarters was on New Year's Day when the Diplomatic Corps travelled down to Tsarskoe Selo. As a man he appeared to be enchanting. It was his … crowning tragedy to be Emperor and autocrat in such times and to be surrounded by sinister and fatal influences which he was probably too kindly-eyed to see, certainly too weak-willed to control.[3]

One Englishman, however, did have unique access to the imperial family and was able to observe them all at close quarters. This was Sydney Gibbes, who in 1908 was appointed as English tutor to Nicholas and Alexandra's three eldest daughters, Olga, Tatiana and Marie. The youngest daughter, Anastasia, joined the lessons a year later, and in 1913 the Tsaritsa asked Gibbes to teach English to the 9-year-old Tsarevich, who had so far refused to speak the language at all. Gibbes continued to serve the imperial family almost to the end. In 1934 he gave his considered view of the character of the Tsar in a sermon on St Luke XII:6–7[4] which he appears to have delivered around the time of his ordination as an Orthodox priest:

Tsar Nicholas II surrounded by his children and a group of Cossacks

I have always felt that the world in general never took the Emperor
very seriously, and I have often wondered why, for he was a man of
no mean powers. I think it must be largely attributed to the fact that
he seemed incapable of inspiring FEAR. He knew very well how
to guard his dignity. One never dreamt of any one taking liberties
with the Emperor, the thing was unheard of. He had a 'presence'
that was second to none, so full of quiet and assured self-possession
and dignity. But it never inspired fear. The deepest sentiment that
it evoked was <u>awe</u>, not fear. I think that the reason for this was his
eyes. Yes, I am sure that it was his eyes, so wonderful were they. Of
the most delicate shade of blue, that looked you straight in the face
with the kindest, the tenderest, the most loving expression. How
was it possible to feel fear? His eyes were so clear that it seemed as
if he opened the whole of your soul to his gaze, a soul that was so
simple and pure that it did not fear your scrutiny, look you as never
you may. This was his great charm and this was politically his great
weakness. For in battle the inculcation of fear is often more than
half the way to victory. This physical advantage he did not possess.
Had he been free to express himself more freely, to say and write
just what he thought, as any ordinary man might do, then, no
doubt things would have adjusted themselves and he would have

found his level. But in his position this was impossible, his utterances were bound to be couched in official terms. Nevertheless he did, on rare occasions, state in a straightforward, manly way, his state policy. I may quote, slightly condensed, the words he uttered when he ascended the throne on the death of his father in 1894:–

> In this sorrowful yet triumphal hour of our accession to the ancestral throne of the Russian Empire ... we make this solemn vow before the Face of the Almighty, always to make our sole object the peaceful prosperity, the might and the glory of dear Russia, and to further the happiness of all our subjects. May Almighty God who has been pleased to call me to this great office give me His help.

Thus in the few words comprising this sacred oath he summed up the guiding policy of his life – peace, prosperity, glory and power for Russia and the happiness of his people, but above all trust in God. But lest he be misunderstood by the foreign powers of the world, he later issued a second Manifesto expressly directed to all foreign powers having diplomatic relations with Russia. In this he declared that he would consecrate all his efforts to the peaceful development of the internal prosperity of Russia and

> never forsake a completely peaceful, firm and straight policy that will powerfully further the general peace. Russia will be unwaveringly faithful to her obligations. She will direct all her efforts to the maintenance of friendly relations with all powers and will, as formerly, consider the respect of rights and legal procedure the best guarantee for the safety of the state.
>
> In the beginning of the reign which has now closed, the declared policy was directed to the creation of Russia, strong and prosperous for her own good and not to the detriment of others. Now at the dawn of a new reign with unchanging sincerity we declare that we will follow the same lead, asking the blessing of the Almighty on its fruitful and unchangeable application during many years.

Thus clearly and simply did the Emperor Nicholas II enunciate the guiding principles of his life from which he never departed. Above everything the Emperor was 'straight'.

By the irony of fate he who was so great a lover of peace was destined to be so troubled by war.[5]

Gibbes also left this pen portrait of the Tsar at the time of the imperial family's exile in Tobolsk, written shortly after their murder at Ekaterinburg in July 1918:

> Extremely honest, cheerful, kind and compassionate, and a devoted lover of his country. He spoke and wrote English and French to perfection; his memory was exceptional. Preferring to study social matters and history he did not worry about light reading. He was slightly reserved and disliked familiarity, though sometimes he chatted with the soldiers. Methodical in his habits, he could not bear anyone to touch his things.

On the Tsarina, Gibbes had this to say in his 1934 sermon:

> Born of an alien race and of an alien faith, the young Empress had had many difficulties to overcome. In spite of the fact that she whole-heartedly accepted the faith of her adopted country and even in the course of time became more strictly Orthodox than the Orthodox themselves, nevertheless she was never able to completely win her way into the hearts of her chosen people. I have often wondered why. I think that the cause of this must be attributed to the Empress's lack of a 'theatrical' sense. The theatrical instinct is so deeply engrained in the Russian nature that one often feels that Russians act their lives rather than live them. This was completely foreign to the Empress's school of thought, which she had mostly acquired under the tutelage of her revered grandmother, Queen Victoria. Left motherless at the age of six, Queen Victoria had supplied the place of her beloved parent, as far as distance and circumstances would allow. They were in constant correspondence, which was continued after the Empress's wedding, in fact until the old Queen died in 1901. When we were in Tobolsk the Empress said that one of the most painful things she had done before leaving Tsarskoe Selo, had been to burn the old Queen's letters. But she held them in too great veneration to allow them to fall into the hands of the Bolsheviks. It is therefore not surprising to find that this fundamental difference between the character of the young Empress of Russia and those of millions of her subjects ... served as the basis of that estrangement which has been remarked upon by almost all persons who have written on the subject. The Empress herself was keenly aware of it without suspecting its real cause. She rather attributed it to her 'shyness', which she so much regretted but could

not overcome. The real cause, as we have seen, was deeper to seek. Be that as it may it was a terrible handicap...

No reference to the Empress, however short, would be complete without mentioning her piety. This she had practised from childhood. Her admission into the Orthodox faith only served to intensify all her religious instincts. She became whole-heartedly Orthodox. She truly made its tenets the guiding rule of her life and faithfully until her death did she scrupulously observe the fasts and festivals of Holy Church. She regularly made her confession and received the Holy Communion and invariably did the same before all the great acts of her life. In this she was always supported by her husband, who was likewise sincerely devout.

In his submission to the examining magistrate who was investigating the murder of the imperial family, Gibbes offered this assessment of the Tsarina:

Formerly very good-looking and graceful (her feet were large). She had wonderful soft grey eyes. She was clever, but appeared to be more so to those who knew her least. Not haughty in the ordinary sense, she never forgot her position; she looked queenly, but I was always at ease with her. Kind-hearted, extremely fond of homely secrets, she liked to prepare surprises. Russia she loved and considered herself a Russian, but she had German traits (and was more economical than an Englishwoman). Her genuinely religious feelings, in the Orthodox way were quite normal and not induced by hysteria. Always a stronger, more aggressive character than the Tsar, she never opposed him; I never saw a single quarrel.

Of the children, Gibbes regarded the oldest, Olga, as 'innocent, modest, sincere, and kind, but easily irritated; her manners could be a little brusque. She liked simplicity and paid little attention to dress. Her moral outlook reminded me of her father whom she loved better than anyone else. She was very religious.'

Tatiana was 'haughty and reserved, dutiful and pensive; it was impossible to guess her thoughts, even if she was more decided in her opinions than her sisters. Though her technique as a pianist was better than the others, she showed no feeling when she played. She painted and embroidered well. I think the Empress preferred her to her sisters; any favour could only be obtained through Tatiana.'

Maria 'was very strong and broadly-built and could easily lift me from the ground. Good-looking with light grey eyes, she ... grew very thin after illness. She could paint and draw, and played the piano competently; less well than Olga or Tatiana. Marie was simple and fond of children; a little inclined to laziness; probably she would have made an excellent wife and mother. She liked Tobolsk and told me she could have made herself quite happy there.'

Anastasia was 'short and stout, the only ungraceful member of the family; she might have been the best-looking had she been taller and slimmer. Her hair was lighter than Marie's, her eyes were grey and beautiful, her nose was straight. Refined and witty, she had all a comedienne's talent and made everyone laugh, without even laughing herself. It seemed as if her mental development had been suddenly arrested; and though she played the piano and painted, she was only in the first stages of either accomplishment.'

Alexis, the Tsarevich (or 'Naslednik' as he was often called), was at the time of the family's exile in Tobolsk 'tall for his age and very thin [and] had suffered greatly in childhood from a disease inherited from his mother's family. He became worse in Tobolsk where treatment was hard to find. A clever boy, he was not fond of books. He had a kind heart – during the last Tobolsk days he was the only member of the family to give presents – and he loved animals. Influenced only through his emotions, he rarely did what he was told, but obeyed his father; his mother, loving him passionately, could not be firm with him, and through her he got most of his wishes granted. Alexis bore unpleasant things silently and without grumbling.'

Later, in his sermon in 1934, Gibbes reflected that it may have been 'the restrictions caused by his social environment that prevented him from being perfectly balanced as in an ordinary child. For this reason he would sometimes appear too old for his years, while on other occasions, on the contrary, it would be just the other way. Casual observers, having no opportunity to strike a proper balance, were therefore not seldom at fault when criticising this extremely lovable child.'

Although Gibbes spent more time with the imperial family than almost any other foreign resident of Petrograd, his path and that of Grigory Rasputin do not appear to have crossed; certainly in his papers there is no record of his ever having met Rasputin, but, later in life, he did tell the historian George Katkov that on one occasion during the war he saw the Tsar opening the mail at the army headquarters in Mogilev; throwing one letter into the wastepaper basket, Nicholas reportedly exclaimed, 'Another of those denunciations of Gregory. I get them almost every day and throw them away unread.'[6]

'The court's evil spirit'

ENCOUNTERS WITH RASPUTIN

Grigory Rasputin, who was born in 1869 in the village of Pokrovskoe in the Tyumen district of Siberia, was a semi-literate peasant who became a starets or mystic in the Orthodox tradition, and in the early years of the twentieth century attracted a large number of followers in St Petersburg society. From 1905 onwards he had access to the court, and in time came to be widely identified as an 'evil spirit', who 'swayed the destinies' of Russia through the 'unbounded influence he wielded over the Empress Alexandra',[7] obtained by his apparent ability to 'cure' the Tsarevich's haemophilia through hypnotism or prayer. Although more sceptical of Rasputin's powers, the Tsar was swayed by his wife's belief in Rasputin's powers as a 'Man of God'.

Rasputin's influence grew after the Tsar took personal command of the army in 1915 and spent much of his time away from Petrograd at army headquarters. This was deeply resented by other members of the royal family and by members of the Duma, who suspected both him and the Empress of being pro-German.

Few foreigners knew Rasputin personally. However, on one occasion, consulting engineer Stinton Jones found himself sharing a train compartment with him:

My only encounter with Rasputin was during a journey from the Ural Mountains to Petrograd, which occupies some three and a half days. At first I had a large coupé to myself, but a short time after, at a small station, a man and two girls entered and took their places. My first thought was that there was some mistake and that a third-class passenger had, by mistake, entered a first-class coupé, as although the two girls were well but plainly dressed, seeming of a slightly better class than the man, the man himself was clothed as an ordinary moujik, or peasant. His clothes seemed very appropriate to the person wearing them, for his general countenance was that of an ordinary coarse and ill-bred peasant, with unkempt hair and a long beard, on which were traces of recent meals.

We had not gone far when the conductor of the train asked me into the corridor and said that he was arranging that I should go into another coupé. I told him I was quite comfortable where I was and, as I had booked my seat, had no intention of removing. He was insistent, but I was obstinate and returned to my coupé. My fellow traveller then went into the corridor and had a heated argument with the conductor, who then again approached me about changing my berth; but I could not see the force of his argument that he should interfere with my comfort for the sake of a common-looking peasant. The 'peasant' returned to the coupé and proceeded to stare at me with his strange eyes. I decided that he was trying to will or hypnotise me into falling in with his wishes.

At the next stopping-place I left the train for exercise on the platform. My fellow-passenger did the same, and I noted that the people on the platform showed him great respect, and as he passed they crossed themselves. I enquired of one of the porters, 'Who is that man' and he replied, 'Georgie Rasputin'.

This was a revelation to me, as, although I had heard a good deal of his unkempt and unconventional man, I never realised that he was quite so ungroomed as I found him, and I was able to appreciate the conductor's anxiety to get me out of the coupé. I now determined to remain where I was so as to see more of this much-spoken-of individual.

Upon returning to the coupé I closely inspected him and was certainly struck by the expression in his eyes, which were deep and piercing, and probably it was in these eyes that his power lay.

Finding that his efforts to have the coupé to himself were unavailing, I was left in peace for the rest of the journey. Upon arriving in Petrograd I saw one of the Court automobiles was waiting for him.[8]

One who claimed to know Rasputin better was British translator and writer Gerard Shelley, who, in his book *The Speckled Domes* (published in 1925) recounts several meetings with the starets, both in Petrograd and in Moscow. Unfortunately, the book contains a number of errors, along with names of followers of Rasputin which are not to be found in other accounts of the period, so, as a contemporary reviewer wrote, 'one is inclined to wonder whether everything happened just as he said it did'.[9] Nevertheless, his accounts of meeting Rasputin have an air of authenticity about them, and his own political and religious beliefs made him noticeably more sympathetic towards Rasputin than many other observers. As with everyone who encountered Rasputin (see Plate 4), it was the starets' eyes which, on the first occasion on which they met, made the greatest impression on him:

> At my reply, he smiled at me with his great eyes. They seemed to emit soft, velvety rays, caressing one almost as one feels the caress of a melodious voice. The power and charm of such eyes, combined with that deep, fluted voice, those massive shoulders and giant frame was obvious. Rasputin was the superman of body and soul. What he would have been if he had been an Intelligent, cannot be imagined. Perhaps he would have lost the secret force that made him what he was. Nature is deeper than science.
>
> Meanwhile he held my hand against his beard and said in a rhythmic manner: '*Utrennaya rossa na nyejhnoy travye raduga radosti, no vyechernaya vlaga slyoz soodby!*' (The morning dew on the tender grass is a rainbow of joy, but the evening damp is the weeping of fate!)
>
> I had been warned he was accustomed to make cryptic remarks so I took this with the proper respect.[10]

Following this initial introduction, Shelley appears to have visited Rasputin in his own apartment on a number of occasions. On one of these,

> Rasputin was standing against the window, reading out of an old book.
>
> I noticed that his hands were perfectly clean, and his nails well cared for. The myth about his dirty finger-nails was just part of the campaign of the Aristocracy against him; their own idea of their position was so exalted that they almost believed they were born

under supernatural laws. A peasant or a bourgeois was something vastly inferior, to be told so on every possible occasion, and made to feel the elevating superiority of the nobles' boot. This vulgar arrogance of the Russian nobles had perhaps no equal in any European country. Aristocracy being for the Russian nothing but a matter of caste and outward show, it was natural Petrograd society should attach enormous importance to manicure. Manual labour was held in the greatest horror. Even during the war no Petrograd 'lady' ever stooped to do work that would soil her hands. So it was natural that the horror of Rasputin the peasant could not be complete without painting his finger-nails black.

The Staretz wore a peasant robe of fine silk. About his waist was a curious girdle, which, I was told, he only wore on very special occasions. It was made of different kinds of human hair. Devoted ladies had insisted on weaving a girdle of locks of hair sacrificed by pious women as a snub to vanity. The dark, fair, golden and white locks showed up all round the girdle. They were loosely spun and woven, while pearls and rubies in gold repoussé settings formed panels at intervals. I suppose the devoted spirit which induced these ardent souls to weave this girdle was akin to that of pious ladies who embroider slippers for their curates. Perhaps the most remarkable thing about the girdle was the lock of the Empress, which was enclosed in a sort of escutcheon, like a relic. The case was richly ornamented, and formed a cover for the buckle. It was stated that people were expected to kiss this 'relic' of the Empress on greeting the Staretz, but no such ceremony ever occurred in my presence, nor do I believe it existed outside the strange imaginations of her enemies.[11]

Shelley thought that,

Apart from his saga-like eloquence and rich, poetic visions, his stalwart physique and velvet toned 'breasty' voice, he did not strike me as being more mystic than other Startzy I had met. At times he struck me as being very much like an Old Testament prophet. I think the secret of his power lay in the sense of calm, gentle strength and shining warmth of conviction. He considered the Russian nation as God's chosen people and the Tsar as God's Anointed, whose task was to restore the Cross to St. Sophia.[12]

Shelley also claimed to have been present on one occasion when the Empress herself visited Rasputin:

The chairs were being drawn up in readiness for the guests when the door bell rang. Two veiled ladies entered. They were both modestly attired in simple black dresses, a fur toque covering their heads. The Staretz moved forward to greet them, saying gently:

'Greeting to Alexandra, the servant of God.'

Throwing off her dark veil, the tall lady stood revealed. It was the Empress. I was astonished beyond words. With her was the Grand Duchess Tatiana, tall, elegant and beautiful in her simple black dress.

I could not help noticing the reverence the Empress showed towards the Staretz. There was a look of religious peace and happiness in her eyes as she returned the Staretz' greeting and, lifting the gold cross he wore on a chain, pressed her lips to it with tender piety. I felt dreadfully embarrassed, and hardly knew what to do. My first thoughts were of flight. I felt sure my presence must be irksome to the Empress, who had probably come to the flat under the impression that only the two ladies in waiting would be present.

The Empress, however, put me at ease immediately. I had already had the honour of being presented to her during her visit to Kharkov in the early days of the war, when she visited the Red Cross Depôt at the House of the Nobility. Furthermore, she was aware of my association with the Grand Duke Oleg, who was killed at the front.[13] Her Majesty had taken a personal interest in the projects of her young relation.

'I feel sure you will appreciate the beauty of our friend's character,' she said, taking the hard chair I drew up for her convenience (there was no sign of luxury in the flat. Nothing but bare, painted boards, hard deal chairs and a simple table). 'It is so refreshing to me. If we are true Christians we must love simplicity. Our friend takes one back to the simple faith of the early Christians, when high and low met together to hear the Word of God from a poor fisherman. The Spirit breathes where it will.'

I ventured to state the platitude that God was no respecter of persons.

'If people would only bear that in mind!' she exclaimed. I could not help noticing the sad look that crossed her face, as though she saw before her mind's eye some disheartening tragedy. Her skin was very red, the complexion beginning to get streaky.

I was very much startled when, with blunt directness and forceful emphasis, she declared:

The Empress Alexandra

'Petrograd society is rotten! There is hardly a soul to be relied upon.'

The Staretz was busy talking to the Grand Duchess Tatiana. I caught snatches of their conversation about helping the soldiers with clothing and comforts.

Finding my views reasonable, and probably because of my connection with the political and other projects of the Grand

Duke Oleg, the Empress told me some of her views about the great problem she had at heart. After the 1905 Revolution she had come to realise that the security of the Throne and Russia could only be assured by a closer knitting together of Tsar and peasantry. The work of past emperors had been too Western, imposing a culture which had merely led to nihilism and atheism. The nobles and merchants were 'rotten.' They had lost faith and worshipped materialism. They were untrustworthy, anarchical, evil-living.

I was aware of a deep meaning when she said: 'Even the highest and nearest are full of revolt and schemes.'

Rasputin was to tell me afterwards that the Tsar lived in daily dread of being the victim of a plot to dethrone him by several of the more ambitious Grand Dukes. Russian history, no doubt, furnished him with plenty of cause for anxiety. The world had been openly talking of the chances of the Grand Duke Nicholas.[14] He was the idol of the Army, and was credited with a strong dislike of the Emperor's pro-peasant policy. Rasputin actually attributed half the propaganda against himself to him.

The Empress appeared to be very earnest in her desire to secure for her son a firm place in the hearts of the people.

'All my thoughts are for him,' she assured me. 'He is to be the Autocrat of Russia and defender of the Orthodox religion. He must be the leader of those who are faithful to the Church and Throne. The middle class is rotten. It is in love with revolution. That is all bad blood. It can never be got out of the body. It is doomed to die. The upper classes are rotten, too. There is hardly anyone who can be relied on. If Russia is to be saved we must look to the simple peasants.'[15]

'Whispers about treachery'

THE OUTBREAK OF WAR

Despite all the deep-seated and long-term causes of the Revolution, there can be little doubt that Trotsky was right when he wrote in 1918 'The Revolution grew directly out of the war, and that latter became the touchstone for all parties and forces of the Revolution.'[16] Failures, both militarily and on the home front, acted as the trigger for all that followed.

By as early as late August and early September 1914 the Russian army had suffered major defeats at the hands of the Germans at Tannenberg and the Masurian Lakes. Their premature and badly executed invasion of East Prussia undoubtedly relieved pressure on the British and French forces on the Western Front, but at a terrible cost to themselves. General Knox, British military attaché, later wrote:

> Possibly the detachment from the Western theatre that the Russian raid wrung from the German Supreme Command saved the Allies in the West and so turned the whole course of the war. No price could have been too great to pay for this relief in the West, but the price actually paid – the crippling of the Russian army – was greater than it need have been, and for this crippling the Allies generally, and Russia most of all, were eventually to pay.[17]

Although Russian armies recorded victories elsewhere against the Austro-Hungarians, they were no match for the better-trained, better-equipped and better-supplied German forces, and as the war progressed the inadequacies of Russia's supply chains became ever more apparent, and of increasing concern, to her Western allies. Following further defeats, including the loss of Warsaw, in 1915, the army commander, the Grand Duke Nicholas, was dismissed, and the Tsar took personal command of the army, thus allowing himself to become associated personally with any further failures.

Yet in August 1914 the war was greeted as enthusiastically in Russia as it was in the other warring nations. One anonymous Anglophile Russian, writing in 1917, caught the flavour of that moment only three years earlier:

Never had the Emperor been so popular as at that exciting time. The day of the publication of his Manifesto was the most triumphant of his reign. When His Majesty, after the religious ceremony in the halls of the Winter Palace, stepped out on the balcony to greet the people assembled in the Square in front of the Palace, the people dropped on their knees, baring their heads before the Monarch, singing the National Hymn, 'Boje Tzaria khrani' (God save the Tzar) and acclaiming him with a thunder of cheering. Patriotism filled all hearts, real patriotism, that made the people forget all past grievances and rally round the Throne, eager to defend beloved and Holy Russia from the invasion of the hated Germans. In the moment of National danger all parties joined. Political contests were forgotten in the unanimous wish to give the Monarch adequate support to crush the enemy.[18]

And Arthur Marshall, a British businessman at that time staying in the Astoria Hotel in Petrograd, wrote to his wife immediately after the declaration of war between Germany and Russia that

The people here are all hugely delighted at the prospect of a scrap with Germany and spent last night in processions with much cheering and singing of the Russian National Anthem which sounds fine when sung by a huge mob of people gathered in the streets with their hats off and finished off as well as started with shouts and cheers.[19]

Two days later Marshall wrote again to describe the dramatic scenes surrounding the sacking of the German Embassy, which was situated close to his hotel:

There has been so much shouting in the streets of late that I did not take much notice when I heard it begin again and hurrah after hurrah came from the crowd (the Russian says 'oorrrah' rolling the r's very much) but as it did not seem to get better ... I decided to investigate for myself and got out on the balcony. There I saw a scattered crowd in the Square opposite us but all the police were facing the Isaac's Square where the German Embassy is situated and of which we can only see the end from here. On the balcony I heard the sound of glass being broken so I decided to go down to the street.

Here I found a mass of people gathered. Some of the windows of the Embassy had been broken and the crowd was being addressed by two or three men, all of whom were haranguing them to the same effect, viz rush the Embassy and destroy it.

There stood the Embassy, gaunt and black, not a light to be seen. All the blinds down, the German Eagle perched on top of the flagstaff and the bronze group of two horses and two men of enormous size shewing up faintly against the dark sky.

The crowd swayed this way and that and shouted themselves hoarse. Then came the whisper 'the police are charging' and in a moment there was an ugly rush. But the police were not charging and the crowd once more settled closer and closer.

Marshall then went back inside the hotel and moved rooms so that he could watch the unfolding drama in comfort:

Sitting here armed with glasses we watched the crowd below who now settled down to grim business. Men, women and boys rushing forward would throw their stones through the windows and then retire to the crowd to get more ammunition.

Apart from this the crowd was quiet and well behaved and kept where the police told them to.

Then suddenly we saw first one, then another, then two or three dozen men on the roof and heard hammering and saw flags waving and the crowd yelling itself hoarse as one man climbed the flagstaff and threw the eagle down to the street below replacing it with a Russian flag.

Others had been at work on the bronze figures for soon we saw one fall on its side and the other was pushed over into the street.

Then we saw a light in one of the top windows and figures moving about and the windows opened and out poured sheets, pillows, curtains, clothes, pictures, books, papers, china, chairs, etc. Then another and another window lit up and the same took place.

Then the police entered and sent the crowd out and the crowd started large bonfires and threw on the flames uniforms, hats and all the fuel they could get.

Then someone shouted 'Set fire to the Embassy'.

No sooner said than done and with an ugly rush the people surged up and did succeed in lighting some curtains but the police pulled them down and put out the fire.

The fire brigade was called up however and proceeded to play first on the bonfire and then on the people. They drenched a General who came up to them mad with rage but the water kept the people back a bit and the police then spoke to them and the crowd thinned out and dispersed a bit.

Thinking it was all over, Marshall prepared to go to bed, but

By the time I had finished undressing the noise was once more as great as ever and slipping on a coat and a macintosh I ran along to the other room and for the next hour or hour and a half sat and watched a most extraordinary scene.

Every room in the Embassy was a blaze of light as if for a state ball but not a curtain was there and soon not a pane of glass and scarcely even a window frame.

The place was full of men working with feverish haste armed with anything they could lay their hands on as an instrument of destruction.

They worked hard and there was the almost continuous sound of smashing china, glass, wood, etc. The windows were used as shutes and out came a continuous stream of things. The huge reception hall filled with men working like demons. Chair after chair, table after table, clocks, ornamental vases, tapestries, pictures, curtains, carpets, mirrors, in fact everything that could be was wrenched away and thrown into the street where it formed a gradually growing mound. Brass pots, plants, bowls, uniforms, robes, stationery, all helped to make the mound grow and what could not be thrown out was destroyed in position.

Then the mob mounted higher and reached the upper floors where the bedrooms were and here as before out came everything, beds, bed-clothes, wardrobes, chests of drawers, clothes, hats, boots, books, papers, desks, chairs, crockery, anything in fact, and still the mounds grew and grew in size and at each extra loud crash the people yelled themselves hoarse with joy.

When the rooms were swept clear of everything intact the people wandered through once more to try and find something more to smash and two or three of the leaders stood on the window sills and bowed to the mob who shouted praise in return.

The firemen played on the heaps below to prevent their being fired by the mob for such a bonfire would almost certainly have spread.

The Astoria Hotel during the 18 May 1917 demonstrations (*The Sphere*, 9 June 1917)

The following morning he noted that

> Except for the frameless windows and missing eagle and figures
> the Embassy looked unaltered ... All the debris had been cleared
> away and all the pavements swept clean, but the Embassy side of the
> square is shut off and the police on guard.

And he concluded his account with the observation that

> The whole thing was well-organised and the crowd well-behaved
> and under control. The authorities had evidently decided that they
> were to be allowed to work their own sweet will on the Embassy
> provided they behaved quietly otherwise and the people evidently
> kept to their part of the bargain.[20]

Marshall himself was not too displeased by the turn of events as
he could see that for the foreseeable future the Germans would be
shut out from any trade with Russia, and he thought he could see his
way to sign various contracts with the Russian government which
would earn him a net profit of £4 million.[21]

A few days later, from the same window in his hotel, he watched the departure of some of the first troops to leave for the front:

In the square opposite my window here a whole regiment was drawn up and a service held prior to their departure for the war. The priests stood in the middle of the square and prayed with them. Then the whole regiment sang the National Anthem which is one of the most stirring pieces of music I know and is typical of the great silent Russian Race, stronger in their silence than others in their shouting. There is a strong passion in the music which cannot be expressed in words, it is like the voice of the people moved with one will and one desire and determined to get it whatever the cost and relying on the help of the Almighty.

The service was fine, although that word does not express it, it was grand and solemn even as death is solemn and its grandness too was similar to the grandness of death itself and one almost expected to hear the 'still, small voice' in answer to their prayers.

Then the priests walked through the ranks blessing them and sprinkling them with holy water.

After this the General made a speech telling them what the war was about, how it had started and that they were going to fight for their lives and wives, their children and homes, their Czar and their God and that God would give them Victory and that defeat was worse than death as it involved others in death and trouble. Let them fight and die if necessary that others might live.

The men cheered and the women wept and cheered, laughed and cried as they said their final adieus and then columns and columns with colours flying and bands playing a joyous march the regiment filed out of the square headed by its officers, with its transport, its artillery and cyclists on the road to the station and the war, that is to and must mean victory for them and for us and a freedom from the military power that Germany has been for years forcing on the world through her desire as expressed by her Emperor for personal and national aggrandisement. A few of the women marched beside their men, hating to say the last farewell, and longing for the chance of still another word, still another smile.[22]

Later in the month, on 23 August, the Tsar and his family went to Moscow to attend the traditional service of prayer at the Uspensky Cathedral in the Kremlin in aid of victory. As the daughter of the British ambassador, Meriel Buchanan was in the procession from the royal palace to the cathedral, and recorded the sight that greeted her as she came out onto the square in front of the Cathedral:

> And then suddenly wide open doors giving out on to a terrace, and the wonderful stone flight of steps known as the Red Staircase, and all the square below as far as eye could reach a vast concord of people! A crowd that thronged up the steps of the surrounding churches, that stretched away to the encircling walls of the palaces, that filled up all the corners between the sacristy and the distant rose-red monastery, leaving in the midst of all that seething darkness one narrow pathway, raised just a foot's space from the ground, covered with a strip of crimson carpet.
>
> And when the Emperor appeared on the top of the long flight of stairs, as if at some unspoken signal, all that great crowd, workmen and citizens, merchants and peasants, soldiers, women and children went down on their knees, and from them rose a sound that broke against the ancient walls like the waves of a tremendous sea, that echoed and re-echoed, swelled, died down, and burst out again. For some of them were cheering, some were sobbing, some – with streaming eyes fixed on that small majestic figure descending the great stairs – were singing the National Anthem, the hymn for the Sovereign's safety.
>
> Slowly between that kneeling throng of people, the Emperor passed, so near that by stretching out a hand those close to the pathway kept for him could have touched him. And there was nobody to guard that path, no policeman or soldier with fixed bayonet to keep back that seething, overwhelming mass of people.
>
> By now nearly all the crowd were singing the National Anthem, singing it in broken, faltering voices, with tears choking their utterance, while here a woman lifted a child up in her arms, there a soldier bent his head low over his clasped hands as if he dared not look, and an old woman near the pathway bent to kiss the ground as the Emperor passed.

The procession then entered the Cathedral:

> The vast nave seemed a living casket of jewels – dim, old mosaics on the walls, carpets of wonderful, faded colours stretched on the cold, stone floors, jewelled ikons priceless in workmanship, little points of candlelight catching the reflection of some precious stone, making it burn with hidden fire. And golden and yellow, black and

silver, deep purple and glowing crimson, the sheen and shimmer of the priests' cloaks, and all pale blue and gold the stiff, high-collared robes of the choir! ...

And then, breaking the hush, the deep low voice of one of the silver-haired priests chanting the beginning of the service, and rising above it, silver clear, unbelievably pure, the young fresh voices of the choir.

A long shaft of sunlight streamed through one of the high glass windows, it glanced across the figure of an old, bent chamberlain, woke to glowing colours the corner of a priest's brocaded cloak, and fell on the fair hair of one of the boys in the choir, making of that young face, framed by the high, jewelled collar, the face of an angel in some old picture.

Up by the golden doors leading to the altar a mass of burning candles made a blaze of orange light amidst the blue haze of incense smoke. And as the dense crowd swayed and shifted, one caught now and then a glimpse of the Emperor's motionless figure, of the huge, bearded Cossack bearing the frail form of the little pale-faced boy, of the Empress's hard, set features, of the wonderful spiritual figure of her sister, the Grand Duchess Elizabeth,[23] clad in the straight white robes of a nun.

On and on went the glorious service, the marvellous music of those boys' voices, falling now to the low, passionate note of an organ, rising now clear and high in the triumph of youth and perfect training.

And then in a sudden hush the rustling of women's dresses as they fell on their knees, here and there the sharp rattle of a sword striking the stone floor, and then in the deep silence above that kneeling multitude the low, deep voice of a gray-haired priest, his trembling hands raised in supplication, his face very pale beneath the weight of his wonderful jewelled crown. A prayer for victory, for strength, for unity, for patience and endurance; a prayer for the arms of Russia and her allies; a prayer for the fulfilment of the world's liberty, and for an ultimate glorious peace.

The beautiful old voice died away, and in the silence that followed a muffled sobbing was the only sound. Then as in a jubilation the clear young voices of the choir breaking out again and a burst of dazzling sunshine as the great doors swung open.

Once more the long procession formed, and as the Emperor left the church a great roar of cheering broke out from the patiently waiting crowd, and high above it against the soft blue sky the mighty clamour of the bells – silver bells that laughed and rippled, great bronze bells that cried a solemn warning to the idle world, golden bells that seemed to call to prayer.

And between that tempest of sound, the hurricane of cheering, that thunder of bells, the Emperor passed out and the dim old church sunk back to its dreams of long dead magnificence, while the walls of the Kremlin echoed and re-echoed to that tumultuous cheering that beat itself out against their strength and died at last to silence.[24]

Nevertheless, unnoticed by Meriel Buchanan, this was, as at the Tsar's coronation in Moscow eighteen years earlier, a day of ill omen. Outside on the square Florence Farmborough, soon to volunteer as a nurse at the front, noted that between the raised walkway on which the procession was making its way to the cathedral and the crowd of spectators

there was a well-defined space of some twelve to fifteen feet. Into that empty space the figure of an old man of the peasant class suddenly stumbled headlong forward. In his hand he held a roll of paper which he stretched towards the Tsar with a beseeching flourish. Then he was on his knees, the paper still held aloft, and then, there were men alongside him, obliterating his crouching figure from view. Then the space was empty again. Not a sound had been heard, no cry, no scuffle, for we were out of earshot, but soon around us an undertone of voices was heard; it rose to a murmur of inaudible words, for each was whispering to each and the keyword of the whispers was 'petition'. The people around us were now speaking clearly though softly. Those who had seen were telling those who had not, and the facts – real or imagined – were being vehemently discussed. Ah! they sighed, the usual thing: an attempt by a peasant to hand the Tsar a petition, but his effort had – again the usual thing – been frustrated. 'Wretched man,' they told each other in hushed voices, 'that means prison for him, perhaps even hard labour, or banishment.' It had happened so quickly, so quietly, the majority of people had not seen, but the Emperor had undoubt-edly seen, though he'd made no sign. Calmly, with undeviating step, he had continued on his way.[25]

It did not take long for the inadequacy of Russia's war machine to become apparent and for disillusion to set in. In little more than a month since the declaration of war Russian forces suffered crushing defeats at Tannenberg (26–30 August) and the Masurian Lakes (7–14 September), leading the British military attaché General Knox, who witnessed much of the fighting, to comment that 'The Russians were just great big-hearted children who had thought out nothing and who had stumbled into a mare's nest.' The enormous losses (around a quarter of the army's strength), he continued, 'dealt a severe blow to Russian morale and deprived the Russian army of a vast quantity of very necessary material'.[26]

Despite successes elsewhere, principally in Galicia against the Austro-Hungarians, the Russian army never really recovered from these early defeats. Under-equipped and poorly trained, they were simply no match for their German opponents, even after additional supplies from their western allies began to filter through the northern ports of Archangel and Port Romanov.

As in all the belligerent countries, military failure led to a search for scapegoats; in Russia the German-born and already unpopular Empress and her associates were easy targets. The anonymous Russian author of *The Fall of the Romanoffs* spoke for many when, in the aftermath of the February Revolution, she wrote:

> Strange reports were circulated about the Empress Alexandra and some of the Grand Duchesses, who were German Princesses by birth. It transpired that Her Majesty was not at all enthusiastic about the war. The idea of an armed strife between her former Fatherland and her present country filled her with pain and distress. Her attitude damped the Tzar's animation in favour of fighting to the end until a definite victory made peace overtures acceptable to all the Allies.

The following anecdote, widely spread at the time, though a fictitious one, is illustrative of this general impression:

> 'I really don't know,' said the little Tzessarevitch to a friend, 'on whose side I am to be? When the Russians are beaten, Papa looks glum and when the Germans are beaten, Mamma cries.'
>
> After two months of war it was whispered that the Empress was endeavouring with all her might to bring about a reconciliation between the Kaiser and the Tzar, and thus ensure a separate peace.
>
> Meanwhile the fond delusion of the Russian people, that the Tzaritza had more of the Englishwoman in her than of the German,

was being rapidly dispelled. The fact was suddenly revealed that at heart she belonged to Germany, and that she bore a serious grudge against England.

Rasputin, too, was accused of being pro-German:

> He made no secret of his pacificatory inclinations, and openly assured everyone that a prolonged war would be Russia's undoing. He would, he assured everyone, never have let things come to such a pass had he been at Court. War would have been avoided. From the first, Rasputine manifested aversion to the bloodshed that was going on, and insisted on the necessity of peace. He even told the Empress that her son's safety depended on its being speedily concluded. This peculiar attitude of his towards the war at a time when the whole country had risen as one man, palpitating with indignation at the insults the German Kaiser had hurled against the Russian Tzar, eager to go to battle in defence of the country and the Throne, made people suspicious of his motives, and the popular belief was that Rasputine must be a German agent, or the tool of some skilful German spy.

Thus,

> Spying and treachery seemed in the air. Petrograd was full of German agents, only one could not lay hands on them. Most of the suspicions seemed to lead up to the Palace of Tzarskoe Selo. The Empress was accused of having a wireless installation secreted in the Palace, which gave her the opportunity of sending and receiving wireless communications from her German relatives. However, the search made after Empress Alexandra's arrest proved this aspersion, at least, to be false. Notwithstanding the minutest examination all over the Palace, including roof, garrets and countless lumber-rooms, nothing of the kind was found.

On the other hand, especially after Nicholas had assumed direct command of the army himself in 1915, many thought that the Empress was able to exert a far greater degree of influence over both the personnel and the policies of the government (although historians now disagree about the extent of this influence), leading to rumours such as this:

[A] plan of the Empress [was] discovered which caused the members of the Imperial Family grave anxiety. The part Catherine II played in Russian History had from the first appealed to the Empress's imperious nature. When the question was broached as to what name she should assume as the future Empress of Russia, the Princess suggested Catherine, but the name was disapproved of by the Dowager Empress, and Alexandra was substituted. The idea had been suggested to Her Majesty that the best way to obtain unlimited power would be to get the Emperor into such a state of debility that he would have to be set aside in favour of the Tzessarevitch, and she would be proclaimed the Regent during her son's minority. She could then direct the course of Russian politics in the way she pleased.

Even after the murder of Rasputin in December 1916, the Empress continued to ignore all the warning signs, and by now even her hospital visits to tend to the wounded were being held against her:

The Empress continued to repulse every friend or partisan, and was steadily sowing the seeds of hatred amongst her husband's subjects, especially among the army, where the most bewildering tales were spread of her predilection for the Germans and her prejudice against the Russians. On her visits to the war hospitals, her attitude called forth the most bitter feelings of animosity; indeed these hostile sentiments had of late been so manifest, that Her Majesty ceased them, and even suspended her daily visits to the Court hospitals in Tzarskoe Selo.

When the Empress entered a ward, she nodded her head stiffly, a forbidding look on her set face. She seldom addressed anyone, but in exceptional cases, her repertory of questions was invariably the same: 'At what battle were you wounded?' 'Which part of your body is hurt?' 'Does it give you much pain?' These visits were always a source of disappointment to the wounded warriors. Her coldness stabbed them more cruelly than the sharpest weapon of the enemy. Her aloofness they were convinced was the outcome of the contempt she felt for them.

On one occasion there was a painful scene. The Empress asked a soldier where he had been wounded. The soldier happened to be garrulous and entered into details of how they had put the enemy to flight.

'Which regiment was it?' queried the Tzaritza.

'The Hessians, Your Majesty.'

'The Hessians never flee before the enemy!' remarked the Empress haughtily. Then, pale with wrath, her lips compressed, she walked out of the ward, leaving everyone in consternation. The miserable soldier burst into tears, and agitation reigned in the ward. Nearly every patient had to receive a sedative to soothe him from the effects of the Empress's dramatic departure. . . .

One of the causes of the wounded warriors' displeasure with the Empress was that Her Majesty spoke German in their presence with one of the doctors. This infraction of the established rules excited the soldiers' bitter indignation; for boards were put up in all public places, bearing the legend, 'One is requested not to speak German.'

Nicholas's own sympathies were never openly questioned, but it was pointedly noted that many of the men he surrounded himself with had German surnames:

The entourage of the Tzar became the subject of severe criticism: Count Fredericks,[27] Count Benckendorff, Baron Meyendorff, General von Grunwald, Baron Hoyningen Huehme, Baron Korff, Count Nieroth, were all Germans. The Minister of the Imperial Court, Count Fredericks, in particular, attracted general mistrust. He was known to be the leader of the German party at the Court, and was suspected right up to the time of the Revolution of further-ing German interests. This distrust and dislike on the part of the people went to the extent of accusing the old Count of being a spy, of using his position at the Court and the knowledge of military secrets he gained to give useful information to the Germans.[28]

Gossip such as this systematically undermined the authority of both the Tsar and the government. However, Sydney Gibbes, who was in a position to know, was at pains to refute any suggestions of treachery on the part of either the Tsar or the Tsarina, when he came to deliver his sermon on the imperial family in 1934:

It was after the Emperor's assumption of the supreme command that one heard more and more persistently whispers about treachery. These rumours, spread without doubt by the enemies of Russia and the Allies, quickly took root in the most unexpected places and certainly did very much to undermine the Emperor's position and authority. They thereby weakened to an incalculable extent

Count Fredericks

the allied resistance to the common foe. No man, not even the Emperor, but has his own particular defects. But whatever defects the Emperor Nicholas had, treachery was not one of them. Above everything the Emperor was straight. Not one of the revolutionary commissions was able to lay anything crooked to his door. His personal sympathies were all whole-heartedly on the side of the Allies. Naturally both he and the Empress had relatives on both sides, but so keenly did they feel the anomaly of their position that they voluntarily refused to receive any communications from their relatives on the enemy side. The Empress in particular felt this separation very keenly but for that very reason she kept the stricter to the rule. The insinuation of treachery was therefore the greatest stigma that could be placed upon them. I have never seen the Emperor so angry as when he referred to it. When I first met him after his abdication he absolutely pounced upon me, for it was from English sources that he had received the severest blows. Stabs from the revolutionary leaders of his own land he realized that he must receive and suffer, but from England, to whom he had been so loyal and true, that was the unkindest cut of all.[29]

'Rumours of discontent'

THE MURDER OF RASPUTIN

By the autumn of 1916 there was a general feeling, not least in aristocratic circles, that things could not go on as they were, and that what was seen as the pro-German influence of both Rasputin and the Empress, and through them of the government ministers, needed to be curbed. A plot was hatched by Grand Duke Dmitri and Prince Felix Yusupov to lure Rasputin to the Yusupov Palace and there assassinate him. The Grand Duke may also have had some thoughts of supplanting the Tsar on the throne.

As always, antiques dealer Bertie Stopford, with his many contacts among the Russian aristocracy, was aware of the conspiracy some time before the assassination took place:

Went on to supper at Schubine's where I found amongst many friends the Grand Duke Dmitri. I had not seen him for many months. He called me aside into another room, where he discussed with me at great length the whole internal political situation. Having had knowledge both of my loyalty and my discretion, he confided to me the steps he thought must be taken to arrest the continued reactionary policy of the Empress; how imperative was the removal of evil counsellors.

LETTER 22 DECEMBER 1916
Are we back in Peter the Great's reign? Where will it all end? I have been warned of a drama which may soon happen. But I dare not breathe a word. Even my frequent visits to Europe might count against me!

DIARY 30 DECEMBER 1916
About 5 pm was asleep when Seymour came. A friend in the police, whom he met in the street, told him Rasputin had been shot three times by Felix Yusupov. He did not know if Rasputin was dead. I telephoned to the Embassy but Lady Georgina was out. She rang me up at 5.40 pm to say she had just heard the report. Meanwhile I had already written to the Grand Duchess Vladimir. In the hotel the rumour was generally known by 7.15. To the French theatre, where in the Imperial box were the Grand Dukes Boris and Dmitri. A cousin of Felix Yusupov's was there, but knew nothing. Nobody knows anything definite. It looks as if the warning I received from Dmitri on December 19 of a tragic *dénouement* before December 31 had come true.[30]

On the same evening Edward Heald, an American working for the YMCA's prisoner-of-war relief programme in Petrograd, was returning home around midnight. He noted in his diary that

the atmosphere of the streets [was] full of terror; people seemed to whisper of terrifying events, and to be looking for the hand of doom from which they were preparing to rush for safety. A four mile walk of alarm and uneasiness.[31]

Prince Felix Yusupov

The news swiftly 'spread like wildfire all over the town',[32] despite attempts to hush it up, and it was not long before it reached the front. Nurse Florence Farmborough gave a graphic description of how she heard the news at Trebukhivsti:[33]

We were sitting quietly in our common-room when a knock came on the door. An officer appeared. 'Ah! here you are!' he ejaculated, 'I have some news for you! Grigoriy Rasputin has been murdered.' We were all looking at him, agape with curiosity and suspense and not a word was spoken. 'Yes,' he said slowly, 'strange as it may sound, it is true. We received the news from a reliable source this afternoon.' In the buzz of conversation which followed, question after question was asked; everyone was eager to hear every available detail of such an amazing crime. We heard that the monk had been missing for several days, but his disappearance had been hushed up; nevertheless, it was known that the Secret Police, together with Rasputin's friends and the Court Officials who had openly supported him, had been searching for him high and low. Now his body had been discovered, half-embedded in ice in the River Neva. The newspapers referred to the 'mysterious crime' in guarded terms; they dared not do otherwise; and the names of the conspirators – even that of Rasputin himself – had not been mentioned. 'Have you any idea who the murderers might be?' someone asked. Our friend hesitated and then replied: 'We all have our suspicions, but it would not be right to brand a couple of patriotic men as murderers until we have proof. One thing we do know – the world is well rid of this treacherous man, who was doing all in his power to bring about the downfall of Russia and to sell his country to the enemy.'[34]

Bertie Stopford noted the effect of the assassination on the royal family when, on Christmas Day (7 January in the Orthodox calendar) he travelled out to Tsarskoe Selo and attended the service in the Emperor's church:

all the family were there, a little worried-looking, after the events of the week – the Emperor very drawn and white; he was very still and looked straight before him all the time; only once he turned and looked into the body of the church, and once, when the sun had come out, he looked up at the dome. Once both he and the Grand Duchess Olga, who always sits next to him, looked down their aisle for a minute or so. Probably the Heir Apparent was doing something to attract their attention, which happens often.

The Empress was all in white and looked *congestionnée*. I had never seen her so flushed before. The Heir Apparent is a beautiful boy and much grown since I saw him last in the summer. He drove away with his father and mother.

He also noted that Rasputin had been buried in the grounds of Tsarskoe Selo, his grave being in the new church that the Empress's confidante Anna Vyrubova[35] (herself one of Rasputin's most fanatical devotees) was building there:

> We all know where the *moujik* was buried and how and when. It is disgraceful. What is really feared for the Imperial family is that the Empress may make herself Regent while the Emperor is away at Stavka [the army headquarters].[36]

On 19 January, Stopford returned to Tsarskoe Selo:

> Since I was there last, on their Christmas Day, the whole place is overrun with secret police, which is something quite new.

He then noted ominously:

> There are all sorts of forecasts of the outcome of the Rasputin tragedy. Though it has been discussed fully and publicly and even in the Press, perhaps nothing serious will happen. There are rumours of discontent in the Guards Regiments, especially the Preobrajenski.[37]

'An old world made young'

THE FEBRUARY REVOLUTION

The visit of the Allied missions served to distract attention for a time from the deteriorating position on the home front, but, once they had left, as Meriel Buchanan noted, 'the cloud gathered again more darkly than ever' as the bread shortage reached a 'critical point'. Despite fears of rioting, plans for the Duma to meet at the end of February went ahead, Protopopov[38] assuring the Tsar that measures had been taken to prevent any uprising on the part of the people. One precaution the authorities took was to secretly place machine guns on the roofs of many of the larger buildings in the city, including churches. If anyone noticed these, it was to be said that they were to repel German air raids, and the police were given orders to fire on the people and clear the streets of any protesting crowds that assembled.[39]

The first protests occurred on 7 March (22 February OS) when workers at the Putilov Factory went out on strike; and on the same day the Tsar left Tsarskoe Selo for the army headquarters at Mogilev, a move subsequently explained by Prime Minister Golitsyn[40] as determined by Nicholas's desire to 'avoid more reports, meetings, conversations'.[41] Already he was demonstrating a weariness and a desire to evade taking responsibility.

The following day the strikers were joined by more crowds, including many women, protesting at the food shortages. A bread shop was looted and the first Cossack patrols were seen on the Nevsky Prospekt. So far, however, there had been few signs of violence, and the goodwill shown between the crowds (by 9 March comprising as many as 200,000 people) and the Cossacks was something noted by almost every observer.

The Empress wrote to the Tsar that she had learned 'unofficially' that 'There were riots yesterday on Vasilievsky Island and Nevsky Prospect because some poor people stoned a bakery, tearing Filippov's bakery to pieces & the Cossacks were called in.'[42]

On 10 March (25 February OS) things became more serious as the police opened fire on the crowds and several people were

Protest at the Putilov Factory, the 'cathedral of the Communist faith', on 2 March 1917

killed. The Empress again wrote to the Tsar, with more than a slight sense of complacency, that 'the city's strikes and riots are more than provoking … it's a movement of hooligans, boys and girls running around shouting about no bread – just to stir up excitement – as are the workers preventing others from working. If the days were very cold, they would probably all be sitting at home, but all this will pass & calm down…'[43]

The following day troops were ordered to fire on the protesters, and for the first time some of them, belonging to the Pavlovsky Guards, mutinied. Cocooned at Tsarskoe Selo, and deeply concerned by the illness of her children, who had all contracted measles, Alexandra still seemed unaware of the true seriousness of the situation:

Much talk about the riots in town … The whole problem is this bawling public, those well-dressed people, wounded soldiers, & so on, girl students & the like, inciting the others. Lili[44] talks to drivers to find out news & they have told that students have come and said if they go out in the morning they will be shot at – what rotten types! Naturally the drivers & carters are striking, but they say it's not like 1905 because everyone adores you & only wants bread...

Rodzianko,[45] the chairman of the Duma, had no such illusions, and on the same day sent the Tsar an urgent telegram:

There is anarchy in the capital. The government is paralysed, trans-portation, food and fuel have reached a pathetic state. Military units are firing on each other. There is random shooting in the streets. You must immediately name someone who has the country's trust to form a new government.... Any delay is akin to death. I pray God that in this hour accountability does not fall on the wearer of the crown.

And, as the situation in the capital continued to deteriorate, he sent an even more impassioned telegram the following morning (27 February OS/12 March NS):

The situation is growing worse. You must take measures immedi-ately for tomorrow will be too late.

In fact Nicholas had sent orders to General Khabalov, commander of the Petrograd Military District, to take action to quell the dis-turbances, but, faced with ever-increasing disaffection among the troops, Khabalov was unable to act decisively; indeed, farcically, he was even unable to post notices declaring a state of siege because of a mysterious shortage of brushes and paste.[46]

Nicholas also determined to return to Petrograd, and set out by train on the morning of 13 March (28 February OS). However, rebels blocked the railway line and his train was diverted to Pskov. Communication with Tsarskoe Selo was lost. Tutor Sydney Gibbes noted in his diary that the Tsarina was 'very troubled at not hearing from the Emperor'.[47]

At Pskov, on the morning of 15 March (2 March OS) Nicholas wrote in his diary:

Ruzsky[48] came and related his very long telephone conversation with Rodzianko. According to him, the situation in Petrograd is such

The Duma before and after the February Revolution (*The Sphere*, 12 May 1917)

that now the Duma ministry will be powerless to do anything since they are being opposed by the Social Democratic Party in the guise of the workers' committees.[49] My abdication is necessary.

Nicholas asked General Ruzskii to find out if this was the view of the army commanders too. Later he continued his diary, recording that

By 2.30 replies had come from all of them. The essence is that, to save Russia and keep the army at the front, this is a necessary step. I agreed.

Later on the same day, two delegates from the Duma, Vasily Shulgin[50] and Alexander Guchkov,[51] arrived by train, bringing with them the instrument of abdication, or manifesto as it was termed,

Alexander Guchkov

for Nicholas to sign. After consulting with a doctor over the state of his son's health, he returned to the railway carriage and signed the abdication on behalf of both of them. Only then was he permitted to leave Pskov, writing:

> At 1 in the morning left Pskov with the heavy sense of what I had been through. Am surrounded by betrayal, cowardice and deceit.[52]

Meanwhile, at Tsarskoe Selo, Gibbes noted that, although he spent the day 'much as usual', constructing model houses and reading aloud with the Tsarevich, 'everybody [was] anxious about the issue of events' and that there were 'no trains to Petrograd since the morning'.

The Tsarevich remained very ill throughout this period; on 4 March (OS) Gibbes noted that he was 'better, but not in very good spirits. [He] knows nothing of passing events, but feels them all the same.' The two of them 'cast lead bullets & built model houses' until 'finally the day passed'.[53]

What is striking from Nicholas's diary is how distanced he felt, not just physically, but also mentally, from the events in Petrograd. For the foreigners in Petrograd the opposite seems to have been the case. They were caught up in the events on the streets, the battles between the police and the army and the arguments between the different contending factions as to what form the new government of Russia should take, but with a few notable exceptions, Bertie Stopford among them, they gave little or no thought to the fate of the Tsar himself. On the other hand their letters, diaries and memoirs present a graphic description of what it was like to live through the Revolution as each day's new developments unfolded; where appropriate the diary entries of Hugh Thornton, who was private secretary to the British Secretary of State for War, Lord Milner, are included to give a sense of how the revolution was regarded by the government in London as it unfolded.

7 MARCH (WEDNESDAY)

From Bertie Stopford's diary:

> Heard there had been disturbances in the streets today and some tram-car windows smashed.

On the same day, remarkably, the American air ace Lieutenant Bert Hall met the Tsar at General Ruzskii's headquarters, where he was to receive a medal from him. He wrote in his diary:

> The Tsar decorated me to-day. He spoke very good English without the slightest trace of an accent. His uniform didn't fit and he wore his hat on the side of his head like a British Sergeant-Major on leave. The Tsar wears facial hair like most Russians, and in some strange manner, resembles King George of England, except the Tsar is not as well taken care of. The King of England must look after his health, but the Tsar has eye-bags under each eye and a very sad, wistful look in his face. He wore a kind of Sam Browne belt with two shoulder straps. His body-guard, or the Konvóy, as they call it, is a damned handsome outfit. They would surely make a hit in the Opera Comique. How I would love to get hold of one of those outfits, particularly the hats, and their knives. They do look fierce.
>
> The ceremony to-day was positively mediaeval and damned impressive. If these folks could organise their armies and carry on the war as well as they carry on their ceremonies and their flag wavings, something might happen. But it looks hopeless, or rather, it sounds hopeless. On every hand, people talk reform, revolution; murder the Tsarina, kill Stummer [sic],[54] or Count Fredericks, or Protopopoff. There are strikes already in Moscow and Petrograd.

8 MARCH 1917 (THURSDAY)

From Hugh Walpole's diary:

> Cossacks charging down the Nevski, so suppose there have been riots.

From Bert Hall's diary:

> There were riots and minor disturbances on the streets to-day – it looks like trouble.

From Edward Heald's letter to his wife, 16 March 1917:

> Little did we secretaries realize a week ago today that the Strike, which had started in the shops here, had such a tremendous significance. The government and military officials seemed to have little more realization of it than we, for the Committee of the Empress

Alexander Protopopov, Minister of the Interior

met on Thursday night with Mr. Harte and laid plans for the war prisoner work as if nothing unusual was in progress.

From General Knox's diary:

> I visited Guchkov at 6pm, driving through Coasack and police patrols on the Liteini for the workmen are commencing to strike for want of food. ...
>
> Questioned regarding the attitude of the workmen in the towns towards the war, Guchkov said that from 10 to 20 per cent would welcome defeat as likely to strengthen their hands to overthrow the Government. The remainder are in favour of the war, and they hate the Germans, but they disclaim any idea of conquest; their motto is national defence, but not offence. They are opposed to the idea of conquering Constantinople or Galicia.
>
> In a pamphlet printed by this latter group it is laid down that 'the whole strength of the country should be mobilised for its defence,' and again, 'the present political regime is not only designed for the oppression of the working classes, but seems also to be an obstacle to the mobilisation of the whole living strength of the people for defence, and is thus leading the country to military disaster.'
>
> The eleven labour members of the Military Industrial Committee, who were arrested by order of Protopopov on the night of February 5th, belonged to this group. They are still in confinement. However, Guchkov, who guaranteed that they had no revolutionary tendencies, has secured a promise that they will be eventually tried.

9 MARCH 1917 (FRIDAY)

From Bertie Stopford's diary:

> Just after crossing the Nicolai Bridge I met a demonstration singing the 'Marseillaise'. They were prevented from crossing the bridge, so turned back and went up the 8th Linea Street. I got out of my sledge, and telling the man to wait, I joined them and went with them as far as the Bolschoie Prospekt. They were accompanied by Cossacks. They were not harassed at all and the Cossacks chaffed them and talked to the children; all were on the best of terms. I wanted to see how they behaved and how they were treated. *Tout était à l'amiable.* When I left them I walked back to my sledge and went on to the hospital.

From Hugh Walpole's diary:

> As I supposed, trouble has broken out. All day crowds walking up
> and down the Nevski. On the whole they seem at present cheerful
> and good-tempered, singing songs and cheering the Cossacks, who
> are also very amiable.

From Bert Hall's diary:

> Things happened today – bread riots – endless mobs of people
> marching along singing wild songs, throwing bricks into street
> cars. I asked a Russian friend of mine why the people didn't go
> ahead and have a revolution and get it over. He said that the church
> dignitaries were unwilling. According to the report, God still loves
> the Tsar and it would be a misfortune to revolt against a ruler who
> stood in well with God.
>
> This kind of fairy story didn't draw much water with me, but I
> had to be serious about it and say some attempted wise things to
> cover up my amusement.
>
> Once this afternoon I saw a procession of workmen carrying
> placards. One of them said 'Give us bread!' Others said 'Give us
> land!', or 'Save our Souls!' At the end of the procession came a little
> girl carrying a tiny banner. On it was written, 'Feed your Children!'
> It was the most pathetic thing I ever saw in my life.
>
> There is no food to be had. Everyone is horribly hungry. A
> woman friend of mine who lives at the Hotel du Nord just across
> from the Nikolai Station has a good supply of sugar. She has given
> me quite a lot.
>
> Just before sundown, the police tried to disperse a crowd of
> workmen and their wives who had gathered in front of the Nikolai
> Station. The police were using both whips and swords. Suddenly
> a detachment of Cossacks appeared. The leading Cossack calmly
> rode up to the Captain of the Police, drew his revolver and shot the
> Captain through the head. As the Police Captain fell to the ground,
> the Cossack leader shot two more shots, both hitting the unfortu-
> nate policeman. There was a wild yell. The policemen, seeing the
> look of certain murder on the faces of the Cossacks, spurred their
> horses and fled in great haste.
>
> Immediately the crowd rushed up to the Cossacks and patted
> their horses and talked very kindly among themselves, the Cossacks
> telling the crowd to go home quietly. From this I judge that the
> Revolution is a serious possibility.

From Edward Heald's letter to his wife, 16 March 1917:

Streetcar traffic became irregular Friday and practically ceased during the afternoon. The sleighs with their drivers likewise disappeared from the streets, so that when Day [a]nd I had to deliver a letter for Mr. Harte to Premier Golitzin on the other side of the city, we had to walk. We were informed at the Palace of the Premier that he was not at home but had gone out to Tsarskoe Selo that day.

Crowds of unarmed strikers and families gathered on the Nevsky Prospect during the day and order was preserved by the Cossacks. We anticipated a repetition of former times of disturbances when women and children were ridden down by the Cossacks. This time, however, they used no violence, but merely rode through the open lanes of the people, while the latter shouted at them 'You're ours' and the Cossacks smiled back.

That Friday night six of us attended the performance of Gogol's *Revisor*, greatest of Russian comedies, at the Alexandrinsky Theater. The house was filled and everybody in a lively humor at this satire on the political weaknesses of the mid-nineteenth century. Few of them realized that a greater drama was at that moment unfolding in real life throughout the capital. The Czar's empty box was guarded by two sentries who maintained their inflexible pose and stare during a theater performance for the Czar, for the last time.

Burri did not go to the show with us but continued his walk up the Nevsky. He says that while we were at the play there were volleyings up and down the Nevsky several times, the soldiers firing upon the people.

10 MARCH 1917 (SATURDAY)

From Bertie Stopford's narrative:

At 1.45 I heard a great noise outside the hotel and saw the Cossacks ride down the Michail Street and clear the people away. But as soon as the Cossacks had left the people came back, and a man addressed a crowd just in front of the hotel. Shortly afterwards I heard a crash, the breaking of the windows at Pekar's – the café at the corner of the Nevski Prospekt under my hotel. The Cossacks then rode back down the street and the people ran away before them. I leaned out of my window and could see into the Nevski.

I then dressed and went to luncheon at Donon's. Returning along the Nevski towards my hotel I talked for a moment to Savinski. The street was full of the usual people one sees of a Saturday afternoon on the Nevski. The Cossacks, unmounted, were posted by the Moika Canal outside the Stroganoff Palace; where the Morskaia crosses the Nevski the patrol was going down to the end of the Prospekt. Returning up the Nevski I went on foot to my hotel. It was a beautiful day. The streets were quite normal and very full. As I turned down the Michail Street I saw, higher up the Nevski, a crowd collected at the Sadovia crossing – whether troops or people I could not make out. Motor-cars and sledges were driving about; there were no people off the sidewalk in the street itself.

Later he was going out to a concert.

I had put on my boots and my trousers when I heard a sound which I knew, but couldn't recall. I opened my window wide and realised it was the chatter of a machine-gun; then I saw an indescribable sight – all the well-dressed Nevski crowd running for their lives down Michail Street, and a stampede of motor-cars and sledges – to escape from the machine-guns which never stopped firing. I saw a well-dressed lady run over by an automobile, a sledge turn over and the driver thrown into the air and killed. The poorer-looking people crowded against the walls; many others, principally men, lay flat in the snow. Lots of people were trampled on, and people knocked down by the sledges or by the rush of the crowd.

He went to try to help but firing had stopped and the street was almost empty by the time he got down, and he continued on his way to the concert.

When I got back to the hotel at 6.50 the manager told me that, after I had gone out, the guns had been firing to clear the street, and that four people had been killed at the corner of the Nevski. Alma, the housemaid who looks after me is well, came to my room and said she had been all the time at a window that overlooks the Nevski, and when the machine-gun had fired a second time she had seen a woman and three men shot.

A crowd had come down from the Sadovaia; and when they arrived at the Municipal Duma opposite my hotel, a man made a speech saying the people wanted the Emperor to know how much they were suffering. The police, not the soldiers, fired, killing three men; the woman was shot at the corner of the street. The bodies were taken away either by the police or the soldiers; one body was put on a sledge and driven quickly away down the Nevski. Alma saw all this.

From Hugh Walpole's diary:

Things have broken out with a vengeance. All trams and izvoscht-chiks stopped. Lunched with Lintor and Brooks and on the way was caught up by surging mob in Nevski and nearly run down by Cossacks. Temper of the people quite different from yesterday, but I don't notice as yet any cry against the war – it's all for bread. Cossacks said to be friendly and determined not to shoot.

From Bert Hall's diary:

This morning I decided to leave the country, but I found I could not get my passport viséd. The street cars are out, the railroads are practically stopped, and the city is starving. Everywhere the people are pleading with the Cossacks, pleading with the soldiers, trying to make the military understand that hunger and cold and wretched-ness and poverty are the reward they have received for their loyalty to the Tsar. It looks as if I am stuck here, and I've decided to see the thing up as close as possible. There are all kinds of rumours. Some say that the Government is inciting the workers to a Revolu-tion which will be suppressed in one cruel swipe as a lesson to the common people.

From Edward Heald's letter to his wife, dated 16 March 1917:

Saturday things became noticeably more unsettled. Streetcar traffic entirely ceased. We learned that the motormen had taken off the grips so that the cars could not be started. We were told that the cordial feeling existing the previous day between the soldiers and the strikers had changed owing to the fact that one of the officers had been killed while protesting against the taking of the grips. Zemmer was called by the Russian Red Cross organization Saturday noon to help protect their stores. One of the office girls was called up at noon by her mother and notified that the police had instructed that she should come home at once as it was getting unsafe to go through the streets in that part of the city (near the

American Embassy). The other girls were not long in following suit, all except Miss Golubeva who stayed to get out the mail and telegrams. Nevsky Prospect was closed to traffic except two blocks at the end of our street. When we had to cross the Nevsky on our way to lunch at the Malo Yaroslavets, Saturday noon, the bridges were heavily guarded by soldiers. We could see a dense crowd of the strikers a couple of blocks further up the Prospect in front of Kazan Cathedral, waving a big red flag at their head.

Saturday evening three of us walked down to the Mayak, but the attendance at the gym class was small. Mr. Gaylord was there and I asked him how this compared with the Revolution of 1905, through which he had passed. He said that there had been more excitement on the Nevsky this time, but less in the rest of the city. But on Saturday the real movement had not yet gotten underway. The police still had control of the situation at least in the center of the city. There were reports, however, that there were three hundred thousand armed strikers on the outskirts in the factory districts, and that when they should break through into the center of the city, nothing could stop them. We also heard that the government had brought in quantities of ammunition, machine guns, armored automobiles, and tanks as well as large numbers of Cossacks to meet the emergency.

From General Knox's diary:

The Nevski was quiet when I crossed it at 3.30 pm, but half an hour later the gendarmes were charging the people. Bruce (the First Secretary) arrived at the Embassy in a state of holy wrath, having conducted to her home a woman who had been knocked down in the scuffle. About 5 pm Head (another Secretary) telephoned from the Hotel Europe that he had just seen two civilians killed and Lady Sybil Gray from the Anglo-Russian Hospital that a civilian had been killed on the Nevski in front of the hospital.

Tereshchenko[55] came in and told us that the labour leaders had been to Guchkov in the morning; they were getting uneasy as the workmen were getting out of hand. Martial law was proclaimed at 11 am following the murder of a police inspector. However, Tereshchenko thinks that the weather is 'too cold for revolution' and that things will settle down.

I dined with the W————s, near the Marinski Theatre, and found them very pessimistic. Madame W————'s brother said he had mingled with the crowd and had found them far more determined than in the disturbances of 1905. I walked back with him at midnight, and found the streets deserted except for Cossack patrols and a few lonely policemen.

From Hugh Thornton's diary:

Police and Cossacks called out to deal with a mob in Petrograd. Chief [i.e. Milner] rather thinks serious trouble may be brewing.

11 MARCH 1917 (SUNDAY)

From Henry Keeling's narrative:

I went out about midday for a walk and could not help noticing that an important addition had been made to the placards and proclamations which ordered the strikers to return to work. I stopped to read it, and although cannot remember all it contained, the sting was in the tail, which said that unless the workpeople returned to work by Monday (or it may have been Tuesday – I cannot remember distinctly) morning without fail they would all be mobilised for active service. No account was to be taken of the kind of work they did, there were to be no 'indispensables' and all would be immediately SENT TO THE FRONT.
This proclamation was signed by the Chief of Police – Obolensky.

This was, as it was intended to be, an ultimatum, and the sequel proved that it was no idle threat. I walked along the Nevsky Prospekt and found that it was extraordinarily crowded with people and, what was even more remarkable, although we did not realise the significance of at the time, was the entire absence of the usual gorodevoy – the Russian policeman. In their places were groups of soldiers fully armed with rifles, bayonets and other military equipment.

Rumours were flying thick and fast; people constantly turned to the soldiers and, talking loud enough for them to hear said, 'Surely they will never fire on their brothers', and made other remarks of a similar kind.

Usually under such circumstances the Russian soldier would have smiled and made some kind of good-natured answer; these men, however, remained stolid, glum and quite immovable. It was not until later we discovered that they were not soldiers, but police dressed and armed as soldiers. I strolled into a cafe and sat for perhaps half an hour or so, and then walked out. The Prospekt was more crowded than ever; it was quite an orderly crowd, there was wonder rather than excitement.

Suddenly, just as I was about to cross the road, an officer drew his sword, waved it in the air and shouted out several times, 'Go away, go away'.

Now as the Prospekt is two miles long, only the tiniest fraction of the crowd could possibly have heard him; it was mere chance that I was near enough to do so. Almost immediately after shouting, 'Go away', he gave another order, the actual words of which I did not catch, but I saw a row of 'soldiers' throw themselves down across the road and straight-away begin to fire volleys into the crowd. I was astounded and too paralysed with astonishment to move. At first I thought the rifles could not really be loaded, and that perhaps they were only firing blank cartridges to disperse the crowd.

It was not long before I realised that the shots were fired to kill, and did kill. The great wide road began to empty like magic, people ran for their lives. They tried to run down gateways, but these had been closed by order of the police, they then rushed down the side streets. I saw numbers fall. One boy not far from me, wounded and bleeding, tried to crawl away from the centre of the road, others lay where they had fallen. In other directions, the 'soldiers' were firing down the Nevsky. By great good luck I happened to be standing just between two groups of 'soldiers', and so was able to escape, as their fire was outwards.

After recovering from the first paralysing shock, my blood tingled with rage and shame, and I thought to myself that if the Russian people stood this without resisting they would never deserve to be free people.

From Bertie Stopford's narrative:

At 2 I went on foot down the Nevski to Donon's. At the corner of Michail Street and Nevski I crossed over to see where the bullets of the police had hit the wall of the Municipal Duma and the shops alongside of it. The police had come up the Nevski from the Kasan Church, and had drawn themselves up under the windows of the 'Europe', which give on to the Nevski. The people were unarmed and peaceable citizens.

Going to luncheon I noticed there were no trams running, but in the Nevski there were a few sledges. The streets were full, and crowds of Sunday people walking down the middle of the street.

There were patrols of Cossacks everywhere. The Cossacks after patrolling would stop at the corners of the streets, get off their horses and talked to the people. I witnessed no unpleasantness at all.

Later he learned there had been shooting at the Nicolai station. He then went to the British Embassy.

On the way back to my hotel I had to pass in front of the barracks of the Pavlovski Guards Regiment. There was much ferment amongst the soldiers at the gates, and a great deal of very animated conversation. The men who had been out on leave during the day were now coming back for the night. Some of their officers were urging them to go quietly into their barracks. Later the police came to the Colonel and asked to be allowed to wear uniforms of his regiment. The soldiers, hearing he had consented, killed him. This was the first Guards Regiment in Petrograd that mutinied. ...

I had words with Boris Golitzin about the police shooting the people who, quite quietly, were asking for bread. He sneered, 'You were very much upset at seeing a few people killed in the street. Tomorrow you will see thousands!' I replied, 'It's damned hard lines asking for bread and only getting a bullet!'

From Hugh Walpole's diary:

Great stories of massacres near Nikolaievsky Station, obviously a number of people killed there.

After some hesitation Anna Androvna, K.[56] and I ventured out to the French theatre. We were allowed to cross the Nevski; wonderful sight, the street quite deserted under the moon save for the picket of Cossacks and their horses. Theatre nearly empty but we enjoyed ourselves.

From Bert Hall's diary:

The city is covered with great posters telling the population not to stop in bunches on the street, as the Tsar has ordered that any disturbance will be handled by the military authorities – the police would shoot to kill, etc. It is impossible to believe anything. My Russian friend who told me how much God loved the Tsar now says that the Revolution might go on at will. It is rumoured that God no longer loves the Tsar. It might even be that God never did love the Tsar, not even long ago, when Nikolai was young and popular, before he married the Princess from Hesse.

Soldiers marching on the Duma (*The Sphere*, 21 April 1917)

From Edward Heald's letter to his wife, dated 16 March 1917:

> Sunday was a beautiful sunshiny day. I attended church in the
> morning, and the English pastor was very much perturbed over the
> conditions in the city. Then I visited the art gallery, and the attend-
> ance was not a quarter of what it had been the preceding Sunday.
> Many people were obeying the warnings to stay off the streets.
> Then George Day and I set out from our apartments for dinner at
> the Malo Yaroslavets about three o'clock. We started in the direction
> of the Admiralty Building but were stopped, along with many
> others, at the end of our block by mounted police who ordered
> us back. We went to the Morskaya and succeeded in crossing the
> Nevsky on that street. I shall never forget the sight looking up
> the Nevsky that beautiful afternoon. For the whole length of the
> Prospect not a person was going along the street, either in the street
> or on the sidewalks, but people were crossing at each cross street.

After dinner we tried to return by the way we came, but the approach to the Nevsky was blocked by a dense crowd of people and by mounted police, who waved us back. So we had to go back through the arch of the Winter Square and try to reach our apartment by the route that was closed when we started out. As we crossed at the end of the Nevsky at the Admiralty corner, there rounded the Square over five hundred Cossacks armed with lances who started up the Nevsky. You could not imagine a more brilliant and martial sight than the Cossack cavalrymen glittering in the sunlight. Three large prospects radiate out from Admiralty Park like spokes from a hub, the Nevsky being one of the three. There had been volleys up the Nevsky as well as on the other two prospects frequently that day, and everybody ran as they crossed the sidewalk where it commanded a view of the prospects. We reached home all right and found Burri excited over experiences he had at the further end of the Nevsky towards the Siberian Railroad station. He had seen the soldiers form lines across the street and fire upon the unarmed crowd. He saw two dead and a number injured. One of the volleys came into the crowd he was with, and he took to his heels with the others into one of the nearby basements. He said that the crowd kept crying 'bread, bread' as they came with outstretched arms towards the soldiers...

12 MARCH 1917 (MONDAY)

From Henry Keeling's narrative:

> Everyone was ... saying that the long-expected Revolution was imminent.

From Bertie Stopford's narrative:

> No street traffic or trams running....
> During luncheon we heard incessant firing....
> At the Embassy I heard that the Olives – who live opposite the Tauride Garden, where the Palace of the Duma is situated – expecting friends for luncheon, had telephoned to say they were quite cut off, and hoped nobody would risk the journey. That immediately excited me to go, so I started off along the French Quay. I had just got to the Liteiny and was in the act of crossing the street, when machine-guns began to fire, so I lay down in the snow, and

a fat woman of the people lay across my legs till the machine-guns had finished firing. With difficulty was I able to extract myself from the snow and the old lady. Plato defined bravery as the knowledge of what one ought – and ought not – to fear. I then bolted across the street and continued my way to the Olives'. Along the Schpaler-naia Street the first troops were coming back from having sworn allegiance to the Provisional Government.

I wanted to get news of the British Red Cross Depôt, over which the Ambassadress presides, and found it had not been looted – shutters up and everything in order. After that I made my way up the quays because the crowd was threatening; and having seen a boy officer killed because he would not surrender his sword, I avoided the broad streets that run towards the Duma, as they were continuously being swept by machine-gun fire. Walking along the edge of the river I witnessed a fierce battle going on across the Neva on the opposite quay.

In my faltering Russian I asked a non-commissioned officer who was walking in the deep snow whether I was to go straight on or turn to the right for the Potemkinskaia. He replied in Russian, 'Straight on'. A few minutes after, to my utter astonishment, he said in purest English, 'This is a hell of a mess!' He then told me that his mother was English, and we continued walking together until he left me at the Olives' house. On the way we looked in at the Duma to see the troops 'swearing allegiance' before they marched off to patrol the streets against the police, though by this time there were no police on the streets – they had either been killed or taken prisoners, or were in hiding. All day there was unceasing firing of rifles and machine-guns.

From Hugh Walpole's diary:

One of the most exciting days in my life. In the morning things seemed quiet and I walked to the office easily enough. About twelve, however, on the way to the Embassy heard gun firing. On arriving at Embassy Lady Georgina Buchanan told me we had taken Bagdad [sic]. Then Bruce burst in with news that four regiments had risen against their officers and seized arms. At lunch Ambassador reported Government in great state of panic. Afterwards walking back heard loud firing. Then about four a terrific noise of firing and shouting in Liteini; went to our window and saw whole revo-lutionary mob pass down our street. About two thousand soldiers, many civilians armed, motor lorries with red flags. All orderly, picketing the streets as they passed. Then Garstin and I went out. Started down the Nevski; fierce battle in Morskaya so turned down Moika, but came to where dead civilian lying in the snow, women screaming, etc. Had to run here for our lives, and ran straight into 'Legitimist' camp who however passed us through. Got to the Astoria, filled with wildly excited officers. Dined there with Garstin and Seale. Left for home about nine. Passed through much firing but safely. At every doorway citizens being given rifles. Got home to hear that provisional Revolutionary Government established, Rodziancko [sic] at head. Last news that Czar has given away about everything and appointed Michael Regent. Don't believe it.

From General Knox's diary:

MORNING

To-day is the critical day. It is grand with about twelve degrees of frost (Réaumur). A biting north-east wind would have been better, as it would have kept people indoors.

Ivan, my orderly, arrives with the news that heavy firing is going on on the Viborg Island, and in the Nevski direction. The sailors have come in from Kronstadt to join the movement. Bands of excited men are motoring about in cars with rifles, cheering and being cheered by the populace. Ivan thinks that there is 'perfect organisation'! He says: 'Orators have been appointed in the Mikhail Manege, and they are lecturing the people. Anyone can come and go as he likes!' This seems to him the summit of human happiness.

The telephone does not work. One can only hope for the best. If the officers would only join the movement! I must go out to try to find out things.

In the evening, Knox was dispatched to the Duma to report on proceedings. He witnessed Mikhail Rodzianko, chairman of the Duma, address the soldiers, and he also heard an address by Alexander Kerensky, newly appointed Minister of Justice, who would later become Minister for War and then Prime Minister of the Provisional Government following the July Days uprising.

I made my way to the Embassy and the Ambassador sent me to the Duma. The Canadian railway expert, Bury, and his assistant, joined me and we started on our two miles' tramp through the snow. Half

Alexander Kerensky

way, a country sledge passed us crowded with peasants in holiday
dress. They waved their arms and cheered, and when we cheered
in reply, they stopped the sledge and offered us a lift, an old soldier,
who smelt strongly of vodka, turning other passengers off the
sledge to make room for us. As we drove along, holding on to one
another to avoid falling, my soldier friend breathed into my ear
that the Emperor was a good man, and fond of his people, but was
surrounded by traitors. Now these traitors would be removed and
all would be well.

We arrived at the Duma at the moment when the Preobrajenski Regiment was being interviewed by Rodzianko. The whole wide street before the building was thronged with lorries filled with joy-riding soldiers. Our self-appointed guide walked in front of us, waving his hat and shouting: 'Way for the British representative!' I felt a fool, and no doubt looked it. The Preobrajenski giants yelled: 'Hurrah!'

Our man conducted us to the great Catharine Hall, in a cleared space in the middle of which I saw for a moment Rodzianko and Guchkov. Then I fell back into the crowd while Rodzianko addressed the men, calling upon them to return to barracks and to maintain order, otherwise they would degenerate into a useless mob. I overheard one soldier near me say to his companions: 'No. We won't return to barracks, for that will mean guards and fatigues and work as before.' Then I noticed an expression of sad bewilderment and disappointment come over the face of my guide, who had been listening intently to another man of the Preobrajenskis. Poor fellow! No doubt his simple, honest beliefs had been shattered and he had begun to understand that a revolution was something coarser than the gentle thing he had imagined.

Rodzianko was succeeded by the pale-faced lawyer, Kerenski, who spoke hoarsely from the shoulders of guardsmen. I could not catch much of what he said, but I am told that he is working loyally with the Duma Committee.

The other Labour members have been less patriotic, and are working on purely party lines for the Sovyet. The first news-sheet (Izvyestiya) of this organisation, which was published to-day, contains nothing objectionable, but a leaflet, signed 'Petrograd Committee of the Russian Social Democratic Labour Party and the Party of Social Revolutionaries' is less pleasant reading for an ally, for it incites to class-war. It commences: 'Proletariat of all countries, unite! Comrade workers, the hour has struck! The movement we long ago inaugurated has grown to fruition, and has cleared our way for the realisation of the eternal longing of the proletariat. The people has overthrown the capitalists and in co-operation with the army has annihilated that hireling of the Bourgeoisie, the Imperial Government. The place of the latter has been taken by the Temporary Revolutionary Government, which should be composed only of representatives of the proletariat and of the army.'

Harold Williams, the Daily Chronicle man, whom I met at the Duma, told me that things last night were very bad – worse even than they are at present – but that the Duma Committee is now gradually getting the upper hand.

The scene in the Duma to-day, however, did not show much sign of the re-establishment of order. Few people were working. Soldiers lounged everywhere. There were only about thirty officers, and they seemed ashamed of themselves. One room was being used as an extemporary cartridge factory. In another, bags of flour were piled up for the issue of rations to the troops as they arrived. In another I found poor Engelhardt trying to function as Military Commandant. He sat at a table, on which was a huge loaf of half-gnawed black bread, and tried vainly to make himself heard above the noise of a rabble of soldiers, all spitting and smoking and asking questions.

Suddenly the late Prime Minister, M. Stürmer, was brought along the corridor with an *opéra bouffe* escort, led by a solemn student with his sword at the carry. The old man, wrapped in a huge fur coat, was unceremoniously hustled along. Later came Piterim of the Holy Synod, and then the Assistant Minister of the Interior. Three parties are out looking for Protopopov, but he has not yet been found.

In my walk back from the Duma, I met Tereshchenko, who told me that efforts were being made to induce the officers to come over in order to restore order. Meanwhile, many officers are being arrested. I am probably the only one in Petrograd that now wears a sword!

From Bert Hall's diary:

All night there was firing. I am told that the police have located machine gun nests on the tops of all the principal buildings. A great number of soldiers from the Volynski regiment have mutinied and killed their officers. Yesterday's posters are covered up with a new lot. To-day we are informed that all workmen who remain away from their respective jobs will be sent to the front at once. The strike must be stopped. At noon I saw a seething mob of men and women running down Nevsky prospect headed by a collection of soldiers waving swords and banners. They were crying 'Down with Nikolai!', 'Down with the Government!', 'Give us bread!', 'We are the masters!', 'Down with the police!' Then I knew that the Russian Revolution was a reality.

It is a Revolution carried on by chance. There is apparently no organisation, no particular leader – just a city full of hungry people who have stood enough and are ready to die if necessary before they will put up with any more Tsarism. As I watched that mob of screaming people I thought of the tired, far-away look in the Tsar's eyes. He must have known that the dry rot had eaten the heart out of things. What a chance for a smart organiser, someone who really has the fortunes of these hundred and seventy millions of Russians at heart. No-one seems to know where the Tsar is. Some say that he has committed suicide and confessed to the most extraordinary crimes against the people.

The slaughter in the streets to-day was unbelievable, I can understand men being killed, but women and children – no. The Astoria Hotel has been practically ruined and many officials with their entire families have been killed. They are said to have suffered terrible deaths. My friend who lives at the Hotel du Nord was wounded yesterday by a stray bullet. It seems that when these folks are shooting at you, you are quite safe, but God help the innocent bystander who is not being shot at. He will get potted. The Pathé movie man is sticking on the job and shooting some of the scenes whenever he can without running a risk of losing his camera.

From Edward Heald's letter to his wife, dated 16 March 1917:

Monday, March 12, was the great day that suddenly sounded the knell of the old regime, though we were slow to realize what was taking place. It was quieter on the Nevsky than the day before. I walked up the Prospect to the Sadovaya at noon and saw nothing exciting though the banks and most of the business places were closed. The center of the action Monday was on the other side of the city, three or four miles from our office, in the region of the American Embassy, the Mavak, the Liteiny, and the Finland Station.

Mr. Harte, who always treated our predictions of a revolution with a smile saying that nothing of the sort would happen, was still planning to go to Sweden the next morning. Penn Davis had to go through the trouble zone this Monday morning to complete passport arrangements and secure documents for Mr. Harte and himself. When he arrived at the Liteiny Prospect, he found barricades and was stopped by the strikers who had some student soldiers with them. After showing his American passport and explaining his business, he was allowed to go on and got back all right.

During the day the sound of firing became louder in our part of the city. Neither Baker nor I understood what was taking place when we started over to the Narodni Dom after tea that evening to hear Shaliapin in *The Roussalka*. There was an atmosphere everywhere of excitement, uncertainty, and danger. Volleys and shots started at every crossing and corner. Around the Winter Palace Square people clung to sides of buildings, and if they came to street intersections where they had to cross, they darted across. The gloomy, somber red buildings seemed to be sitting in judgement on the country's doom.

When we reached the middle of the Nikolaievsky Bridge over the Neva, we stopped on the high middle and looked back over the city. We saw flames rising over the Liteiny region, which we afterwards learned were burning law courts. Machine guns were keeping up an incessant rat-a-tat-tat in a dozen different quarters of the city. It was particularly loud in the direction of the Narodni Dom. At the further end of the bridge was a squad of soldiers forming a line across. I went up to the officer and asked if there was any objection to our proceeding on to the Narodni Dom. He asked for passports and when I showed them he said, 'All right.' As we neared the bridge over the Little Neva, a little further on, another squad of soldiers stood facing us. When we were about fifty paces off, the crowd of women and working people in front of us broke and ran, and looking ahead we saw the guns raised in our direction. We immediately reversed our direction, and while we didn't run, we never walked faster until we put a building between us and the raised guns. We decided to hear Shaliapin some other evening. Later we learned that no performance was held at the Narodni Dom that night.

We saw no policemen during this walk. It was the first time that they had not been on the streets in the center of the city. We haven't seen any since. They disappeared from the streets late that afternoon.

The real surprise awaited Baker and me when we got back to Mr. Harte's room at the Grand Hotel. He had given up his trip to Sweden the next morning. But not until he and Day had taken a trip to the station that had been full of thrills. They had loaded the trunks and baggage on one of the high freight-carrying sleds, known as lomoviye, to take to the station for checking purposes the night before the train leaves, according to the Russian custom. As their lomoviye passed the big square in front of the Winter Palace, they were fired upon. As they continued down the narrow Millio-naya Ulitza, they were fired upon again. They ducked their heads, and Mr. Harte prayed while George used his Russian on the driver to speed him up. The driver didn't need any coaxing. They arrived at the Liteiny Bridge only to be surrounded and held up by a crowd of about a hundred fifty strikers, students, and soldiers. The leader was a student. The strikers thought that Harte and Day were trying to take ammunition over the river to the enemy and demanded that the trunks be opened for search. There were these two Americans standing up on the high sled with the crowd of revolutionists thronging around them from every side. What Mr. Harte feared most was that some of the Czar's cavalry or police would suddenly appear on the scene and proceed to fire upon them in which case Mr. Harte and George, standing high above the crowd, would be the best targets.

Another thing was troubling Mr. Harte. He had forgotten to bring one of the trunk keys which he had left with Penn Davis at the hotel. What would the strikers think when he told them that he did not have the key? But he had one of the keys and opened the trunk it fitted. After carefully searching it, the mob was satisfied and did not ask to look in the other trunk. They provided an escort of soldiers to conduct him to the station. As soon as they got their trunks off the lomoviye at the station, the driver disappeared with his horses and sled. Then Mr. Harte could find no one to take charge of their baggage. The customary crowd of porters was nowhere in sight. No officials were to be seen. The platform was almost deserted. Finally a lone official appeared who looked at the Americans in wonderment and told them that there would be no train in the morning; that the officials had been disarmed by the strikers; that no one was in authority; and that there was no one to look after their trunks.

It was in vain that Mr. Harte and Day searched for another vehicle of any kind to take them and their baggage back to the hotel. They were almost giving up hope of finding a place to store their baggage when a man appeared who showed them a closet where they could lock their things up. It was characteristic of Mr. Harte that the excitement did not keep him from seeing to it carefully that his wardrobe trunk was set up in the right position, doubtful though it was that he would ever see it again. Then he and Day walked the four miles back to the hotel, arriving there shortly before we returned. Mr. Harte was ready to acknowledge that the situation was serious. Half of the area that he had been through was in the hands of the strikers.

The next big surprise awaited us at ten o'clock when Day and I returned to our apartments. A Russian sailor was there, who was a friend of Madame Stepan. He gave us the astounding news that the old government was overthrown, that a new government had been established with a committee of twelve at its head responsible to the Duma, and that the entire city was in the hands of the revolutionists, excepting the police districts which were all under the fire of the revolutionists. He lived in the Morskaya Police District. Most of the soldiers had already gone over to the strikers, and the people and the others were rapidly following suit. Not until then did we realize that we were in the midst of the great revolution that so many of our friends had talked about and dreaded.

One of the pieces of information which our marine friend gave us, which was later verified, was that the same Monday morning the Czar had appointed Minister Protopopov dictator, ordering the dissolution of the Duma. But the Duma ignored the orders of the Czar and immediately went into executive session, thus defying the Czar and his government. That was the point where the real revolution began.

Our marine friend said that he could not get home on account of the siege against the police district near his home. He said that most of the firing then going on in the city was at the police districts and also by boys who had secured firearms and were shooting them off in the air for sport. Crowds of sailors and strikers were holding jubilee meetings over the city, as comrades in a common cause, adopting the red flag of the revolution. Officers who stood by their oath of loyalty to the Czar were being arrested. One of the first efforts of the revolutionists was to clean out the Police Department, and the lives of the police were unsafe if seen on the streets. The wrath of the movement seemed directed chiefly toward this institution, the records of which were dumped out of the windows on to the streets and sidewalks below and burned. Russians with whom we talked called the police system a treacherous German institution that had been foisted upon the people back in the time of Peter the Great and used as an instrument to keep the masses in ignorance and bondage ever since.

The next piece of news came when Burri arrived home at midnight. He and Gott met an officer in the block in which our apartments are located. Across the street is the building of the War Ministry. This officer asked Burri and Gott if they were English. They replied that they were Americans. The officer replied 'Good,

I also foreigner. I Finnlandsky. Tomorrow that building is ours,'
pointing to the War Ministry. He spoke in Russian and Burri and
Gott knew just enough of the language to guess that he said that
they were going to blow up the building. We accordingly wondered
as we turned in that night whether we would be awakened by
an explosion. The Finn was as happy as a boy. Immediately after
talking with Burri and Gott, he went over to the building and
passed into the court between lines of soldiers who evidently held
the building for the revolutionists.

A half hour after midnight, Eric Christensen came home. Ordi-
narily he is very calm, but this time he was dancing and shouting
with excitement. He had just shaken hands with a couple of men
who had been released from the famous Peter and Paul Fortress.
Both the prisoners were Finns. They had a thousand rubles each,
furnished by some Finnish revolutionary committee, to pay their
expenses home. The fortress had been taken by the soldiers that
evening, and all the prisoners who were there for political and
religious reasons were released, including nineteen soldiers who
had been imprisoned during the last few days.

It was hard to shake off enough of the excitement that night to
get to sleep.

13 MARCH 1917 (TUESDAY)

From Henry Keeling's narrative:

Very early [in the] morning I was awakened by wild shouts of joy
from the populace, mingled with near and distant shooting. Above
everything could be heard the cry, 'We have taken the fortress of
Peter and Paul', everybody shouting it out. Excitement was continually at fever heat as the name of one regiment after another was
given who had come out openly on the people's side. When it was
definitely known that the Cossacks had come over, the enthusiasm
reached its climax. . . .

Many of the streets were quite impassable owing to the great
crowds of soldiers and workmen, all armed, who were going about
looking for the hiding-places of the police and well-known supporters of the old régime. Every few minutes the crowds opened out to
let through motor cars and lorries filled with soldiers, workmen,
and even boys, all armed to the teeth and waving red flags who
were rushing off to take part in the 'siege' of one or the other
police stations which had not yet capitulated.

18 D

PRINCE EDWARD   CZAR NICHOLAS II.   PRINCE OF WALES
THE CZAREWITCH.

DEBENHAM & SONS,
COWES.

ROTARY PHOTO, E.C.

1 Tsar Nicholas II and the Prince of Wales with their respective sons, 1909

ЕГО ИМПЕРАТОРСКОЕ ВЫСОЧЕСТВО НАСЛѢДНИКЪ
ЦЕСАРЕВИЧЪ И ВЕЛИКІЙ КНЯЗЬ АЛЕКСѢЙ НИКОЛАЕВИЧЪ.

42.

2 Tsarevich Alexis: 'His Imperial Highness Tsarevich Heir and Grand Duke,
Alexei Nikolaevich'

Е. И. В. Вел. Кн. Елисавета Ѳеодоровна

Начальница Мароо-Маріинской обители въ Москвѣ.

grand Duchess Elisabeth.

3 The Grand Duchess Elizabeth as abbess of the Convent of Saints Martha and Mary in Moscow, c. 1910

4 Grigory Rasputin

Петроградъ.   Германское посольство и Маріинская площадь.

WINTER PALACE, ST. PETERSBOURG.

5 The German Embassy and Mariinsky Square

6 Postcard of the Winter Palace

7 The Nevsky Prospekt in July 1917

8 The Astoria Hotel

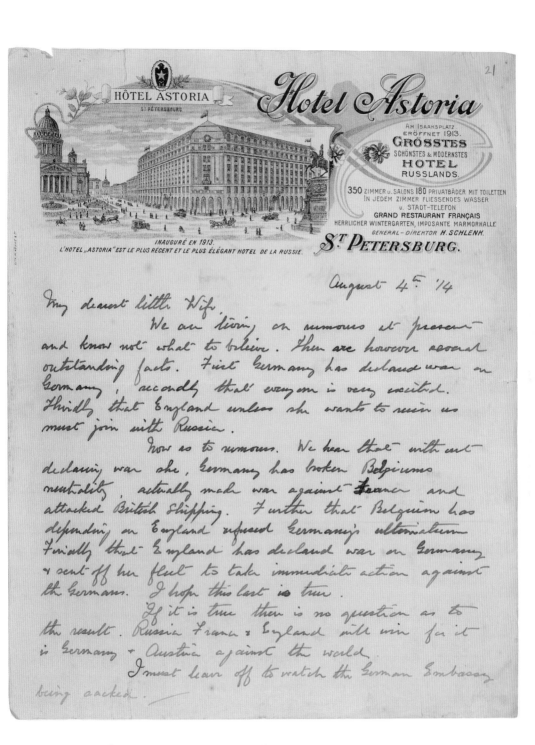

HÔTEL ASTORIA
ST-PÉTERSBOURG

Hotel Astoria

AM ISAAKSPLATZ
ERÖFFNET 1913.
GRÖSSTES
SCHÖNSTES & MODERNSTES
HOTEL
RUSSLANDS.

350 ZIMMER u. SALONS 180 PRIVATBÄDER MIT TOILETTEN
IN JEDEM ZIMMER FLIESSENDES WASSER
u. STADT-TELEFON
GRAND RESTAURANT FRANÇAIS
HERRLICHER WINTERGARTEN, IMPOSANTE MARMORHALLE
GENERAL-DIREKTOR H. SCHLENK.

INAUGURÉ EN 1913.
L'HOTEL „ASTORIA" EST LE PLUS RÉCENT ET LE PLUS ÉLÉGANT HOTEL DE LA RUSSIE.

St PETERSBURG.

August 4ᵗ '14

My dearest little Wife,

We are living on rumours at present and know not what to believe. There are however several outstanding facts. First Germany has declared war on Germany, secondly that everyone is very excited. Thirdly that England unless she wants to ruin us must join with Russia.

Now as to rumours. We hear that without declaring war she, Germany has broken Belgiums neutrality, actually made war against ~~France~~ and attacked British Shipping. Further that Belgium has depending on England refused Germany's ultimatum Finally that England has declared war on Germany & sent off her fleet to take immediate action against the Germans. I hope this last is true.

If it is true there is no question as to the result. Russia France & England will win for it is Germany + Austria against the world.

I must leave off to watch the German Embassy being sacked.

9 Letter from Arthur Marshall to his wife, 4 August 1914, written while he was staying at the Astoria Hotel

10 Postcard written the day after Nicholas II's abdication on 3 March 1917

11 Postcard with the caption 'National Funeral for the Victims who died for Freedom, 23 March 1917, Petrograd'

12 Postcard of the Winter Palace and the Admiralty

13 Postcard of the Peter and Paul Fortress, 1902

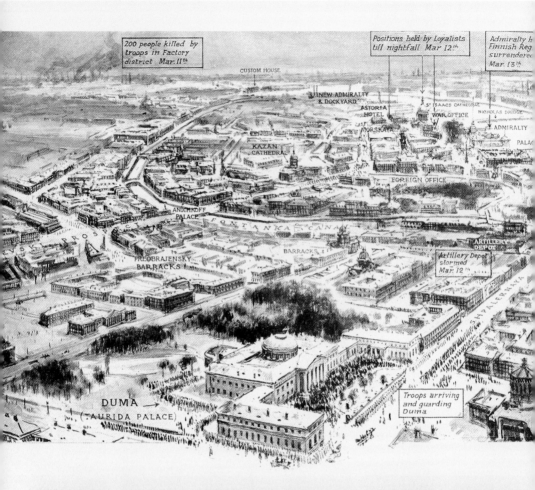

200 people killed by troops in Factory district Mar. 11th

CUSTOM HOUSE

Positions held by Loyalists till nightfall Mar. 12th

Admiralty h Finnish Reg surrendere Mar. 13th

NEW ADMIRALTY & DOCKYARD

ASTORIA HOTEL

ST ISAACS CATHEDRAL

NICHOLAS BRIDGE

WAR OFFICE

ADMIRALTY

MORSKAYA

PALAC

KAZAN CATHEDRAL

FOREIGN OFFICE

ANICHKOFF PALACE

FONTANKA CANAL

ARTILLERY DEPOT

BARRACKS

NEVSKY PROSPECT

PREOBRAJENSKY BARRACKS

Artillery Depot stormed Mar. 12th

SHPALERNAYA

DUMA (TAURIDA PALACE)

Troops arriving and guarding Duma

M. Rodzianko

Mikhail Vladimirovich Rodzianko is fifty-seven years of age. Before the Tsar granted a Constitution he was Marshal of Nobility for his province. He was elected President of the Duma in 1912

M. Gutchkov

M. Gutchkov is a Russian of Moscow, and before the revolution was engaged in energetic organising work. His ability and strength of character are everywhere recognised

The Grand Duke Cyril

The Grand Duke Cyril Vladimirovich commanded the Sailors of the Imperial Guard, and his accession to the national cause was an important factor in the success of the revolution

Prince Yuri Lvov

Prince Yuri Lvov has been President of the Alliance of Zemstvos (Local Parliaments), and to his exertions Russia owes all that was effective in the organisation of hospitals and supplies

Prince Yussupov

With the name of Prince Yussupov is inseparably connected the strange story of the removal of the notorious Rasputin. He is connected by marriage with the Grand Duke Michael

Dr. Shingarev

Dr. Andrei Shingarev is one of the members for Petrograd. He is well known as a student of economic questions, and his appointment as Minister of Agriculture is evidence of his reputation

14 Map of Petrograd from *The Sphere*, 24 March 1917

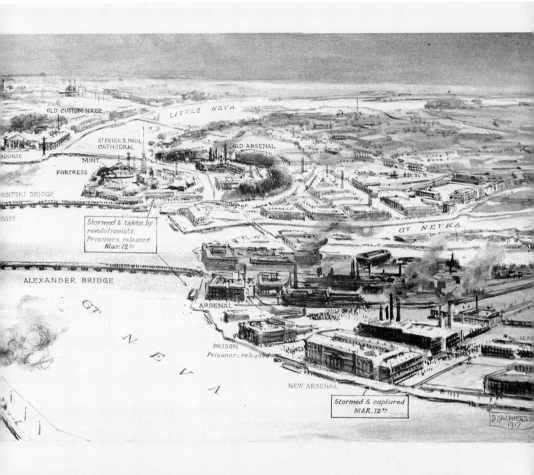

M. Protopopov

M. A. D. Protopopov was Minister of the Interior at the time of the revolution, and is believed to have deliberately provoked an outbreak by starving Petrograd in order to quell disaffection in blood

M. Goremykin

M. Goremykin, an old bureaucrat and Court official, was at one time President of the Council of Ministers. He was a typical reactionary of the old school, and the revolutionists did not leave him long at liberty

M. Bark

M. P. Bark had been during the greater part of the war Minister of Finance, with, so far as is known, considerable success. He has shared the fate of his colleagues : but the precise charges against him are unknown

General Rennenkampf

General Rennenkampf headed the army which gained the Battle of Gumbinnen in 1914, but was later removed from command. He is bitterly hated for his cruelty and overbearing habits, often shown during internal troubles

General Sukhomlinov

General V. A. Sukhomlinov was War Minister until the Russian disasters in 1915. He was tnen superseded and inquiries made into his administration, which resulted in his disgrace. His execution has been fiercely demanded

Prince Golitzin

Prince N. D. Golitzin was the last of the reactionary Prime Ministers of the Court clique. He is a bureaucrat of the old school, but has not otherwise a bad reputation ; in fact, he was regarded as a good administrator

15 Portraits of the main representatives of the Provisional Government from *The Sphere*, 24 March 1917

16 Cover of Florence Farmborough's book *Nurse at the Russian Front*

17   Cover of Rodion Markovits's book *Siberian Garrison*, 1929

Nicholas II as the Czar of Russia.
Hon. Colonel in Chief the 2nd Dragoons (Royal Scots Greys)

The

"GREYS"

20 for **1/3**
50 for **3/1**
100 for **6/-**
Of High-Class Tobacconists
and Stores everywhere

The Big CIGARETTE with the choice Flavour

SILK CUT
VIRGINIA

PLAIN, but good—big, yet easy smoking —"GREYS" meet to-day's call for *the real thing.* Smoked by men of thought and men of action.

Actual Size,
Round, not
Oval.

FOR THE FRONT

Post and Duty Free, and packed in Tins containing 50.
200 for **6/-** ; **500** for **14/-** ; **1000** for **27/-**
Place your Order with your Tobacconist now, and give him your card for insertion in the package.

Manufactured   by   MAJOR   DRAPKIN   AND   COMPANY,   LONDON,
Branch   of   the   United   Kingdom   Tobacco   Company,   Limited.

Printed by EYRE & SPOTTISWOODE, LTD., *His Majesty's Printers*, at East Harding Street, London, E.C., and Published Weekly by THE SPHERE AND TATLER, LTD., Great New Street, London, E.C.—June 9, 1917. Entered at Second-class Matter at the New York (N.Y.) Post Office, 1903.

18   Cigarette advert featuring Tsar Nicholas II from *The Sphere*, 9 June 1917

19 The Church on the Blood, Ekaterinburg

20 (*overleaf*) The Grand Duchess Vladimir Tiara, which was saved and sold by
Bertie Stopford after the Revolution

The hunt for the police was carried out with particular zest. No one was allowed to escape, they were generally shot or bayoneted on the spot. To get out of the range of a machine-gun I ran into a doorway and along a passage, almost into the arms of two policemen who were crouching with Brownings in their hands. I quickly dodged back, whilst the small crowd which followed me in rushed forward, and, discovering the policemen, shot them, afterwards flinging their bodies out into the street.

Near where I lived I saw that a police station was being besieged; very soon it was on fire and although the fire engines were only next door the crowd would not permit anyone to make an attempt to put out the flames. 'Smoke the dogs out of their kennels', they cried, and any unfortunate policeman who tried to escape was at once shot down by the revolvers and rifles of the crowd which surrounded the building upon every side. The wives and families of the police were allowed to come out, bringing with them a few of their treasures, but no men were allowed to escape their vengeance. Afterwards great bonfires were made of all the dossiers, some of which were burning for days, soldiers standing guard over them so that no one should be able to rescue even one leaf from the flames.

From Bertie Stopford's diary:

This morning between 9 and 10, as an orderly demonstration was passing by the Hôtel Astoria, a shot was fired from one of the upper windows of the hotel. The crowd immediately opened fire on the hotel, stormed the entrance and swarmed all over the building on every floor. None of the women was molested, but several officers were killed and the whole of the ground floor was completely wrecked ... From there I went to Potsdam Street to see General Fredericksz's house, looted and set on fire by the mob this morning. It was completely burnt out, only the outside wall remaining. Even their collie dog was bayoneted in the hind quarters. Countess Fredericksz only just got away in time. Returned to the Embassy. Great excitement – fighting in all the streets. Everywhere rifle and machine-gun firing, especially on the other side of the Neva. ...

Walked back to the hotel, keeping close to the houses for fear of being shot. So to bed and had just gone to sleep when the new military police came and made me get out of bed while they searched my rooms for hidden firearms. Interludes of rifle and machine-gun fire all night.

From Hugh Walpole's diary:

Revolution developed into full size. My thirty-third birthday! A strange way of celebrating it. Left about ten and walked to office. Streets crowded with orderly and very cheerful mob, all wildly cheering soldiers, who rush everywhere with red flags. First revolutionary paper published, announcing new Government, at head Rodziancko, Milyukoff,[57] etc. No signs of disorder anywhere except looting of Priestoff's houses. Arrived at office where I was joined by Dickinson. Much firing during morning, a machine-gun here. Afternoon got down with some difficulty to Embassy where I found everyone in deep depression ... Most unpleasant walk with D. by Fontanka. Firing all the way and we couldn't tell where from. Our street appears to be a particularly dangerous bit. Settled down, preparing to sleep on a sofa in the office when invaded by revolutionaries, who demanded to search building for police. Scene à la French revolution, French flag, bayonets, etc. All very polite. After they left, attack on our building – machine-guns, etc. At last to sleep.

From Bert Hall's diary:

The Revolution is now looked upon as a success. The people have killed off so many police and taken the machine gun nests that finally there can be very little resistance. The Fortress of St. Peter and St. Paul is the Revolutionists' Headquarters. All the political prisoners have been released. The courts of justice and the near-by jail houses have been destroyed and all the convicts released. All the prisons in Siberia have released their exiles. The streets are full of soldiers and Cossacks going to the Duma to take the oath of allegiance. I can't understand what they are taking the oath of allegiance to, but there must be a new organisation of some kind...

The soldiers march along with fixed bayonets and red flags or red kerchiefs attached to the bayonets. It is reported that some of the convicts want to go back to jail; they think life in the streets of Petrograd is too hazardous. I almost agree with them. There is a newspaper being published now named *Izvestia*. It is a single-sided sheet and tells its story in short cryptic paragraphs.

[Later] There was a fire in the street in front of the Passport and Criminal Records Bureau. All the records in Russia were destroyed.

This rumour about the Tsar committing suicide seems to be a well-founded one; but then there are rumours about everything. The prison of St. Peter and St. Paul is being filled up with ex-ministers and royalists.

From Edward Heald's letter to his wife, dated 16 March 1917:

Tuesday, March 13, dawned a beautiful clear day. We were awakened by volleys and artillery fire at an early hour, which increased in intensity. People hugged the courtways in the street below us, and if they crossed the streets, they did so with a dash. If they began to take to the sidewalks, a sudden volley would send them scattering for shelter. We were told that our dvornik (house-porter) had given orders to stay in that day.

At nine o'clock, however, I started out as usual for the office planning to stop at Mr. Harte's room in the Grand Hotel on the way. As I reached the end of the block, at the corner of Gogol Street and Vosnesensky Prospect, an imposing sight was before me. Directly ahead, a block away, the square opposite the Astoria Hotel (head-quarters for the officers) was full of soldiers. Down the Morskaya came column after column of soldiers, in martial order, greeted with the rousing shouts of the people assembled in the square in front of St. Isaac's Cathedral. The sun shining on the masses of soldiers made a brilliant spectacle. The soldiers stopped short when they came even with the statue of Nicholas, where they faced the Astoria Hotel.

Suddenly there was a tremendous volley and the sidewalks and squares were emptied of people in the twinkling of an eye. I was half way across Gogol Street when the volleys came, and I had that naked feeling soldiers are said to have when they go over the top. I wasted no time covering the remaining half of the street and was soon in Mr. Harte's room. While we stood at his window looking out on the street, soldiers began to come along the middle of the street leading officers to the Duma to swear allegiance to the new government. These were the officers who surrendered and said they were willing to swear allegiance to the new order. Some of them looked downcast and others happy.

During a lull in the fighting, I crossed the street to our office building and with some of the other secretaries looked down from our sixth floor directly on top of the Astoria Hotel roof at the end of the block, on the opposite side of the street, and on the fighting in the street and square in front of the hotel. We could see the marines lying down on Gogol Street in front of St. Isaac's shooting at the hotel. We saw several men fall, and some of them afterwards crawled off dragging a wounded arm or leg. The Red Cross automobiles came and went rapidly. The famous storming of the officer's headquarters was in full swing. More and more detachments of soldiers came along leading officers to the Duma. Some of the officers offered resistance and were killed on the spot. Others shouted 'We're for you,' and were allowed to keep their swords and arms and often given commands. At the height of the fighting we noticed a commotion on top of the Astoria Hotel roof. A machine gun had been placed there and the officers had begun firing down on the sidewalk below. It did not take long for the soldiers to spot the mischief and put an end to it with short shrift for the unfortunate officers.

While we were watching this affair from our windows, Burri and Gott had an exciting time down on the street. They were on the Morskaya under the Astoria Hotel when the machine gun began its work from the roof. In the rush for shelter Burri fell and had many a kick and cuff before he regained his feet. He said he got all the excitement he wanted that time.

We saw the soldiers smashing bottles of liquor on the sidewalks, and we saw the contents running down the street. We saw only a few soldiers carrying off or drinking the liquor.

The battle lasted about a half hour. By that time the soldiers had everything in their own hands, and the officers had flung out the white flag. This was the day of the private soldier. They told their officers to go home and stay out of sight until things were quiet again. The officers, having taken their individual oath of allegiance to the Czar, considered themselves more bound to it than the soldiers who took allegiance in groups. For the officers it was a great moral struggle, many of them being in sympathy with the revolution. Caught as they were in a situation where they had to make instant decision, there was a variety of reactions on their part, many paying with their lives for their hesitation.

The way the soldiers took things in their own hands was a revelation. They showed perfect confidence, tackled most difficult tasks with a practical efficiency and did all with a buoyant, smiling assurance and mastery that gave everyone confidence that they knew what they were doing. The 'children of the Czar' this day stepped forth as their own men and masters.

Probably the predominant impression that an American received from the events of the day was the self-restraint and order of the soldiers, as well as of the workingmen. There were cases of killing and bloodshed, and during the day many were taken to the hospitals; but considering the size of the revolution and the number of men and soldiers engaged in the struggle, the amount of bloodshed was small. Outside of the destruction of property in the police districts, the officer's quarters, and the homes of the suspected aristocracy, there was little looting. And this order was maintained despite the fact that there was an indiscriminate distribution of firearms to workingmen and boys. This was one time when prohibition was a blessing to Russia. If vodka could have been found in plenty, the revolution could easily have had a terrible ending.

One of the problems of this day were the snipers. The soldiers quickly handled such cases by bringing up an armored car or tank against the building from which the shots came and playing the machine gun upon it. Many of the police were in hiding, concealed often through the connivance of dvorniks, who formed a part of the old police system. The Hollingers had an exciting experience in their apartments. Shots were fired into the court from some upper floors. A group of fifty or sixty soldiers immediately came in and made a thorough search of every room at the point of a gun. The starshy (head) dvornik was almost shot, but was saved at the last moment by one of the captors who had an argument that had an effect upon the other soldiers.

The center of action was transferred from the Liteiny District to the Gogol and Morskaya District. We had the full benefit of it. In the afternoon the magnificent palace of Baron Fredericks, the German sympathizer who was the Czar's personal advisor and chamberlain, was in flames. It was in plain view up to the Gogol from our office and was completely burned out.

Towards evening of this day I picked up on the streets a news sheet entitled Izvestia, Number 1, of the Petrograd Soviet of Workers' Deputies, dated February 28, 1917, and calling upon the working-men of all lands to unite. It announced that the bourgeois system had been overthrown and the capitalistic class destroyed, and urged the workingmen and soldiers to elect deputies for a central labor council or soviet. This was the first printed matter that had appeared in the capital for several days. It was also the first announcement of, or by, the Soviet. The newspapers had all been closed since Friday. We didn't know what was going on in the rest of the world or empire. The wildest rumors were afloat. One rumor had the Kaiser overthrown and a revolution successful in Germany. Another had the Czar's army on the way from the front to put down the revolution. The discovery of five hundred machine guns on the roofs of the buildings in Petrograd, carrying an apparent threat of a St. Bartholomew's massacre to put down the revolution if necessary, did not dispel our nervousness. The minister Protopopov had ordered one thousand machine guns placed, according to report, but had only succeeded in getting five hundred up when the plan was discovered. The plan was for all the machine guns to begin playing upon the multitudes at the same instant, the signal for which was to be an airplane that would come over the city from Tsarskoe Selo. Rumor had it that the Czarina was to give the fatal order that would start the airplane, but that she lost her nerve at the last moment. Well, to pick up this red revolutionary bulletin on top of these rumors did not quiet our nerves. All restaurants and stores were closed. At night the streets were pitch dark and the street lamps not being lighted. It was a disquieting evening.

From Hugh Thornton's diary:

Serious news from Russia giving account of revolution in Petrograd. Mutiny in several Guards' regiments. At 4.50 wire received to effect that mutineers were practically in control of Petrograd and rifles are being handed out to the mob. Chief rather perturbed at last telegram...

14 March (Wednesday)

From Henry Keeling's narrative:

Near the Touchkoff bridge a policeman was caught by the crowd ... as he was taking his two little girls out for a walk. He was dressed in civilian clothes. It was a pitiful sight to see the two poor little children taken away crying whilst their father was being led away to be shot. This so worked upon my feelings that I became bold enough to suggest to one or two who were holding him that perhaps he was not so bad as some and might be allowed to go. Two or three took up the suggestion, moved, no doubt, by the children's tears, and after they had given the ex-policeman a number of blows over the head he was allowed to depart.

On another occasion I saw a lad standing and chuckling over the body of a policeman which was lying in the road. As I passed the lad turned to me and said, 'He chivvied me out of the market the other day; he won't do it any more.'

All the prisons were captured; I saw several burned down. The prisoners were first brought out, pale and trembling, and nearly all looking very ill. As they came out, they were asked by the crowd, 'What were you in for?' If it was a political offence they were cheered; many shook their hands and it was difficult to suppress tears on seeing some of the touching incidents. The kindliness was overwhelming. If the prisoner admitted having been imprisoned for some criminal offence, particulars were asked, and in many cases they were thrashed and told they would forfeit their lives if they were caught again. All were allowed to go. One poor fellow had been in prison twenty-seven years; when he found himself free he did not know what to do. He sat down on the snow and cried. Except for the killing of the policemen the whole atmosphere seemed to be one of an old world made young.

From Bertie Stopford's narrative:

Snowed all day. I heard no firing before 8.50. Streets quiet, but many soldiers walking about. . . .

I looked in at the Votive Church for the Emperor Alexander II's requiem. Only I and a few moujiks were present; last year the Court was there.

[To the Embassy from where] we saw quantities of troops crossing the Troitze Bridge, who turned along the quay in front of the Embassy on their way to the Duma to support the Government. In the night all the Krasnoe Selo troops, and all the Tsarskoe Selo troops, had marched or come in trains to Petrograd; also many of the Kronstadt sailors. There were batches of sailors marching about, mostly orderly.

[Learnt that new Ministers had been chosen.]

Knox told me at luncheon that Protopopov had had machine-guns out on all the corner houses of Petrograd, and that the troops had taken forty-four machine-guns off the roofs yesterday; but there are evidently still some left, for I had heard one close to the Ours at midday.

In the hotel I was told 3000 people had been shot in all. One wonders how many more the police would have killed unless the troops had joined the people!

From Hugh Walpole's diary:

7TH DAY OF REVOLUTION. Things seemed quiet in the morning, and there is obviously no question of a divided army. Another split however is occurring between the Duma Government and the red-hot revolutionaries, the former insisting on a regency, the latter on a Republic and Stop-the-War. This may be a very serious division for us. Lunch was interrupted by a lively battle in the street under our windows. Finally had to run down the street for my life, an unpleasant experience. Afternoon, much firing round us. Twice invaded by revolutionaries who insisted on searching our place as a policeman is hidden somewhere. Went down the Nevski to the France; wildly excited groups everywhere, women generally in the centre of discussion ... Garstin arrived from a massacred Astoria.

From Bert Hall's diary:

It is rumoured that the name Petrograd will be changed very shortly. Count Fredericks' household has been destroyed; his wife and another woman were found in the place alone and were beaten nearly to death. All the furnishings and valuables were either carried off or burned. Fredericks has been chief of the Tsar's domestic organisation for many years. Fredericks is a German of the Prussian type and the people hate him terribly. They mean to kill him if ever they lay their hands on him. More fires in the streets! The workers are burning up the wooden royalty insignia – eagles, crows [sic], etc. The Soldiers' Committee posted the city to-day in favour of giving up strong drink. Everywhere I looked there were signs asking all the comrades to refrain from liquor.

A Provisional Government has been formed. The names signed to the posters are Kerenski, Rodzianko, Milyukoff. I hear the people talking about two women who have just been turned out of Siberia. They have been in exile; one since eleven years. Their names are Katherine Breshkovsky,[58] known as babushka, and Spirodonova.[59] Spirodonova killed a Russian Governor named Lupjenovsky and did eleven years for it. The Governor apparently needed killing though. He was a brutal bastard, according to rumour.

Alexander Kerensky and Ekaterina Breshkovskaya (Catherine Breshkovsky),
the 'grandmother of the revolution'

From Edward Heald's letter to his wife, dated 16 March 1917:

Wednesday conditions became more normal. At 10:30 I started
afoot for the American Embassy. Cheering on the Morskaya attracted
my attention, and when I arrived on the street, I found a great
parade in progress: all revolutionists carrying the red flag and
the bands playing the Marseillaise. I followed the parade along
the Nevsky and shall never forget the wonderful sight. From the
Morskaya to the Liteiny, over a mile and a half, the great Nevsky
Prospect was packed with people from the buildings on one side to
the buildings on the other side.

The parade itself consisted of soldiers, officers, marines, and
workingmen all marching in order, and every division hoisting
the big red banners. The marching columns stretched from the
curbstone to the middle of the broad prospect. The spectators
packed the rest of the street, and a continuous deafening cheer
greeted the marching columns along the whole route. Now and

95

then armored cars darted along with soldiers armed to the teeth. I never expect to see a more thrilling sight in my life.

During the whole time I saw only one drunken man and heard only two shots fired. The order was wonderful. The people were not so much wild with enthusiasm as they were joyously, freely, intensely, spiritually happy. There was an exhilaration to it that was thrilling and indescribable. One felt that it must be a dream, that it was impossible that such things were happening in Russia. Well dressed people were in evidence and apparently as happy as the bent gray-haired workingmen who looked about with a dazed sort of happiness, while their faces shone with a rapturous glow. There seemed to be the best of feeling between the officers and soldiers.

When I reached the Embassy, I learned that the Czar was expected to be at the Duma that afternoon to proclaim a new constitution. The people at the Embassy thought he could still save his dynasty if he would grant the constitution and appoint new ministers who would represent the people. But the Czar never appeared. He let this last chance slip by. Sixty thousand soldiers at Peterhof this day gave their allegiance to the Duma. This same day Grand Duke Cyril [Kirill][60] went out to the Duma and tendered his allegiance and the service of the marines under his command to the new government. We also got our first outside telegraph news this day, to the effect that Moscow was also in the hands of the revolutionists. The struggle there had been brief and an easy victory for the revolutionists. The Mayor of the city was a liberal. The police took refuge in the Kremlin but had to surrender speedily.

While I was at the Embassy word came that Protopopov, the former Minister of the Interior, had surrendered. He had been in hiding with the other ministers of the old regime at the Admiralty since Monday. At 11:15 Wednesday, he appeared at the Tauride Palace, where the Duma meets. A student was at the entrance. Protopopov went up to the student and said, 'You are a student?' 'I am,' was the reply. 'I have always been interested in the welfare of our country,' said Protopopov, 'and, therefore, I come and give myself up voluntarily. I am former Minister of the Interior Protopopov. Lead me to whatever person is necessary.' The student led him to the Temporary Executive Committee. On the way the soldiers, recognizing him, gave vent to their indignation and threatened him, and when he arrived at the committee he was pale and tottering. Kerensky, the new Minister of Justice, pacified the crowd and prevented violence.

At noon this day the Admiralty passed into the hands of the revolutionary soldiers, and the ministers who had been in hiding either fled or gave themselves up.

On my way home from the Embassy, I saw armored cars racing through the streets filled with armed soldiers who were scattering bulletins. I picked one up. It was called *Prikaz* (Order) Number One, was dated March 1, and was signed by the Soviet of Workers' and Soldiers' Deputies, the uniting of these two groups apparently having taken place during the preceding twenty-four hours. This order called upon the soldiers not to salute their officers except when on duty. All titles were to be dropped. Soldiers could no longer be addressed by their officers with the familiar 'Thou' but only by 'Sir' and the polite 'You.' The day before (Tuesday) there had been no saluting, but during the big parade Wednesday morning saluting was general. With the appearance of *Prikaz* Number One, however, saluting stopped.

From Hugh Thornton's diary:

Worse news from Russia. Protopopoff's house sacked and that of Minister of Justice. Troops brought in from Moscow but many of them went over to the insurgents. Further troops being sent from the front. Emperor has put a General in charge of Petrograd and has ordered the President of the Council and other ministers to obey his orders. Emperor on his way back from Headquarters. Railway stations in hands of insurgents. Supplies held up. Imminent danger of Petrograd being starved in a few days if it continues. Buchanan (Ambassador, Petrograd) wires if rebellion is put down by force the material damage in Petrograd will seriously affect the war. Position appears to be about as bad as it could be. Buchanan states if only the Czar would get rid of some of the Ministers all might yet be well.

15 MARCH 1917 (THURSDAY)

From Bertie Stopford's diary:

Seymour came to see me and told me the situation was getting serious – not in the streets, which were quieting down – but amongst the Social Democrats, who were throwing printed inflammatory manifestos out of automobiles. We discussed, and he agreed to, a proposal I made to acquaint the Social Democrats of the Allied nations with the gravity of the position here, and ask them to telegraph their Russian comrades. We went down together to the Nevski, which seemed quite normal; people walking, but no traffic. . . .

He learnt of the Emperor's abdication at the Embassy, and went to the Foreign Office where he was told that the situation was 'most critical'.

[Heard] that the Empress has been placed under guard by a friendly officer, who thus prevented any question of soldiers or people molesting her. The soldiers of Tsarskoe Selo looted all the wine-shops, but next morning asked their officers to take them to Petrograd. The trains did not go yesterday to Tsarskoe Selo for the first time.

From Hugh Walpole's diary:

Things quiet again. Posters and leaflets everywhere urging a Republic, and one persuading soldiers not to salute their officers. That way ruin lies. At the Embassy in the afternoon. Everyone very nice and cheerful again. Ambassador has asked me to write the official account of the Revolution. Harold [Williams] there rather hysterical with forebodings of a Commune. Walked home. Outside the Winter Palace watched a procession, melodramatic riders with bare sabres and high caps on caracoling horses, leading eight policemen to be shot. A crowd followed but very quietly. Also saw a fine old general with a pointed beard very smart and aristocratic led off to prison, his hand on a soldier's shoulder. Very glad to get back. K. glad to see me. Spent the evening looking at drawings very happily.

From Bert Hall's diary:

Condition of Revolution same as yesterday, perhaps worse! Shooting everywhere – dead Russians everywhere – mostly dead policemen!

From Edward Heald's letter to his wife, dated 16 March 1917:

Thursday noon Zemmer showed up at the office. All his enthusiasm for the new regime was gone. 'Everybody is out for what he can get for his own profit,' said Zemmer. 'There is no patriotism.

Everything was beautiful the first two days, then differences arose and harmony disappeared.' Zemmer had been at the Duma the preceding day to swear allegiance to the new government, along with two thousand other officers. He was worried as to the outcome as out of eight thousand officers in the city only two thousand had shown up at the Duma. It was reported that a large number had gone out to Tsarskoe Selo to the Czar. Others were in hiding. Moreover there was a serious struggle going on between the radical revolutionists who wanted a social revolution and the conservative liberals who wanted a constitutional monarchy. Zemmer was afraid that they might split and give the old regime its opportunity to regain control. It was reported that a large army loyal to the Czar was on the way from the front to put down the revolution. Regarding *Prikaz* Number One, Zemmer said that it had been despatched with haste by the truck-load to the front and that it would ruin the discipline of the whole army.

In the evening we heard that the Czar's army had arrived from the front and was engaging the revolutionists in a great battle at the edge of the city near the Baltsky Station. Burri, Day, and I walked over that way but heard and saw nothing out of the ordinary and concluded that the rumor was false.

From Hugh Thornton's diary:

Long and rather tiring day. Grand Duke Michael (Czar's brother) is staying in a private house in Petrograd with a guard supplied by Duma. He sent for Buchanan. Buchanan asked whether he knew where the Czar was. Grand Duke said he was expected soon but later news came to hand saying his train had again been held up by insurgents. Grand Duke said he regretted very much that the Czar had not given way sooner as he had advised him to do. Insurgents appear to have complete control of the situation. Two Grand Dukes were presenting petition to Czar begging him to hand over control to Rodzianko and allow him to appoint responsible Ministers. If only he would do that all would yet be well. Empress received two representatives of Duma but we have no news as to what happened at this meeting. Troops brought in from the front appear to have gone over to insurgents. Chief thought news on the whole was better in so far as it seemed the insurgents were making a clean cut of the business. Buchanan says the organisation set on foot by the Duma is very good. No wavering about the war.

16 March 1917 (Friday)

From Bertie Stopford's diary:

[Skirmunt (Conseiller de l'Empire) told him the new government was] composed of the most intelligent men in Russia.

[In the afternoon he walked down the Moskaia where] Jewish students were pulling down the eagles over the shops and over the Yacht Club. ...

We heard the Emperor had abdicated for himself and his son (which is not legal), and that Michael Alexandrovich had refused the Regency ... [walked to the Winter Palace] where the Red Flag is flying and the eagles on the big gates are covered with red cloth. The big coat of arms is still on the large entrance gate. We then went on by the Millionaia to the Palace Quay. The flag of the Imperial Navy is now flying on the Peter–Paul Fortress in place of the Emperor's flag. From the Palace Quay we heard volleys being fired across the river. I afterwards understood it was the police being shot against a wall. ...

I never saw Petrograd look more beautiful – brilliant sunshine, a cloudless sky, and yesterday's snow not swept away.

From Bert Hall's diary:

Nikolai Romanoff the Second signed the abdication last night. (It seems the suicide story was all bilge.) I discovered this tremendous piece of news to-day through a friend of mine who is in the French Intelligence Department. A committee from the Duma called at Pskoff where the Tsar had been with general Russky and the Imperial Guards. The Committee demanded action and action in a hurry. So the Tsar, refusing to abdicate in favour of his son, left the throne to his brother Michael. They say that in the last moments the Royal Bodyguard deserted Tsar Nikolai. The city is plastered full of new posters. This time they tell the soldiers that they are free and that they are not required to salute their officers any more. This means nothing though, as most of the officers around Petrograd are already murdered. Nearly every soldier I have talked to says that he wants the Grand Duke Nicholas for Tsar. 'He is our friend', they say. 'He hated Rasputin and loved the people, the Mujik and the workers.'

I would say that fifty per cent of the soldiers are on their way back to their homes. They think that the Revolution constitutes a verbal armistice with the Germans. I saw a General murdered. He was in a railway station trying to get something to eat. Some soldiers were making remarks which he resented. The General sent for an armed guard to arrest the offending soldiers, but when the guard came they arrested the General instead. They took the old General outside and a crowd gathered around. The soldiers and the crowd looked at the General like half-witted people. Finally, someone said, 'What shall we do with him?' 'Let's hang him; he was once on the side of the Tsar!' And they hung him. He was a good old man, and one of the few artillery experts in all Russia.

A soldier said to me yesterday, 'Comrade, we should be living in the Winter Palace. It belongs to us now. It is our right. Indeed, it is our duty. Do you not think so, comrade?'

Another soldier offered me a brand new motor-cycle for 200 roubles. I could have bought a cannon or a machine gun for considerably less. They think everything belongs to them. I shudder to think what the Germans are going to do with this outfit unless some strong hand takes charge of matters and drives ahead toward an allied victory.

Tonight I heard some men saying the Tsar would be brought to Petrograd and marched through the streets for all the world to see.

From Edward Heald's letter to his wife, dated 16 March 1917:

Friday morning we were thrilled to see in the windows of the *Novoye Vremya* newspaper a bulletin reading that Nicolai Romanov (all titles removed) had abdicated at three o'clock that morning for himself and his heir, Alexei, in favor of Michael Alexandrovitch, the Czar's brother and next in line for the throne. Alongside it another bulletin read that Michael Alexandrovitch declined to accept the throne, stating that the people wanted a republic, and that he wanted to get back to the front where he belonged. The abdication of the Czar had been written on his special train near Pskov, after it had been shunted back and forth in vain efforts to elude the revolutionists.

With the appearance of the morning bulletins, the new Cabinet was announced. The new Minister of Justice is Kerensky, a socialist, and his first order was that any important papers or documents which were found in the Police Headquarters and were worthy of saving were to be transferred to the Academy of Science. He seems to know how to attract the attention and seize the imagination of the people. There was also appointed a new Minister, one for Finnish Affairs, to take the place of the old Governor General of Finland, who has been arrested. Also the man who was responsible for the new restrictive and repressive measures in Finland in 1905 is in custody.

In the same bulletins the Cabinet announces that it will be guided by the following principles: 1) full and immediate amnesty in all political and religious affairs; 2) liberty of word, press, assembly, unions, and strikes with extension of political liberty to those in military service within the confines permissible by military technical conditions; 3) abolition of all class, religious, and national limitations; 4) immediate preparations to convoke on the basis of universal, equal, direct, and secret suffrage, a Constitutional Assembly which will establish the form of administration and constitution; 5) substitution of national militia in the place of police, with elected leaders and subject to local administration; 6) elections to local administration on the basis of universal suffrage. On the following day a proclamation was issued removing all restrictions from the Jews.

On Friday the old flag of Russia was replaced by the red flag in all quarters of the city. Soldiers were busy all day pulling down the coats of arms of the old regime, including those on the Winter Palace. The Singer Sewing Machine Building protected the American eagle on its top by having it wrapped in the American flag, but all other eagles in the city came down.

Little Alexander, our office boy, when asked what he thought of the revolution, said 'Czarya ne nado' (No need of a Czar).

From Hugh Thornton's diary:

The news from Buchanan yesterday that the Czar had abdicated (which was announced in the House by Bonar Law on the adjournment last night) was today contradicted by a further telegram from him to the effect that his former wire was a mistake. The fact was that the abdication of the Czar was announced by the President of the Duma as an action which they would insist upon. The truth appears to be that no-one knows where the Czar is at present ... Chief rather depressed at situation today. He thought Czar might be dead. On the other hand, he very much doubted whether the new regime would be stable. He rather expected it would fall within a week although its personnel was admirable from our point of view. Buchanan in a further wire referred to the Socialist anti-war party which was beginning to assume threatening attitudes and to demand a Republic. Stayed at office till 9.30 pm but no further news came through.

17 MARCH 1917 (SATURDAY)

From General Knox's diary:

I walked to see the Ignatievs.[61] He was very pessimistic. He told me that the Preobrajenski Battalion had elected three commanding officers in a single day, and one of them was an ex-suisse from the Sergievskaya Street. The commander nominated by Rodzianko had been placed under arrest by the men. Ignatiev said: 'I have served with the troops for thirty-two years, and they can say what they like, but they will never be able to discipline these men again.' I fancy the Government understands this, but it is desperately afraid of bringing matters to a head; and besides, it has no power. Ignatiev took me to the window and pointed out the barricade in the Liteini, saying that Guchkov had ordered its removal, but the men had refused to comply. Poor Countess Ignatiev gave me her jewellery in a parcel and letters to send to her mother and children in Switzer-land if the worst happened. I am sorry for them, and tried to cheer them, but it was difficult to pretend that they are in no danger. . . .

Lavergne[62] tells me that the commander of a brigade due to embark for France in a month came to him to-day and said that of the 3,500 men he had at Peterhof only fifty remained; about 1,000 were in Petrograd doing nothing, and some 2,000 had probably gone home!

Another colonel told him that his men were being corrupted fast by socialist or anarchist speakers.

From Bertie Stopford's diary:

Deep snow fell in the night; still snowing hard, with high wind. I found a sledge at the door and drove to the Embassy. Flurries of snow – almost impossible to see. Lady Georgina [Buchanan] gave me some sardines and jam, there being nothing to eat at the hotel. . . .

There have been no arrests maintained of those who were not directly responsible for reactionary politics. In Moscow they say only two people were killed. . . .

I walked home at midnight up the Nevski – everything quite peaceful. On the windows of the newspaper offices was posted up in large letters 'Nikolai Alexandrovich Romanov has left for Livadia'. How are the mighty fallen!

From Hugh Thornton's diary:

Chief still sceptical as to whether new Russian Government will last. Buchanan wired that Emperor had agreed to abdicate in favour of his brother Grand Duke Michael. Long report from General Hanbury-Williams to C.I.G.S. giving a text of a letter which he had sent to the Czar on his own initiative practically urging him to abdicate. He attempts to justify his action on the ground that it was urgently necessary to bring things to a head as war preparations were being affected.

18 MARCH 1917 (SUNDAY)

From Bertie Stopford's diary:

After luncheon alone at the hotel I decide to go to Tsarskoe Selo and drove to the station. The train was very full. When I arrived I took a sledge and drove along the long avenue and crossed the Petrograd *chaussée* by the old fountain and went through the Convoy Cossacks' quarters to the Feodorovski Sobor, where I have so often been to services with the Emperor and his family. I heard there had been much fighting here, but all was quite quiet now – like any other Sunday. The streets everywhere were full of soldiers and the public. Before the church I stopped and got out. A child on skis was playing in the snow; the trees sparkling in the brilliant sunshine. I then continued by the road along which the Emperor comes from the palace to the church. The roadway, cleared of snow, was as well kept as before. My old friend who sweeps the leaves was not at his corner, but the mounted Cossacks were in their places, and the usual policeman at the park gate – which is rarely or never used – and at the palace gate three policemen in their gray uniform; each of them had a white armlet.

[Visited Prince Paul] *énervé mais pas abbatu*. He told me that it was he who had announced to the Empress that the Emperor had abdicated – that she had known nothing whatever – that the little boy and the two younger daughters had quite got over the measles

– that the Grand Duchess Olga had bronchitis as well as measles, and Grand Duchess Tatiana was also very ill.

From Hugh Thornton's diary:

> Ex-Czar will probably go to Crimea but will be got out of the country as soon as possible. Difficulty at present is that the idea of the new Government is to hold elections to ratify grand Duke Michael's accession. Buchanan pointed out this would be dangerous in middle of a war. Hanbury-Williams wires situation is better as regards output of munitions. There was, however, a great danger of mutiny in the Baltic Fleet which was, however, averted.
>
> [In a discussion with Milner] We both went into hysterics of laughter over the general chaos. Chief said 'Well, there's one thing, you won't have to bother me with many more papers if Russia goes wrong, because we will have to make peace at once which will be quite simple.'

As this discussion makes only too clear, Britain's primary interest was in ensuring that Russia continued to contribute to the war effort and did not make a separate peace with Germany. His subsequent diary entries illuminate the government's thinking.

19 MARCH 1917

> Czar has returned to Petrograd. He appears to be treated with every consideration but is not allowed to communicate with the outside world. Mutiny in the Russian Navy, two or three Admirals being murdered. But it seems to have been fairly soon put down. Buchanan says there are still practically two governments in Russia – the Duma Committee (Moderates) and the Labour Committee (Extreme). Hanbury-Williams, the General of the British Military Mission, appears to be playing an important part; he had 1½ hrs. interview with the Czar and promised to do everything in his power to protect him personally.

20 MARCH 1917

> Nothing further about the elections in Russia. Buchanan has been given authority officially to recognise 'de facto' Government if necessary without referring further to Foreign Office.

21 March 1917

News from Petrograd still fairly good except that French Ambassador lost his temper with Russian Committee because they would not use the phrase 'war à l'outrance' in their proclamation. Buchanan appears to be a great power there. The Committee hinted to him that he ought not to fraternise too much with the Royal Family. He replied that he was not in the habit of deserting his friends when they were in trouble.

22 March 1917

News from Petrograd not quite so good today. General Hanbury-Williams sends a long account of interview with Emperor. He appears to be taking a prominent part in affairs and does not appear to be acting much under Buchanan. Cabinet have instructed Buchanan that Hanbury-Williams is not to accompany ex-Czar to Tsarskoe Selo unless definitely ordered to do so. Buchanan also instructed to be careful about consorting too freely with Royal Family. Buchanan thinks revolution amounts to more than one month's delay in war in Russia. ... Small riot amongst the troops on the Northern Russian front.

23 March 1917

Rather disquieting news from Russia. Workmen's Committee having heard the Czar is thinking to leave the country have ordered his arrest. Cabinet decided last night to invite the Russian Government and his family here, we to see that he does not leave the country during the war.

25 March 1917

More disquieting news from Russia. Trouble in navy; also men seem to be out of hand on Northern part of front.

27 March 1917

Russian news still more depressing today. Hanbury-Williams wires that he has just received a memorandum from Alexeieff (Chief of Staff) saying that owing to the disintegration caused by the revolution Russia will not be able to start her offensive before June or July. Buchanan also wires in pessimistic vein. Respect for officers in Navy and Army is rapidly decreasing.

These were disquieting omens for the future, but by this time Petrograd itself had largely returned to a state of 'normal quiet'. The ambassador's daughter, Meriel Buchanan, noted that

> The streets were crowded with people all wearing red favours, red flags fluttered from all the houses. In many places the wires of the electric trams had been cut and broken by shots, and the trams were not yet running, nor were there yet any cabs to be had, and no motors were allowed to circulate without a special pass from the Duma. Low peasant sledges with straw at the bottom were the only means of locomotion, and one saw them filled with a strange medley of soldiers, well-dressed women, officers, and workpeople. The Imperial arms that hung over some of the shops were torn down and burnt. A crowd assembled on the Square before the Winter Palace to watch a red flag hoisted on the staff from which the Emperor's yellow flag with the Imperial eagle had been wont to float. And in all that silent crowd just one man clapped, while the others stood stolidly looking up at that scrap of red that fluttered against the sky, so small a symbol of an overwhelming change.

She also considered the future:

> And what was it the people wished? A Republic? The word they were being taught by the Socialist party who day by day were becoming more powerful. But how little the people understood it must be judged by the conversation overheard between two soldiers: 'What we want,' declared one of them, 'is a Republic.' 'Yes,' returned the other, nodding his head, 'A Republic, but we must have a good Czar at the head of it!'[63]

Nevertheless, despite concerns over what the future might hold, there seems little doubt that most Russians at this time would have echoed the thoughts of Nicolai Markovitch, a character in Hugh Walpole's novel of the Revolution, *The Secret City*. In this, Markovitch walks through the city's streets at the height of the Revolution and sees them 'filled with poor people, all free and happy':

> And here they were! ... with the snow crisp under their feet, and the sun shining, and the air quite still, so that all the talk came up, and up into the sky like a song. But of course they were bewildered as well as happy. They didn't know where to go, they didn't know

Soldiers leading a crowd on the Nevsky Prospekt – according to Stinton Jones
they are singing the 'Marseillaise'

what to do – like birds let out suddenly from their cages. I didn't
know myself. That's what sudden freedom does – takes your breath
away so that you go staggering along, and get caught again if you're
not careful. ...

Ah, what a wonderful evening that was! You know that there
have been times – very, very rare occasions in one's life – when
places that one knows well, streets and houses so common and
customary as to be like one's very skin – are suddenly for a
wonderful half-hour places of magic, the trees are gold, the houses
silver, the bricks jewelled, the pavement of amber. Or simply
perhaps they are different, a new country of colour and mystery ...
when one is just in love, or has won some prize, or finished at last
some difficult work. Petrograd was like that to me that night.

It was a day, in short, when 'the world was suddenly Utopia'.[64]

The February Revolution

A BOLSHEVIK VIEW

Interestingly, the view that the February Revolution represented a moment of almost unalloyed unhappiness was shared by Maxim Litvinov,[65] who, in an account of it written less than six months later, provided an assessment which has stood the test of time remarkably well:

It was not the capitalist middle classes who made the revolution. On the contrary, strongly as they detested Tsardom, they still more strongly detested the idea of a revolution, and none other than Miliukoff, the well-known leader of the Russian Liberals, publicly stated in the Duma, in reply to a taunt by the Monarchists, that 'rather than organise the country for national defence, if that should help the organisation of the revolutionary forces, he would leave her as she was,' that is, defenceless against the Germans. The utmost these classes were prepared to do was to depose the Tsar by means of a secret Palace revolution, and to put up another in his place who would drive away the Rasputins from the court and surround himself by better men 'enjoying the confidence of the nation,' that is, Liberals. For such a 'revolution' they, indeed, began actively to conspire with certain Grand Dukes and high officers when it became known that the court was intriguing for a separate peace with the enemy. But, happily, the masses of the people, acting spontaneously, forestalled them. They looked at the situation from quite a different point of view. They did not want to save the State of the Tsar and the capitalists. They did not care a jot for the conquest of Constantinople and Galicia. What they saw was that the Socialists had been right in denouncing the war as an Imperialist enterprise and predicting from it untold calamities. They saw in the Tsar but a worthy emblem of the war and of the capitalist State, and in striking a blow against him they were intending to strike a blow also for peace, for bread, and for liberty against all forms of exploitation.

The blow, as is well known, fell on March 12, and two days later the Tsar was no more. The women of the people, standing in queues in front of food shops, began the dance which soon developed into skirmishes between the police and the crowds in the streets. Then Cossacks were sent to make use of their whips, but they partly refused to do so and partly were met by soldiers of certain regiments of the Guards who took the part of the people. Street fighting rapidly developed, more and more regiments went over to the people, the arsenals were sacked and their contents distributed among the crowds, and, before anyone was properly aware, the capital was in the hands of the workers and soldiers. In vain did the Liberals send wire after wire to the Tsar, who was then at the front, imploring him to save the situation by dismissing his old advisers and appointing a new Government from their own midst and other persons 'enjoying public confidence.' While he hesitated and tried this measure and that, the people of Petrograd were acting, seizing one Government institution after the other, and setting up a Council of Workers' and Soldiers' Delegates (Soviet) as a sort of Revolutionary Convention, thereby compelling the Liberals, assembled as an executive committee of the Duma, to establish a Provisional Government and to proclaim the deposition of the Tsar. Of course, the Liberals did not want a republic, and, while deposing the Tsar, they at the same time appointed his brother, the Grand Duke Michael, to succeed him. But the Soviet and the people of Petrograd would not hear of any new Tsar, and the Grand Duke had to sign, simultaneously with the Tsar himself, an act of abdication 'pending the meeting of a Constituent Assembly.' An attempt was then made by the Liberals to establish at least a military dictator-ship, with a view to the further prosecution of the war, under the Grand Duke Nicolas Nicolayevitch, the former Generalissimo, but this, too, came to naught. Eventually the Liberals withdrew all opposition to the revolution, which now spread to Moscow and all provincial towns, meeting nowhere with any resistance, but being greeted everywhere with the utmost enthusiasm. Those were, perhaps, the happiest days in the history of Russia.

Nevertheless, Litvinov also considered that, owing to the absence from Petrograd of most of the Bolshevik leaders, the February revolution 'contained the germs of all future complications':

It must again be borne in mind that at that time there were practi-cally no Bolshevik leaders in Russia, and that most of the Socialists acting in Petrograd belonged to the more opportunist and wholly or partly 'patriotic' party of Mensheviks, with just a dash of that

Prince George Lvov

moderate wing of the 'Socialists-Revolutionaries' (a party of Peasant
Socialism and Political Terrorism, at that time small, but destined
to grow large in the near future), which under the name of the
'Group of Toil' formed a small body of Duma parliamentarians,
and counted as its leader Alexander Kerensky, a young, enthusiastic
barrister, with no political experience. When, therefore, the first
Soviet was formed, men like Tchkheidze,[66] the parliamentary
leader of the Mensheviks, and Kerensky became its natural heads,

and their followers constituted the main leaven of the new and inexperienced revolutionary organisation. This explains the singular circumstance that though the revolution was made by the working class and the soldier-peasants, and though the actual power was concentrated in their hands, the Soviet allowed the exercise of that power to pass into the hands of the propertied classes, as represented by the Provisional Government which had been appointed by the committee of the Duma. That Government had at its head a Prince Lvoff,[67] a colourless politician of the moderate Liberal school, and included, along with a number of 'Cadets,' Miliukoff, the Imperialist Liberal, as Foreign Secretary, and Gutchkoff, a gentleman of the same type belonging to the rich manufacturing and financial bourgeoisie, as Minister of War. Kerensky, who had never been a revolutionary and who had no authority among the masses, was the only representative of the new democracy in the Government, having joined it on his own initiative, though subsequently allowed to remain there by the Soviet. Tchkheidze himself, who was President of the Soviet, though invited to take a seat in the Cabinet, wisely declined to do so, being opposed to any coalition with the bourgeoisie. Such an opposition was perfectly correct, but one may ask, was it at all necessary that a bourgeois Government should come into existence? Was it at all necessary that the proletariat should abdicate its power in favour of a class which had been opposed to the revolution and which was well known to entertain totally different views on the war from those held by the great masses of the people? The action of the Soviet in shrinking from the assumption of Government power by itself at a time when it was omnipotent and the bourgeoisie was 'simply nowhere' constituted a disastrous blunder that can only be explained by the Menshevik infatuation with their dogma that the revolution was and must remain a 'bourgeois' one.[68]

This view that the revolution was 'incomplete' was echoed by Litvinov's predecessor as Soviet Commissar for Foreign Affairs, Georgy Chicherin,[69] who, in an article for the British Socialist Party newspaper The Call, wrote:

The Russian Revolution is a Janus. Imperialism exploits it all over the world, with its help fans war-imperialism in Europe and in America. In this action in Russia Imperialism operates with reminiscences of 1793, it mobilises intellectuals with their elaborate machinery of seductive ideas, honey-tongued Social-Patriotic imposters, old figurants of remote stages of the revolutionary development to whom the new problems are a book with seven seals. The future will show which force will be the stronger. Either it will be imperialism; in which case the result will be that a great new imperialist state will increase the number of existing imperialist states, the enthusiasms of the revolutionary movement will abate, the obsolete economic forms will soon dissolve, and a period of purely imperialist rule will have to be faced. Or the revolutionary class-conscious proletariat will be strong enough to withstand all the machinations of capitalism, will be the driving power of all the popular forces against imperialism; that will mean that a period of great revolutionary struggles will follow. The Russian revolution is a Janus; of its two natures which will prove the stronger? The rulers manipulating the masses or the masses opposing the rulers?[70]

'What a revolution feels like'

THE FIRST EYEWITNESS ACCOUNT
TO BE PUBLISHED IN ENGLAND

The consulting engineer Stinton Jones left Russia very shortly after the February Revolution, and was the first Englishman to have witnessed the events in Petrograd to arrive home in England. He subsequently wrote a number of articles in the English press relating his experiences, which were then syndicated all over the world. Under the headline

> What a Revolution Feels Like.
> Days and Nights of Terror in the Streets of Petrograd

he wrote in the *Daily Mail*:

> One morning a few weeks ago I left my home [in] Petrograd to go to my office, like a London business man living in a suburb leaving his house for the city.
> There was nothing in the daily paper to lead me to suppose that I was about to witness one of the greatest events in the world's

history; but when I got to the place where the tramway cars stop I found they were not running and that they had been derailed. The control handles had been taken away and the collector bows were tied down.

This meant that there was serious trouble coming; but I had seen it done several times during the riots and revolts which periodically occur in Russia.

On this morning I could not find a cab, so I decided to walk the five miles to my office.

On my way I noticed a very large number of mounted police and that crowds were collecting at different points.

The workmen at numerous works were on strike, and there was evidently going to be grave disorder. The shops were all open, and I was able to attend to my business in the ordinary way. I heard that there had been disturbances, but I walked home that night without coming across any trouble.

The next morning the postman called at the usual time. All vehicular traffic had ceased, and the tramway-cars had been removed to the sheds. Large numbers of Cossacks and police were patrolling the streets, but that was not remarkable.

What was strange was that the Cossacks seemed to be in a good humor and they were smiling at the people. We could not understand that.

Cordons of soldiers were drawn across the streets. They were unfamiliar-looking soldiers. As a matter of fact, they were police dressed up as soldiers. The effect was rather like what it would be if one morning Londoners found Metropolitan police in the uniforms of the Grenadier Guards lining the Strand, only, of course, it would be unfair to compare the genial London constables to the police of Petrograd.

The crowds were cheering and shouting, 'We want bread; give us bread.'

I was stopped and asked where I was going before I was allowed to proceed.

When I left my office in the Nevsky Prospekt there were vast crowds, and the Cossacks were galloping through them and guiding their horses so skilfully that nobody was hurt. That was a miracle.

I was in the crowd all the morning when the police fired and killed many people. Orders had been given that the injured were not to be removed, and doctors were forbidden to attend them.

Journalists working at the Duma after the February Revolution during a period of relative freedom of the press

The dead bodies were to be left where they were; the mortuaries were shut. All the shops were closed; no food could be bought. Fortunately, I had some provisions in my office.

I remained in the streets until midnight, and then I managed to get home. All this time, with the exception of the traffic, the other public services were going on as usual.

It was remarkable that during the whole time of the revolution the telephone system was not interrupted. The girl operators remained at their duties as if nothing serious was happening. When sometimes you failed to get a reply to a call, you guessed that it was because the wires had been cut by the bullets.

I came down early to the city on the Sunday, when there was much bloodshed. It is a weird experience walking through the streets in the midst of revolution.

When I came down on the Monday I was stopped at a bridge where nobody was allowed to pass. I got through by saying that I had an appointment at the British Embassy, and an officer told a soldier to conduct me there. From there I went by a roundabout way to my office, and heard the crowds had broken into the small-arms arsenal and armed themselves, and that the soldiers were joining the people. An armed rabble was parading the streets, firing indiscriminately. Every officer was stopped and disarmed. I saw one retired General – a grey, old man – stopped by a knot of civilians and soldiers. With a gesture he refused to give up his arms. Immediately he was struck down with the butt-end of a rifle and his body left lying in the snow.

That evening I decided to return to the house of a senator on whom I had called earlier in the day. On the telephone he told me that it would not be safe to return to my office, as the police were working machine-guns from the roof of the building, so I thought I would go to an hotel near a railway station. It was hopeless to attempt to get home. But to get to the hotel I had to pass this particular danger zone. The journey was accomplished in the company of my partner, Mr. Merrett, by traversing backstreets and standing in doorways whenever a fusillade of bullets came along. On our way we came across the dead bodies of men, women, and little children lying in the snow. In one church square I counted 15 dead bodies. Appalling sights like these were enough to make you lose your nerve, but your own personal danger kept you moving quickly and ever on the alert. By this time the new regime was so far established that the hospitals were all open and Red Cross cars were taking away the wounded, and all cars had been commandeered by the Revolutionaries.

In spite of all this vast upheaval we were able to sit down that evening to a meal in an hotel unmolested.

On the Tuesday we ventured to visit our office, although for all we knew to the contrary the police were still operating machine-guns from the roof of the building.

I was stopped because I was not wearing a red ribbon, but when I showed the Union Jack under my coat and explained that I was English there was a shout of 'Three cheers for the English.'

Just after we entered our office there was a tremendous fusillade. It was the machine-guns on the roof above us. The police were firing on the crowd below. A shot fired from the street crashed through our window and missed my partner by a few inches.

Very soon afterwards the door of the room was thrown open and in rushed soldiers and civilians, all armed. They presented their rifles and shouted 'Hands up,' and then searched the room for firearms. Satisfied that there were none, they withdrew. Within the next hour or two the door was thrown open on five different occasions by other parties of soldiers.

One man demanded that the safe should be opened, but when he was going to take the money he was reproved by another soldier, who said: 'This is an Englishman's office; they must be left in peace,' and no further attempt was made.

I was outside the Astoria Hotel when it was sacked by the Revolutionaries. The hotel had been taken over some months previously by the military as a residence for officers, and at the time was full of not only Russians, but also officers from the Allied Armies.

The crowd at first was only boisterous, but not dangerous, and demanded the surrender of all Russian officers, with their arms, and also all papers and records. While a deputation from the crowd was in the hotel a Russian General fired on the crowd from one of the windows, and at the same time a machine-gun opened fire from the roof, killing a large number of people.

Then the fury of the crowd was uncontrollable. The soldiers outside fired at the hotel and then rushed through the door. They broke every window in the place and smashed everything. The foreign officers were allowed to leave, and were supplied with motor-cars, but the Englishmen declined to go so long as there were women there. They remained until the crowd threatened to bring up artillery and raze the building to the ground. The Russian officers were all placed under arrest, disarmed, brought out into the street, and a number of them shot.

The General who had deliberately fired on the people was shot, and his body thrown into the canal. All documents found on the premises were burnt.

It was on this day that the Provisional Government issued its first newspaper. A car came by me and threw out a bundle of them, and we learnt of the happenings at the Duma.

Some of the English residents had terrifying experiences, for in the revolution, remarkable as it was for the splendid composure and bravery of the Russian people, there were bound to be groups of individuals who showed violence when there was no reason for it.

It must be remembered that with the political prisoners who were liberated when the prisons were thrown open were dangerous criminals, who secured firearms. They were subsequently disarmed.

After the soldiers had gone over to the people there began a great hunt for the police. They were shown no mercy and cleared out of their hiding-places and shot down instantly in the streets. Nobody attempted to remove the bodies. 'They are only fit for food for the dogs,' was the comment made.

I think one of the most impressive scenes of the revolution was when the news spread that several regiments of loyal soldiers were about to arrive from Finland to restore order and to clear the city. At once preparations were made to deal with them. Three 6 in. howitzers were placed behind a hastily-constructed barricade, and loaded, and trained on the bridge by which the newly arriving soldiers would have to enter the city. They also commanded the bridge from both sides by machine-guns.

When the troops came and they heard of the situation, they arrested all their own officers, and handed them over to the crowd. The new soldiers swelled the crowd, while the particularly unpopular officers were shot.

The same thing happened when two regiments of Siberian troops arrived at the Nikolai Station to restore order. The Revolutionaries at once gathered together a complete regiment of soldiers, who lined up in front of the station. At each end of the line was stationed an armored car, with its guns trained on the station. The Siberian troops were quick to declare their sympathy with the revolution, and their officers, after being disarmed, were allowed to go free.

Late at night strange motor-cars without lights would suddenly dash down the street and fire into the people. They were called the 'black automobiles,' and because of them people were asked not to remain out of doors after ten o'clock. Effective measures were soon taken to put an end to these intruders.

When the news came through that the soldiers all over the Empire were joining the new movement, and only a few of the police remained to be dealt with, the city became calm and the streets were thronged with happy crowds. The extraordinary spectacle of an armed mob of soldiers and civilians and small boys with a weird medley of weapons disappeared. The red flags flew from the public buildings, and in a little more than a week people were going about their ordinary occupations again just as if nothing had occurred, but with a new look on their faces.

One of the events I think which made us realise that the old regime was perishing was when walking along a street we saw great columns of smoke rising into the air. The Courts of Justice and the prison were in flames, and it seemed that the ashes that remained were all that was left of the old Russia.[71]

'The women became like savages'

EXPERIENCES OF A JOCKEY IN MOSCOW

The Australian jockey 'Brownie' Carslake had had an adventurous time since the outbreak of the war in 1914. He was riding in Vienna on the day war was declared and was subsequently forbidden to leave the country (although not interned). In 1916 he managed to escape, disguised as a fireman on the footplate of a railway engine, to still neutral Romania, from where he made his way to Russia, where, unlike in Britain, racing was still in full swing, although taking place under somewhat unusual conditions. He later recalled that

> The racing in Russia was a complete farce, anyway from the spectators' point of view. The authorities at first wished to ban it altogether, but eventually decided that their bloodstock industry, very important from a military point of view, would be ruined without it. They compromised by limiting it to Moscow alone, where we raced three times a week.
>
> Another strange thing about racing in Russia during the war was that the sport was conducted without any of the public being admitted. The rules and regulations were strictly observed, and the competition was keen, but instead of the large crowds that are an integral part of the sport all over the world, our only spectators were owners, trainers, and other jockeys.
>
> I shall never forget the strangeness of riding in complete silence. The meetings started at 8 o'clock in the morning, and finished at 11. There was supposed to be no betting, but I saw bigger sums change hands in private wagers than I have ever seen through the medium of bookmakers.

However, this strange calmness was soon shattered by the onset of the Revolution:

> I had not been in Russia a fortnight before the Kerensky revolution broke out.
>
> In Moscow, unlike Petrograd, it was a more or less bloodless affair, and most of the people of the racing community were strictly non-political and were unable to understand what the

demonstrations and meetings that were being held all over the town were about.

The whole revolution broke out in about an hour. There was no fighting to speak of, though hundreds of people, soldiers included, were rushing round the streets, seemingly raving mad, letting off their rifles and creating an absolute panic. The women, I believe, were the worst of all, for they became like savages, and tore around literally pulling off their clothes in their frenzy and waving flags and shrieking at the tops of their voices.

While spared most of the horrors, I saw some sights that literally sickened me. I was staying at the time at the Hotel Fvort on the Petrogradski Schoose, a big wide road that led out of Moscow. The morning following the excitement I was looking out of my window, and I saw about a quarter of a mile away, an ordinary farm cart passing down the road, which was lined with people, and I noticed a very extraordinary thing. As the cart went by, the people, standing beside the road, seemed to fall down, just as if they had been shot. I never heard a sound of any firing, and although there were several Cossacks walking beside it they did not seem to be molesting the population in any way.

I could not make it out at all, and I thought I would go down and have a look myself.

I walked along the road towards it, and it was not until I was about 20 yards away that I saw what was the matter. The cart contained about 20 bodies, all of them soldiers, and in the most revolting condition I have ever seen.

I discovered afterwards that they were Russian soldiers who had been caught raiding by the Cossacks and had been summarily dealt with in this fashion.[72]

Despite events such as these, Carslake and his fellow jockeys were left alone and racing 'went on as usual' until the Bolshevik Revolution later in the year.

Nevertheless, there were some subtle changes to the jockeys' lives. Also riding in Moscow at this time was the famous African-American jockey Jimmy Winkfield. Known as something of a dandy, he now

threw out the carefully selected suits he always wore to the track and dressed down... He deliberately sought out old clothes and kept them dirty. If he'd dressed as usual he would have been pegged as a rich man – the enemy – and thus subject to arrest or murder.

'Nobody bothered us as long as we stayed dirty and wore old clothes', he explained. 'But if we'd ever dressed up, they'd have figured we were aristocrats.' He had to remember to keep his finger nails dirty too. What worker ever had a manicure?[73]

'Never have I seen such perfect order'

BURYING THE VICTIMS OF REVOLUTION

On 5 April the victims of the Revolution were buried in a common grave on the Champ de Mars. British antiques dealer Bertie Stopford watched the procession go by:

> The burial procession of the victims of the Revolution in the Champ de Mars began to pass the end of Michail Street along the Nevski at 8.40. During the next three hours I saw only four coffins go by, and there were in all only twelve coffins in the procession which passed up the Nevski. An automobile with four people in it was in the procession; it contained the Grandmother of the Revolution.[74] Opposite the Municipal Duma three stripling Militia youth rushed up to it and stopped it. An officer who was at the head of the next company quickly walked up to them, very red in the face, stamped his foot, and ordered them off.
> The procession was organised extremely well in companies, and to regulate the distances between them there were men and women carrying small white flags who signalled down the line for advancing or halting. At times the procession would be on only one side of the Nevski, but generally there were distinct companies on either side who halted or advanced simultaneously. At the end of Michail Street seven or eight onlookers linked together and joined in behind the different companies. This I afterwards learnt had been allowed and was announced in the newspapers. I regret not knowing it, as I would have joined them.
> There were many bands; I only heard played the 'Marseillaise' and Chopin's 'Funeral March'. The people constantly sang a song with a simple, harmonious tune but sad, and from time to time the Prayers for the Dead were chanted. When the captains of the different companies gave the order all heads were uncovered. Some

Public funeral for the victims of the Revolution, with Prince Lvov and Miliukov among the mourners (*The Sphere*, 28 April 1917)

one in the procession called out to a man in the crowd near me to uncover.

The Peter–Paul Fortress cannon were fired for each coffin placed in the grave. I believe many of them were empty, the relatives and friends having already buried their own dead. Sometimes a single plank of wood was carried alongside of the coffins to represent another victim who had already been buried. The dead were not all carried together, but in different parts of the procession as they happened to come from different parts of the town.

Never have I seen such perfect order, not a procession or demonstration of people better organised. The proceedings from beginning to end bear striking witness to the self-control of the Petrograd populace. No trams, carriages or sledges were allowed all day. The procession went on until 5 in the evening.

The following day Stopford went to see the graves for himself:

I went this morning to view the common grave on the Champ de Mars, which is quite close to the Embassy. The coffins were still uncovered. I counted 150. I believe there were in all 168 – anyhow there were not 200. Cement was all ready to be put over them, and soldiers were placing planks along, across the coffins. A woman kneeling by a coffin, which she frequently kissed, was saying her prayers and crossing herself. I was surprised at no part being played by the clergy on the route, but heard afterwards that they had not been invited to attend, as they had allowed machine-guns to be placed by the police on several churches.[75]

'The capitalist must pay'

ADJUSTING TO THE NEW SOCIETY

In the weeks and months after the February Revolution observers noted the sometimes curious ways in which the Russians exercised their newly obtained freedoms. One of the first to do so was American airman Bert Hall, who on 2 April wrote in his diary that

> To-day I asked one of the chambermaids at the Hotel how the Revolution had affected her life.
> 'Well, Comrade', she said, 'the most trying problem is my husband and his two brothers. Before the Revolution they were mechanics and worked every day. Now they refuse to work, saying that the worker is supreme and the capitalist must pay!'
> 'What do your men folks do with themselves now that they no longer work?'
> 'They just sit', she said, 'just sit!'[76]

However, the hotels were not exempt from these trends either. The forester Edward Stebbing, who was in Petrograd during the summer of 1917, wrote that

> Amongst other classes of workmen who 'came out' after the Revolution were, of all people, the waiters and women servants of the hotels, etc., in Petrograd. They had the usual processions and banners inscribed – 'No tips.' It is a fact! Most travellers would have rejoiced to see it, though they would have deemed such an inscription incredible. But these people did not think so. They

were demanding equality in the management of the hotels which, according to them, now belonged to the servants as much as to the proprietors. They demanded a share of the profits and no tips. Before this, in the large hotels at least, they depended for their wages on tips, as is customary. During the period the waiters were 'out' the guests of the hotels had to make their own beds, so I was told, clean their own rooms, and downstairs, they had to fetch their own plates and other articles, and go to the kitchen to get their food, and, most objectionable task of all, clean their plates, etc., after the meal.

Stebbing was also told an amusing story of what happened to one particular street orator on the Nevski:

A woman Socialist, well dressed, was holding forth on the equality of all men and women, that all wealth should be equally divided up amongst all, and so forth... One of her male listeners... went up and said: 'You say we are all equal?' 'Yes', and she broke forth again into perfervid periods. Her interrogator waited patiently till breath failed the orator. 'And you say we should divide all wealth equally?' Again she agreed and started afresh. At the next enforced pause the man produced three roubles from his pocket. 'I agree with you', he remarked; 'you have convinced me.' Turning to a bystander, he asked him to change one of the roubles for him. He obtained two fifty-copeck notes. Facing the lady orator he said: 'This is all the money I possess. I will halve it with you,' and he held out the 1.50. She had to take it. She was about to commence her oration again when her questioner continued: 'No, no. How much have you in your purse? We must now divide that, since we are to share equally our wealth.' Reluctantly she produced her purse. It was opened and found to contain forty roubles. The spectators were now thoroughly enjoying the lecture. The forty roubles were carefully counted and divided, twenty of them being given to the man who had shared his three. He pocketed them, thanked the orator for her interesting discourse, and departed.[77]

Others told similar stories. The author of The Fall of the Romanoffs, known only by the initials 'W.B.', recorded the following:

A small boy sent by his mother to take his turn in the inevitable queue waiting for bread, endeavoured to use his diminutive size and slip unperceived to the front of the row. His manoeuvre, however, was noticed by a bearded mujik (peasant). 'Back, youngster, where are you stretching to? Your place is behind.' 'I am not a youngster,' retorted the boy, beating his chest with a small clenched fist, 'I am a free Russian citizen,' to the evident delight of the bystanders.

A country yokel was caught by the guard under the bench of a third-class railway carriage intent on taking his journey without paying for his ticket. The indignant guard dragged him out of his retreat and obliged him to descend at the next stopping place. Full of rancour at this enforced exit, the youth continued his journey on foot along the rails, brooding revenge. He was caught in the act of pulling out the sleepers which support the rails. The express train was expected and the impending catastrophe was prevented by a hair's breadth.

On being questioned as to his motives, the country bumpkin answered sullenly that he wished to be revenged on the guard who had turned him out of the train. 'But the accident would not have concerned him; this is another train with different guards.' 'Leave me in peace! What are you badgering me for? Liberty reigns now, and everyone can do as he likes,' was the unexpected answer of the fellow who had nearly caused the death and suffering of many travellers. His way of appreciating 'liberty' is, alas! not an uncommon one. Many uncouth minds share his opinion.

A gentleman is in the habit of taking his dinner daily at one of the best and oldest restaurants in Petrograd, where the same waiter always attends him. The habitué entered the restaurant a day or two after the great change. On seeing the waiter, the gentleman gave him a cheerful nod.

'How do you do, Simon?' he remarked.

To his astonishment the up-to-then obsequious waiter drew himself up to his full height and with nose well in the air, replied: 'I am no more Simon, I am Simon Ivanovitch now.'

'Oh, very well,' said the gentleman, as he seated himself at the table and prepared to eat his meal. On leaving the restaurant he politely went up to the waiter and shaking hands with him (without giving the usual tip), said, 'Good evening, Simon Ivanovitch.' The next day and the day following the scene repeated itself; the gentleman on entering and on leaving the restaurant shook hands with the waiter, adding invariably: 'How do you do, Simon Ivanovitch' or 'Good-bye, Simon Ivanovitch.' On the fourth day the gentleman was met by a deprecating waiter with the appeal: 'I am tired of being Simon Ivanovitch, I want to be Simon again.'

A lady's maid came to her mistress who happened be the wife of a Senator and a Princess by birth.

'We are equals now, Madam,' quoth the maid with an impertinent toss of the head.

'I congratulate you,' was the quiet reply of the lady, taking up her book and continuing to read.

When Easter arrived a few weeks subsequently, the lady, who had a large establishment, prepared the Easter gifts for the servants. She divided the allotted money into equal parts and putting each into an envelope wrote on it the name of the recipient. A few hours after the distribution the deeply offended lady's maid entered and, in a tearful voice, reproached her mistress for putting her on the same level as the laundress and kitchen maid.

'I could not act differently,' responded the lady, 'for you are all equals now.'

'There will always be a difference – the kitchen maid is not my equal.'

'Nor are you mine,' was her mistress's reply, 'and yet not so very long ago you pointed out to me yourself that henceforth we were all equals.'

'I see, Madam, that you evidently don't understand anything about the differences of position,' and the irate damsel flounced out of the room.[78]

Some scenes were less amusing, however. Henry Keeling noted a 'constant succession of lynchings'. On one occasion he was on a tram and saw a lady

who cried out suddenly that she had had her purse stolen. She said that it contained fifty roubles and accused a well-dressed young man who happened to be standing behind her of the theft. The latter most earnestly protested his innocence and declared that rather than be called a thief he would give the woman fifty roubles out of his own pocket. Nothing availed him; perhaps they thought he protested too much. He was taken outside and promptly shot.

The body of the poor fellow was searched, but no purse was found. The upholders of the integrity of the Russian Republic returned to the tramcar and told the woman that she had better make a more careful search. She did so and discovered that the

Postcard of the Fontanka river, Petrograd

missing purse had slipped down through a hole in the pocket into
the lining. Nothing could be done for the unfortunate victim of
'justice', so they took the only course which seemed to them to
meet the case and leading the woman out, shot her also.

Another time he saw three merchants who had been accused of
burglary thrown into the half-frozen Fontanka river, after which

> From the house where the burglary had taken place an elderly man
> rushed forth hatless and without his coat, crying that a mistake
> had been made. The real burglars had got clean away and three
> entirely innocent men had been lynched. In a moment the crowd
> had turned on the newcomer, and crying, 'No doubt he is an
> accomplice', seized him and threw him in after the others. When
> the crowd had partly dispersed several of us tried to get the poor
> unfortunates out. We managed to get two of the bodies out, one
> was that of the old gentleman. Later it was clearly proved that he
> was the owner of the house and had spoken quite correctly.

Keeling himself also 'had two very near squeaks … through being
close to people who were accused of theft, and only escaped once
after having been rather severely beaten'. He believed that this form

of summary 'justice' could be attributed to two factors: the first was
the abolition of the death penalty, 'which caused people to think that
there was no redress for wrongs done' and in particular that there
were no checks on 'social crimes', and secondly, there was 'a belief
that no-one had the right to commit crimes now that the Revolution
was a fact':

> Under the Tsar much might be forgiven, but nothing could be
> forgiven a man who spoiled the Revolution.[79]

And Bert Hall asked one soldier what the attitude of the Revolution
was towards the church:

> He said that God was out of the running at the present, because
> in the olden days God had been above the people and now that
> everyone and everything was equal, God was entirely discounted. I
> asked him what would become of the churches and the cathedrals.
> He thought they would be made over and used by the people as
> community homes.[80]

'Time is the tardy advocate of kings'

THE FATE OF THE IMPERIAL FAMILY

In the immediate aftermath of the Revolution Bertie Stopford paid
several visits to Tsarskoe Selo. On 24 March he noted that

> The Emperor is allowed to walk in the park, but always accom-
> panied by an officer. He sweeps the snow off the path to occupy
> himself. He has the face of a dead man, though his fine eyes still
> gleam; he shows no emotion at all – he has never shown emotion
> even during the most trying situations of his life. I grieve to write
> it of so good a man, but as Emperor, through all this terrible time,
> he has not made un seul beau geste. The Empress is quite calm. They
> are not separated as the newspapers say. Her evil genius, Madame
> Virbova, is ill with measles in the palace. She will be taken away
> under arrest as soon as she recovers.

And a week later he added that

> The Emperor is a fatalist. He is so pleased to be with his children, and to have the heavy burden of responsibility he had inherited from his father lifted from his shoulders, that he does not realise the great danger both he and the Empress will run when the State trials of the former Ministers begin. The uneducated masses will never be able to distinguish between the treasonable designs of the Ministers and the Emperor's unconscious acquiescence, or realise his great love of Russia. He thinks he will be allowed to leave as soon as the daughters have recovered. He would like to go to Norway.[81]

In fact, during the early weeks of the Tsar's confinement England seemed the most likely destination for the dethroned monarch, but, as diplomat Hugh Thornton's diary reveals, this was by no means as straightforward as it at first may have seemed:

22 MARCH 1917

> Provisional Government of Russia are anxious that ex-Czar should leave the country as soon as possible and suggest that he should come to England. Cabinet considered this yesterday and decided to wire to the effect that the Government as at present advised were not at all sure that England would be the best place for him. Had he considered Denmark or Switzerland. Provisional Government intimated that if he came to England they would like a guarantee that he wouldn't be allowed to leave during the war. Dowager Empress feared the journey.

23 MARCH 1917

> Rather disquieting news from Russia. Workmen's Committee having heard the Czar is thinking to leave the country have ordered his arrest. Cabinet decided last night to invite the Russian Government and his family here, we to see that he does not leave the country during the war.

24 MARCH 1917

> Hanbury-Williams wires Czar and his family are under arrest and he rather fears for his safety. FO to wire to the effect that it is essential that no violence should be offered to the Czar. They wire that he and his family should sail for England at the earliest possible moment.

25 MARCH 1917

Buchanan wires it will be impossible for Czar and family to come to England until they have recovered from measles.

14 APRIL 1917

Foreign Secretary instructed by Cabinet to inform Buchanan that they did not think it advisable that the Czar should be invited to come to England. They suggested the South of France or Spain (in the event of her joining the Allies) as a better place for residence.[82]

In fact, as is now known, it was King George V personally, rather than the British government, who vetoed the invitation, and the opportunity to remove the imperial family to a place of safety was lost.

The broad outlines of what happened subsequently to the imperial family, from their initial confinement in the palace at Tsarskoe Selo, through their removal to Tobolsk in Siberia to their ultimate murder in Ekaterinburg by local Bolsheviks, thought by some to be acting on orders from Lenin and Sverdlov, are too well known to need repeating. However, one account by an eyewitness of most of the story, the Englishman Sydney Gibbes, who was tutor to the Tsarevich Alexis at the time of the Revolution, is less well known than some others. Gibbes was absent from Tsarskoe Selo in Petrograd on the day the revolutionaries occupied the palace and on his return from the city he was not allowed back in, only being able to collect his own possessions at the time the family was transported to Tobolsk. He accompanied the family into exile voluntarily and continued to give English lessons both to the Tsarevich and to the Grand Duchesses, as well as helping to devise entertainments such as plays for them. In May 1918 the Romanovs were moved to Ekaterinburg, but although Gibbes, along with the French language tutor Pierre Gilliard, accompanied them once more, they were, perhaps fortunately for them, not allowed to leave the train and spent the next few weeks living in a fourth-class carriage, which eventually became part of a refugee train to Tyumen. He was thus not in Ekaterinburg at the time of the murders, but returned soon after and assisted the Sokolov Inquiry, not least by identifying some of the remains found by White forces after they occupied the city at the end of July 1918.

In the immediate aftermath of the February Revolution, Gibbes appears to have been relatively sanguine about the general outlook, although naturally worried about his own position. On 15 April 1917 he wrote to his uncle W.J. (Will) Fisher:

> Since the receipt of your letter a month ago our world has been completely upset. In most things the change is for the better although personally the opposite is the case. If only things settle down we should go on all right, although what will happen to myself I do not know. . . .
>
> I am still living in the Palace, although I have not been permitted to join my pupil who is in a different part.[83]

Initially, before the idea was vetoed by King George V, it was thought that the family might be able to travel to England, and Gibbes hinted at this possibility in a letter he wrote to his aunt Hattie, shortly afterwards:

> you will doubtless by now know the position in which we are placed here from the turn of political events. It therefore seems out of the question at the present time [to return home] for nobody knows what is going to happen and my duty as well as my interests call for my presence here. Out fortunes are completely broken and it is more than possible that I shall leave Russia & return to England with my 'pupil'. But when that might be I cannot say, at the present time they cannot leave.[84]

Among the Gibbes papers, copies of which are held by the Bodleian Library, is a narrative of the exile of the imperial family to Tobolsk. This appears to have formed part of the sermon which Gibbes delivered in 1934 after his ordination as a priest in the Orthodox faith. It begins:

> The idea of a Revolution and the weighing of its pros and cons had gradually crept into general conversation. So that little by little it began to appear almost everywhere. I was often amazed to hear persons who had everything to lose by a revolution intellectually playing with the idea. And then it came suddenly and crushingly. It was like the sudden death of a person who has been lying sick for years and years, when it does come, a quite unexpected and

unbelievable event. Then after the excitement and the tension there
succeeded a dull calm. The Empress and the Imperial family seemed
to become very human – From the first one noticed a change in
the palace. The servants did not seem quite the same and of course
there was the isolation. No longer was there the coming and going
of the outside world – the pace of life had stopped. Naturally it was
a sad, sad time for all concerned. The children were all sick and
the Empress completely worn out. The Emperor himself was away
at the Staffka. Then came the last home-coming – how different
to when we had returned at Christmas a few months since. With
the Emperor's advent the Palace was closed. Their home which
they all loved so dearly had now become a prison. Then came the
exile to Tobolsk, that little Siberian town to which thousands of
exiles had preceded them. Strange to say it proved to be a nice little
town, full of quaint churches. Its people, descended from exiles
sentenced by their Imperial ancestors, were found to be kindly and
well-disposed, without any revolutionary bias. Presents of food and
delicacies found their way in and served not only to feed but to
comfort. At the same time they augmented the comparatively frugal
fare, which was now the rule. Their first gaolers also proved to be
not so bad in practice as they had at first appeared. The Provisional
Government had sent certain comforts. There were pictures for
the walls from home and even wine. Unfortunately one box was
dropped and the bottles smashed and the Emperor's wine ran into
the river. Perhaps some had got into the Tyrant's house before the
accident happened. The house must be searched. In the house itself
great perturbation. One box had been safely delivered: what was to
be done? It was hastily unpacked and the precious bottles put into a
basket. The Commission arrived to search the house and rigorously
went from room to room right through the building and – one
room behind the Commission – followed a faithful lackey carrying
a heavily laden basket with the only remaining bottles. Finally all
were satisfied, the Commission, the lackey and the Emperor, who
was not deprived of his glass of red wine for lunch and dinner for
the length of his stay, but the supply was too small to permit of its
being served to anybody else. . . .

But even with these few extenuating circumstances the life at
Tobolsk pressed very heavily on the Emperor and Empress, particularly the latter. With the children it was different, for the Empress
had planned a time-table of lessons which kept them exceedingly
busy for the greater part of the day and so their 'intervals' between

lessons was never too long or too tedious. The only one of the Grand Duchesses who seemed dull was the Grand [Duchess] Olga who didn't have any lessons. The Grand Duchess Marie once said to me that she could live at Tobolsk for ever if only they would be able to walk out a little. The Emperor found it harder to fill up his leisure time. During his hours of exercise he would walk up and down the yard forty or fifty times in an hour, and when that proved too monotonous he would see some of the firing. At the beginning of the winter we made an ice hill in the yard. It wasn't a very good one but still it was a hill. It was soon forbidden, however, being observable from the street. A[lexis] N[icolaievich] seldom played with his sisters. He had his own amusements and at first Dr. Deverenko's son was allowed to come and play, afterwards this was stopped for fear of our communicating with the outside world. There was also one other boy on the staff – the cook's scullion, but in manners and intelligence he was not above his station so he didn't often join in. Just occasionally he would snatch a moment for snow balling or similar games.

With the advent of Yakovleff[85] at the end of March everything turned to the worse. All those living across the road were obliged to find quarters in the Emperor's lodgings. Food was now strictly rationed and we had to forego our third dish at table on account of the lack of sugar. During the early part of the year we had amused ourselves and others by getting up playlets that were acted every Sunday evening, everybody being invited. The Emperor acted only once in 'The Bear' by Chekoff, when O[lga] N[icolaievna] and M[arie] N[icolaievna] took the other two roles. In English I generally selected a very light comedy or still better a little farcical nonsense – something to laugh at, with plenty of movement, the dog also being 'engaged' on one occasion. Of course there were occasional rehearsals, but it was the unrehearsed effects that were sometimes screamingly funny.[86] These pleasures came to an end with the beginning of Lent and our theatre was then closed. On the first four days the wonderful Canon of St. Andrew of Crete was read, and with her usual thoughtfulness the Empress provided a copy of the Canon in Russian for everybody present. As time went on the Commissars and/or the 'guard' found different ways of repression for the Imperial family. The Empress mostly kept her room and therefore came into little contact with the outside world. The one to suffer most was the Emperor. He was obliged to remove his epaulettes, with the monogram of his father, the Emperor

Alexander III. His hours of exercise were curtailed. Nobody was allowed to speak to any of the sentries and eventually the sentries were replaced by Magyars[87] for the most part.

Despite all these difficulties, Gibbes made some attempts to inform the outside world of the conditions under which the imperial family were being held. On 15 December 1917 he wrote to a Miss Margaret Jackson, who was living in a home for governesses in Regent's Park. He clearly hoped that the Bolsheviks, when they censored the mail, would not realize that Miss Jackson had been the Empress's governess in Darmstadt, and he equally hoped that she would pass the letter on to King George V and Queen Mary, although whether she did in fact do so is uncertain. He wrote:

> You will have read in the newspapers of all the many different changes that have taken place. In August the Provisional Government decided to change the residence from Tsarskoe to Tobolsk, a small town far away in Siberia, 300 versts from the nearest railway station. The change has now been effected and we are in our quarters, the residence of the former governor. The town itself is perhaps better than one might expect, but is nevertheless extremely primitive. It is grouped round the foot of a steep hill leading onto a high plateau on which are situated the principal cathedral, containing the local shrine, the Bishop's palace, and a great building now used as the Assize Courts. Although the town contains but 25,000 inhabitants there are more than twenty churches and their spires and towers, often of quaint and curious design, give the town a light and pleasant aspect. By custom the churches are generally washed white and the roof painted a pale green, being sometimes further embellished with a tiny cupola and cross of burnished gold, and against the clear blue sky they make a charming picture as they sparkle in the brilliant northern sunshine. Our House, or rather Houses, for there are two, one on one side of the street and one on the other, are the best in the town; that in which the Household proper lives is entirely isolated and possesses a small garden besides a piece of the road way which has been railed in to make a recreation ground. The other house, which is almost exactly opposite, is occupied by Government Officials and contains quarters for the Suite. The House itself is not very large, but the rooms are pleasant and bright. As in almost all Russian houses on mounting

the principal staircase you enter the saloon on one side of which there is the study and on the other the drawing room. After these come the principal bedroom and a room which the four daughters use as a dormitory. The latter is bright and cosy with its four camp beds round which are arranged the most treasured possessions of each. The youngest has a room to himself on the other side of the corridor that serves him for bedroom and class room too. The dining room is downstairs being more conveniently situated to the kitchens. The days do not vary very much except for Sundays and Holidays ... when there are prayers read by a benign old priest in whose parish we live. On Sunday we are generally permitted to go to the Parish Church to the Communion Service, but otherwise prayers are read at home. The Services are very nice and sympathetically performed and there is now a small choir which sings really well. The younger members of the family have lessons in the morning before lunch, after which we all take exercise and recreation in our small railed-in plot. It is difficult to obtain much variety in so small a space, walking and sawing wood and similar occupations help pass the time and afford the exercise necessary for health. Fortunately all keep well and in good spirits in spite of the times in which we live. Of the outside world we only know what we can gather from the newspapers which in this remote spot come slowly and at irregular intervals...

Later in the letter he refers to 'David' being back from the front in France and asks after his parents. 'David' was, of course, the Prince of Wales, and thus Gibbes dropped a hint to Miss Jackson that she should pass the letter on to Buckingham Palace.

Amongst Gibbes's papers are two notebooks that contain the exercises in English composition or dictation which he set two of his pupils, the Grand Duchesses Marie and Anastasia, during their time in Tobolsk. The majority of the subjects are unexceptionable, descriptions of the photographic process, the first five books of the Bible and elephants, prose renderings of English poetry or accounts of historical figures such as King Canute or Robert of Sicily. But on one occasion Gibbes must have asked Anastasia to compose a letter in English describing their journey to Tobolsk. Unlike the Tsar and the Tsarina's diaries of their imprisonment, this account by one of their daughters is relatively little known, and, in the light of later events,

Charles Gibbes tutoring the Grand Duchess Anastasia

is almost unbearably poignant in its naivety (the original spellings have been retained in the extract below):

My dear Friend, I will describe to you [how] we travelled. We started in the morning and when we got into the train I went to sleep, so did all of us. We were very tired because we did not sleap the whole night. The first day was hot and very dusty. At the stations we had to shut our window curtanse that nobody should see us. Once in the evening I was looking out of the window, we stopped near a little house but there was no station so we could look out. A little boy came to my window and asked: 'Uncle, please give me if you have got, a newspaper.' I said: 'I am not an uncle but a anty and have no newspaper.' At the first moment I could not understand why did he call me 'Uncle' but then I remember that my hear is cut and I and the soldiers (which were standing next to me) laught very much. On the way many funy things happened, and if I shall have time I shall write to you our travell farther on. Good by. Don't forget me. Many kisses from us all to you my darling. Your A.

Gibbes also provided some dictionary definitions for Anastasia to copy out. Among them are the following:

Monarchy is government by a single ruler who may be a man or a woman. The English monarchy is governed by King George V. The Russian monarchy is governed by the Czar. Anarchy means the absence of all [?rules] or law. Chaos is the state the world was in when all was in confusion before God put it in order.
A tyrant is a harsh and cruel ruler.

But this relatively tranquil existence was soon to be rudely interrupted. Gibbes's narrative continues:

Suddenly the worst blow of all fell upon them – they were to be divided. Yakovleff the new Commissar announced that he had orders to take the Emperor away. The poor Empress was completely distracted and shed bitter, bitter tears. After lunch the Emperor and Empress proposed to Yakovleff that she should also accompany the Emperor, to which he replied that it was not in his instructions but that he would not offer any obstruction if she wished to do so but would take the responsibility upon himself. That terrible day! The Caesarevich was very sick, tossing and moaning on his bed of pain. Always sighing for his mother, who couldn't come. It was almost 5 when at last she appeared and then she told us that the Emperor and she would be going away that night. She was also taking with her the Grand Duchess Marie, who was always so kind and bright and willing. 'My legs', the Empress had called her when she, the last of the Imperial children, fell ill of the measles in January 1917. 'I have lost my legs', she said.
    On that fatal night the Imperial family dined alone upstairs with the Empress, while we all had our meal as usual in the dining room. To tea, which was served at about 11 pm, all were invited, a most melancholy meal. After this the Family were again left alone to make their last preparations. About 2 am the conveyances began to draw up in the courtyard. Only one tarantass with a hood, the rest quite open. Between three and four o'clock in the morning they descended into the Yard. Every member of the Imperial

household thronged round them to say good-bye. The Emperor had a handshake and a word for everybody, and we all kissed the dear Empress's hand. And then they started, away into the unknown. The Emperor had wished to ride with the Empress, but this Yakovleff would not allow, the Emperor had to [ride] with him. Why? Did they have a secret conversation? That perhaps we shall never know. Then days passed and only a post-card with no indication of their whereabouts. Then a second – this time from Ekaterinburg and giving their address. Afterwards we found out that they had gone to Tiumen from Tobolsk and there entrained for the east but before entering Omsk Yakovleff had left the train and had a conversation by direct wire to Moscow, in consequence of which their direction was changed and they retraced their steps to the west. However, they got no further than Ekaterinburg, for here the train was stopped and the whole party incarcerated in a private mansion, which had been hastily evacuated by its owner, and fortified from the outside to convert it into a prison.

The rest of us remained at Tobolsk for yet another month, pending the Caesarevich's restoration to health, and then we too made the same journey. However by this time the ice had disappeared and we were able to make the journey by boat. The poor little boy was very sick, but Rodionoff,[88] our new Commandant, had little pity. He was by nature rather officious and I am sure was worried by his responsibilities. First he ins[is]ted on the doors all being open and then he would have them locked and altogether he made himself a great nuisance. Great excitement was felt at passing Pokrovsky and the 'Starets's'[89] house was pointed out to me. When we got to Tiumen Rodionoff assembled us all in the Saloon of the ship and from his list read out the names of the company. As each name was read out the owner had to get up and make his or her way to the train, that was standing opposite the landing place. After General Tatescheff, Countess Hendrikoff, Mlle Schneider, and E.N. had all gone, the Baroness Buxhoeven said 'What about me?' Rodionoff looked at his list and then said all right you can go too. Then the Imperial children were taken away, the Naslednik being carried by Nagorny his valet. I much wished to try and get a photograph of them as they went up the hill, but I was afraid to make the attempt.

After this Rodionoff turned to the rest of us and said now you can all go. But when we got to the train we were placed in a 4th Class carriage apart from the Imperial children. We started immediately and [the] journey lasted several hours, so that it was past midnight when we got to Ekaterinburg. All night long the train was shunted from station to station up and down Ekaterinburg, finally between six and seven it was brought to a standstill between two of the town stations at a road which led direct to the Ipatieff house. The Imperial [children] were jostled out of the train, each being compelled to carry their own things. Nagorny who tried to help them was roughly handled. We could only watch from our railway carriage window and say a silent prayer. Other help we could not give. Soon they were driven away and we never saw them again.

At that time we little knew that their sufferings would not long be protracted. Their murder took place on the night of the 16th–17th July, 1918, and is now known to all. It exceeded in horror and brutality, anything know[n] in history. Blood, there was so much blood that they swept it up with a broom! Then came the bonfire and the trumped up mystery to hide the traces. Thus it remained until the investigation undertaken by Nicholas Alexeievich Sokolov in 1919, when their scanty relics were first discovered and collected, and little by little the full tale of the crime exposed.[90]

Gibbes also kept a copy of a prayer in verse, which is thought to have been composed by Countess Hendrikova, the Empress's lady-in-waiting:[91]

Grant us thy patience, Lord,
In these our woeful days,
The mob's wrath to endure,
The torturers' ire.
Thy unction to forgive
Our neighbours' persecution,
And mild, like Thee, to bear
A bloodstained Cross.
And when the mob prevails,
And foes come to despoil us,
To suffer humbly shame,
O Saviour aid us!
And when the hour comes
To pass the last dread gate,
Breathe strength in us to pray,
Father forgive them!

Gibbes did not know it, but the Tsar's last words, as recorded by one of the executioners, Commissar Peter Ermakov, completed the saying of Christ on the Cross:

You know not what you do.[92]

Gibbes concluded his sermon on the fate of the imperial family with these words:

Later years have seen some slight reparation done to their memory. Works have appeared by many members of their circle, but the authoritative book has yet to come. Come it will some day, but perhaps not in this generation – verily TIME IS THE TARDY ADVOCATE OF KINGS.[93]

Although it took longer than Gibbes may have anticipated, the 'whirligig of time' did, in due course, lead to the rehabilitation of the Tsar, as he had hoped. In 1981 the imperial family, along with their servants who were murdered alongside them, were canonized as 'new martyrs' by the Russian Orthodox Church Abroad, and in 2000 the Moscow Patriarchate canonized the family as 'passion bearers', meaning people who face death with resignation in a manner similar to Christ, rather than those who are killed for their faith; and the site of the Ipatiev House in Ekaterinburg is now covered by the Church on the Blood, which was consecrated in 2003. The altar is directly over the site of the executions, and there is also a museum devoted to the imperial family.

'Reddest of the Red'

THE ARRIVAL OF LENIN

When the February Revolution broke out the majority of the Bolshevik leaders were in exile, far from Petrograd and unable to influence events directly. Kamenev, Sverdlov and Stalin returned from internal exile by the end of March, and on the evening of 16 April Lenin arrived back in Petrograd from exile in Switzerland, following his famous journey by 'sealed train' through Germany.

Lenin had been living in various different Western European countries, including England, France, Switzerland and Finland, since his exile to Siberia following arrest for sedition in 1895, returning to Russia on only a handful of occasions. During this time he became a prominent member of the Russian Social Democratic Labour Party and published various political tracts, including *What Is to Be Done?* (1902). The party was banned in Russia, but its journal, *Iskra*, was smuggled into the country. When the party split into Bolshevik and Menshevik factions Lenin emerged as the leader of the Bolshevik faction, which eventually formed its own party in 1912. In the early years of the First World War he had called for ordinary soldiers to turn against their commanders and transform the conflict into an international socialist uprising. The February Revolution and the Provisional Government's seizure of power had given him the opportunity to return to Russia and campaign for a Bolshevik-led form of government.

Lenin's arrival at the Finland Station, following that of his great rival Plekhanov[94] five days earlier, was witnessed by Jean Schopfer, a Swiss-born Frenchman who was a reporter for both *Le Temps* and *Le Petit Parisien*. Schopfer's diary of these events reveals that, as with many English and French socialists, he had great hopes that Plekhanov would use his influence to help keep Russia in the war, but it soon became obvious that Plekhanov, who had lived in exile since 1880, had little or no influence over events in modern Petrograd, whereas Lenin rapidly became a key figure in the continuing debates over the future course of the Revolution, and whose anti-war stance in particular (funded, it was alleged, by Germany) made him an object of both fear and loathing for the representatives of the Allied nations in the Russian capital. Schopfer's diary entries also show that Lenin's message was, at least at first, not universally popular among the soldiers, and that he had, on occasion, to adopt a lower profile:

12 APRIL 1917

Yesterday evening, the French and English Socialist Delegates and Plekhanoff arrived. They were welcomed by the President of the Executive Committee and the representatives of the parties. They came to endeavour to make their Russian comrades understand the evident truth that there was no necessity more urgent than that of making war to the bitter end and of overthrowing Germany. Plekhanoff would employ all his influence in the same sense.

17 APRIL 1917

The famous Social Democrat Lenin arrived yesterday evening at Petrograd, from Switzerland, where he had been living. He is the reddest of the red. And what road had he and his comrades who escorted him taken to regain their fatherland, if I dare employ a word so denuded of sense in speaking of the place which had witnessed the birth of these Social Democrats? They had passed across Germany, which, as one might expect, had opened her doors wide to this ill-omened company. Ah! Germany had made no difficulty about allowing Lenin and his friends to pass. She would have no better allies than they. She introduced the enemy into the fortress. It was a skilful stroke of policy.

But, surprising thing! These men, returning from Germany were very well received here. No one seemed disposed to seek a quarrel with them about the way of return that they had followed. I do not speak, that goes without saying, of the Extremists. But a Kerensky, a Minister, said: 'It was difficult to prevent them from passing through Germany. We could scarcely object to that.' But a certain V———, member of the Council of the Empire, professor at the University, likewise was not shocked by that which disgusted us. In France, in default of men, if they had failed in their duty, the women would have cut in pieces these creatures without a country, returned from Germany! Here there was no indignation. Was this people lacking in patriotism? Must one end by believing the many

Russians who, for years past, had not ceased to assure me that such was the case?

This Lenin is what one calls, in the horrible Socialist jargon, a 'Defeatist', that is to say, one of those who prefer defeat to the War. He wanted peace, peace at any price, and without delay, and no matter what kind it might be. That was the thesis which he came to defend in the frightful confusion of the present hour in Russia.

Well, Lenin and his acolytes had been received at the Finland Station with the same enthusiasm, and by the same delegates of the Committee, as had Plekhanoff and the English and French Socialists. Affecting speeches were delivered, while to-day there were grand demonstrations in the streets, with red banners, and the citizen Lenin was delivering a speech in the Duma at the very time I was writing these lines.

Our French and English Socialist friends were greatly disgusted. They began to understand in what amazing anarchy we were living here – political anarchy, military anarchy, administrative and economic anarchy, which had, as it basis, anarchy of minds.

The day after his arrival, Lenin set out his 'April Theses' in which he argued that to move from the Soviet of Soldiers' and Workers' deputies to a form a parliamentary government was a step backwards and that the aim should be a Republic of Soviets of Workers, Poor Peasants and Peasants' deputies. This in effect was a restatement of the doctrine of uninterrupted revolution which had caused the split between the Bolsheviks and the Mensheviks in 1903, but, with the Soviet still largely composed of Mensheviks and Social Revolutionaries, initially this message had little success, as Schopfer noted:

18 APRIL 1917

Lenin did not triumph yesterday at the Congress of the different fractions of the Social Democratic Party.

22 APRIL 1917

During this Sunday, the Nevsky was in an excited state. Orators held meetings at the street corners. They were Anarchists who were advocating the looting of the banks. As the Revolution had given liberty of speech to the people, they were allowed to preach in peace civil war. In the Ligovskaia there was a quarrel between armed soldiers, who fired, and several persons were killed. And at the Kamenoostrovski Prospect, from the top of the balcony of the Kchessinskaia, the Communist Lenin continued to harangue the people and to incite it to revolt.

26 APRIL 1917

[Schopfer met an NCO, who said about the Bolsheviks:] 'What is it that they have come to do here, these people? Now we have the Revolution; the Old Régime is overthrown; we are happy, we are free, and this wretch Lenin must needs come to create disorder. Ah no! … I will tell you plainly that we soldiers do not want it. We had decided to go and seize this comrade who is stirring up the people … Yes, we were going in two companies… But our leaders restrained us, explaining to us that, up to the present, he had done nothing but talk, and that people had the right to speak, even to talk absurdities. But let him take care what he is doing! We are keeping an eye on him. Let him try and budge, and we shall settle his account. And that will not take long!'

1 MAY 1917

Before the Palace of the Kchessinskaia there was a meeting. From a 'pergola' in the open air, the citizen Anarchists harangued a light-hearted crowd, which was not moved by their eloquence. The majority of the people had come there, like myself, out of curiosity to hear the lion roar; but Lenin hid himself and allowed his lieutenants to do the work.[95]

Edward Heald also noted the impact of Lenin's arrival in the diary of his time spent in Petrograd working for the YMCA prisoner-of-war-relief programme:

2 MAY 1917

The sudden burst of radical propaganda, which has developed during the past week, is attributed to a man named Lenin, who has just arrived from Switzerland. He came through Germany, and rumor is that he was banqueted by the Emperor who is said to be back of his designs here. As he entered the country through Finland, he harangued the soldiers and workingmen along the way with the most revolutionary propaganda. One of the Americans who came

Lenin spoke to the crowds from the top balcony of Kshesinskaya Mansion, commandeered by the Bolsheviks as their headquarters in Petrograd

through on the same train told us how disheartening it was. Lenin's first words as he got off the train at Petrograd were 'Hail to the Civil War.' God knows what a task the Provisional Government has on hand without adding the trouble that such a firebrand can create.

Soon after arriving in the city, Lenin gathered four or five hundred of the workingmen together in a street parade with banners that read: 'Down With the Government,' 'Down With the Capitalists,' 'Down with the War,' and down with everything else. 'There is the poison that will destroy the democratic revolution,' was my comment to one of the secretaries.[96]

The British socialists in Petrograd, who were largely supportive of Kerensky and the Provisional Government, and who, like their French counterparts, wanted to keep Russia in the war, were wary of Lenin, and attempted to place him in the tradition of Russian revolutionaries who had turned out to be *agents provocateurs*. They also recognized his utter ruthlessness. Alex Thompson wrote:

I have met no-one who knows Lenin, and very few who have even seen him. He keeps himself, like a spider, well concealed. But the best-informed people agree that Lenin is a peculiarly Russian blend of honesty and venality, quite sincere in his fanaticism, but Jesuitically ready to accept help from anybody 'and no questions asked'.

And Julius West saw him as

a queer person. Some people say that he is a German agent, but it is more likely that he is one of those curious products of the Russian revolutionary movement who have ceased to live on the moral planes of the rest of the world. So many revolutionists have turned out to be police agents, who in their own heart of hearts did not know which of their employers held the first claim on their allegiance. Azev,[97] and Father Gapon,[98] and the detective who shot the Premier, Stolypin, are all examples of the type ... I think that Lenin is under the same shadow. To him the future of humanity, and its realisation by his methods, are everything – matters infinitely more important than the sources of the subscriptions to his funds or the character of his allies. To him the end justifies the means. If Lenin could sell his own soul for a sufficient guarantee of success, he would do it.

Although West failed to recognize the degree of control Lenin had over the Bolshevik Party and thought that Bolshevism 'was not a conspiracy quite so much as a rabble, not a theory quite so much as an easy acceptance of the doctrine of least resistance, and the cash that goes therewith', he did realize all too clearly the threat posed by Bolshevism:

Numerically the Leninites and their allies have about 20 per cent of the organised working-class movement. But it is the most dangerous section; indeed it is the only dangerous section. Essers [i.e. Socialist Revolutionaries] and Mensheviks may have their little differences, but while they control the machinery of the C.W.S.D's all is well. But when the others begin ———![99]

The Bolshevik headquarters was the former mansion of Matilda Kshesinskaya,[100] the prima ballerina at the Mariinsky Theatre and a former mistress of Nicholas II before he became Emperor. Here, according to one hostile account, there were strange goings-on:

Amongst all the strange happenings associated with the revolution in Petrograd perhaps the strangest was the forcible seizure by the Leninites and militant anarchists of the splendid palace of Madame Kshesinskaya, Russia's foremost ballerina, and the favourite of the ex-Tsar Nicholas.

The gift of her royal lover, who also had it furnished for her regardless of expense, the Kshesinskaya Palace was one of the landmarks of the capital, and was among the first buildings of the kind to be invaded and sacked by the revolutionary mob. Later it was occupied permanently by the Leninites, who made it their headquarters, and herein were enacted scenes that are unparalleled since the days of the first French Revolution.

In the grand salon, with its ebony and silver decorations, its rose silk hangings, and its famous green malachite doors, the scum of Petrograd ate, drank and made merry. Every night and all night there were music and dancing, punctuated at intervals by the rattle of the machine guns planted by the anarchists on the roof, and the answering volleys fired by the troops in the streets.

It was an orgy such as Hogarth never pictured, nor Balzac imagined. Death danced with the dancers. Powder-blackened men and half naked women drank champagne from silver flagons, and died even as they drank, their life blood staining the golden wine a vivid crimson.

Then the wild riot would cease suddenly for a brief period, while the survivors, shouting imprecations and curses, rushed to the windows and fired wildly up and down the street. But only for a few minutes. Afterwards the music struck up again, lilting Russian dance airs played upon Kshesinskaya's four thousand rouble piano – with its silver gesso work and Vernis-Martin decorations, the gift of a Grand Duke – and the feet of the wine-maddened dancers whirled anew, and with seemingly unflagging zest, amid a litter of broken glass and torn tapestry.

Anon the story would get about that Leninite sailors from Cronstadt were marching to their relief, and that the hours of the Provisional Government were numbered. Whereat cheering would break out and run through all the many rooms of the vast building, crackling down corridors and from one apartment to the other like a musketry feu de joie.

The cheers came full-throated in all tongues, for anarchy knows no country. There were American sailors there, having as they expressed it, 'the time of their lives'; 'there were Germans – secret service agents, no doubt – Rumanians, Lithuanians, Serbs, and scores and scores of pretty filles de joie, culled from half the capitals of the world during the old, gay, pre-war days. Why should they, and such as they, not make merry? they asked one another. Death might come tomorrow. On then, with the dance today.

However, there was also a more sinister side to what went on at the Kshesinskaya mansion:

This is one side of the picture, but there was also another. The Leninite leaders, at all events, had a certain method in their madness. Anarchy was their watchword, but even successful anarchy requires a certain amount of organisation. So it came about that, side by side with all this riot and debauchery propaganda work went on unceasingly. In Madame Kshesinskaya's pink and gold bedroom a printing press had been set up, and anarchist proclamations were struck off and an anarchist newspaper prepared for the Press. Her Roman bathroom of Parian marble re-echoed to the click click of typewriting machines, operated by little, short-haired revolutionaries. The great dancer's holy of holies, her silver and blue boudoir at the door of which under the old regime Grand Dukes had knocked in vain, was transformed into a telephone exchange.[101]

Meriel Buchanan recorded that

A monster red flag waved from the roof, every night lights blazed from all the windows, every day crowds surged all round the house, while, from a little kiosk at the corner in the garden, Lenin spoke to them, inciting them against the war, against the Government, against the Allies.[102]

'You will fight for Russia'

WITH KERENSKY AT THE FRONT

Of all the changes instituted by the February Revolution perhaps the most fateful was Prikaz (Order) number 1 of the Petrograd Soviet. Intended to protect those soldiers who had taken part in the Revolution from reprisals by their officers, it declared that soldiers and sailors should obey their officers only if their orders did not contradict the decrees of the Soviet. It also called on the soldiers of each unit to elect representatives to the Soviet and to elect local committees which would control each unit. Furthermore, soldiers no longer had to stand up or salute their officers when off duty.

Although the Order itself made no mention of soldiers electing their own officers, the Bolsheviks encouraged soldiers to elect their own commanders, and action was certainly taken against officers who were judged to be insufficiently sympathetic towards the Revolution.

The Order was widely seen, both at the time and subsequently, as undermining Russia's war effort. Florence Farmborough noted the effects of the reforms on the soldiers at the front:

> They were intended to create a closer relationship, a more friendly atmosphere; they seem, however, to be doing exactly the reverse. Strangely enough, it is the soldiers who appear disgruntled; they are moody, even morose, and often astonish their officers by pertness and effrontery. Soldiers can now sit – even smoke – in the presence of their officers. They are free men now and they insist on every new privilege as their bounden right. But even privileges, never before dreamt of in military service, produce a rapid deterioration in morale and discipline quite foreign to the rigid military training of the Russian rank-and-file.

Kerensky's response to this was to make a series of tours to the front, speaking to the soldiers directly and attempting to appeal to their patriotism and to persuade them to continue the fight. His reputation as a 'born orator' had gone before him, so when, in May 1917, it was announced that he would be coming to Florence Farmborough's sector of the front she was keen to go and hear him:

149

13 MAY 1917

During breakfast the Order was brought to us: Kerensky was coming to Podgaytsy! He would come and harangue our soldiers with heartening words. Pray Heaven that his influence would succeed in re-organising the already disorganised Front Line troops. We had no doubt that at Podgaytsy he would be given as hearty a welcome as on other sections of the Front. We were all most eager to hear him. In small groups we wended our way through the dusty streets and up the hill outside the town. What an enormous mass of military! It was amazing that so many could collect together in so short a time! Our first thought was, 'We shall never catch a glimpse of him in such a crowd.' But we pushed our way forward and fortune favoured us. Some regimental doctors of our acquaintance spied us and helped us through into the very front row.

The hill-top spread out like a wide arena and on all sides were tightly-packed masses of soldiers. The hill-slopes were literally bristling with military. I noticed cameras in the hands of some officers, who, every now and then, would look anxiously skywards. My eyes followed theirs – dark clouds were slowly rising, drawing nearer the sun. I studied my camera; it was in order. 'If he comes now,' I thought, 'I can get a snapshot before the sun disappears.' But in the excitement of his arrival I forgot all about my camera! As he stepped out of the car, a great roar of welcome rose. He approached the high platform, mounted it and stood there confronting the multitudinous assembly. At first glance, he looked small and insignificant. He wore a darkish uniform and there was nothing about him to indicate the magnetic power he was able to wield. I remember clearly a feeling of disappointment. Was this man really the Kerensky? He looked less than his 36 years and his beardless face made him even younger. For a while he stood in silence; then he began to speak, slowly at first and very clearly. As he spoke, one realised immediately the source of his power. His sincerity was unquestionable; and his eloquence literally hypnotised us.

He spoke for about twenty minutes, but time seemed to stand still. His main theme was freedom; that great, mystical Freedom which had come to Russia. His words were often interrupted by wild applause, and, when he pointed out that the war must, at all costs, continue to a victorious end, they acclaimed him to the echo. 'You will fight to a victorious end!' he adjured them. 'We will!' the soldiers shouted as one man. 'You will drive the enemy off Russian

Russian soldiers at the front (photographed by Scotland Liddell for *The Sphere*, 23 June 1917)

soil!' 'We will!' they shouted again with boundless enthusiasm. 'You, free men of a Free Country; you will fight for Russia, your Mother-Country. You will go into battle with joy in your hearts!' 'We are free men,' they roared. 'We will follow you into battle. Let us go now! Let us go now!'

When he left, they carried him on their shoulders to his car. They kissed him, his uniform, his car, the ground on which he walked. Many of them were on their knees praying; others were weeping. Some of them cheering; others singing patriotic songs. To the accompaniment of this hysterical outburst of patriotic fervour, Kerensky drove away. His car was soon lost to sight. We were told that more than 12,000 soldiers had gathered to acclaim him. We were all greatly impressed by him and his marvellous influence over the men. He had promised them that the Offensive would not be long delayed and had assured them of the renewed strength of batteries, heavy artillery and ammunition at their disposal. ... So we all felt confident that ... all would go well.

But the moment was lost. A month later, and 'no Orders from the Russian High Command have been received', and Nurse Farmborough noticed the changed mood amongst the troops:

These leisured weeks have given the men – 50 per cent of whom are illiterate – time to think. Their thinking has been their undoing, for their thoughts were concerned – not with Russia, nor with the foe confronting them – but with their new-found liberty. Freedom, for them, is a wonderful, inexplicable thing which has suddenly been thrust upon their country and upon them. 'Freedom,' they argue, 'implies liberty to say, think and act as each individual thinks fit.' 'Freedom gives us the privilege of deciding things for ourselves.' And so they have thought things over among themselves, and the word 'freedom' is bandied from mouth to mouth, and ever the taste of it to these simple, credulous peasant-soldiers becomes sweeter and sweeter.[103]

Nor was Kerensky's reception by the troops always as enthusiastic as that witnessed by Florence Farmborough. General Knox was present when he addressed 'one of the worst divisions in the army', the 2nd Guard Infantry, and noted in his diary:

When Kerenski visited the 2nd Division of the Guard yesterday the men formed into two groups, 6,000 surrounding him, cheering, while 4,000 held another 'meeting' some hundreds of yards distant. Kerenski said he wanted to speak to all of the men, and asked the hostile group to come over. They refused, called him a 'bourgeois,' and said they only wanted to fight the bourgeoisie. They refused a hearing to an officer who tried to persuade them. They yelled: 'Down with the war!' 'Down with everything!' Kerenski was with the division two hours and very few of the opposition crowd strolled over. The Grenaderski Regiment is the worst regiment in the division, partly because it has lost more officers killed than any other Guards regiment and partly owing to the activities of a Polish ensign, who was educated near Lemberg. Of the 1st and 2nd Divisions of the Guard, the Preobrajenski, Semenovski and Izmailovski Regiments are said to be all right, but the other five regiments are all bad.

It is well that Kerenski has had a rebuff, as it will show him the present state of things, of which ... he seemed to be ignorant.[104]

Later in the year one Red Guard put the view of the ordinary soldier even more bluntly to British translator and writer Gerard Shelley, who had asked him why he chose to fraternize with the Germans but to make war on his own people:

'It is like this,' he answered. 'I prefer to fight against the bourgeois than against the Germans. We can make peace with them, but we shall always have our bourgeois. When we have finished fighting against the Germans, we get our little money and go home. So it is better to beat the bourgeois and have all their riches. That is a better payment for fighting.'[105]

In July 1917, whilst still at the front, British Military Attaché General Knox had a meeting with Count Ignatiev, an old acquaintance of his, who was equally pessimistic about the situation:

He took me into his small tent to have a quiet talk. He was very pessimistic, and as he is a man of good digestion, with plenty of robust common sense, his opinion is valuable. He thinks there is no hope.

I put three questions to him, whether Russia would:
1. Fight as she fought before the Revolution;
2. Fight as she has fought since the Revolution till the general peace; or
3. Make a separate peace.

To the first question he said emphatically, 'No.' He was inclined to say 'Yes' to the second, but with hesitation, and he was unable to deny the possibility of a separate peace.

He pointed out that peace is essential for Russia, and that if there is not peace soon there will be a general massacre. The prolongation of the war is drawing Russia to the brink of economic ruin. Even at the beginning only an inconsiderable number of the peasants wanted war. The educated classes did, but the one dream of the peasant soldiers at the front has long been peace.

He said: 'If you were now to go out on the village square and to proclaim that the war will end at once, but only on one condition – that Nikolai Romanov returns to power, every single man would agree and there would be no more talk of a democratic republic.

I asked if he thought that the reconsideration of the objects of the war would have any effect on Russian public opinion. He said that it would on the conscientious people, but that the mass of the soldiery only wanted an excuse for saving their skins – they were not Bolsheviki or Mensheviki, but simply 'Shkurniki' (fearers for their own skins).[106]

Alex Thompson also witnessed Kerensky's attempts to rally the troops, and, looking back some years later, offered this assessment:

What he said in effect was: 'I think you had better fight and suffer, but you needn't if you'd rather not. I love my country, my countrymen, and sacred liberty too well to impose compulsions on you. Therefore you won't be compelled to obey orders till you have freely discussed them amongst yourselves. And, of course, you will rank as equals with your officers.'

Beautiful sentiments, beautiful words, but tragically cruel in practice. The soldiers applauded, and then, as soon as Kerensky had departed, those advocates of self-determination who had had enough of martial glory went over to the German trenches to drink the profusely offered vodka, or shot their officers and captured transport trains to take them home.

He then neatly summed up the difference between Kerensky's approach and that of Lenin:

Lenin, when he came to power, found a shorter way with dissenters. He gave them the choice between submission and starvation – with the result that he, the anti-militarist, formed the biggest army in the world.

In short,

Kerensky failed because he was a democrat, Lenin won because he wasn't.[107]

'Contradictory views'

THE HENDERSON MISSION

In April 1917 Arthur Henderson, the leader of the British Labour Party and a member of Lloyd George's wartime Coalition Government as paymaster-general, learned that Dutch and Scandinavian socialists proposed calling an international conference in Stockholm to discuss war aims and the possibilities of peace. Initially opposed to this proposal, Henderson put forward a counter-suggestion of a conference in London and agreed to lead a delegation to Russia to try to persuade the Provisional Government to support his own initiative rather than that of the socialists in neutral countries. Lloyd George supported the idea of Henderson travelling to Petrograd, partly perhaps because he felt that as a fellow socialist Henderson might carry more weight with Kerensky than the British ambassador, Sir George Buchanan, and, critically, stiffen his resolve as to staying in the war; more cynically, it has been suggested that Lloyd George also saw the mission as a means for getting a potentially troublesome Cabinet colleague out of the way, at least for a time.

Henderson arrived in Petrograd at the beginning of June. His letters provide an insightful picture of Russia during the period of 'duality' following the February Revolution, but before the first trial of strength between the Provisional Government and the Bolsheviks during the July Days. It was a time of confusion and uncertainty, and Henderson's letters reflect that feeling.

On 19 June, for instance, he wrote three very similar letters to friends back home in Britain. The first was to Jack Gilbert Dale, which is particularly interesting in showing that already some elements in Russia were proposing to allow the 'Maximalists' or Bolsheviks into power, only so that they could be seen to fail and be overthrown in favour of some more authoritarian regime. To his credit, Henderson was opposed to this line of thinking:

> Since my arrival here I have had a most interesting experience, though I have found the situation most perplexing owing to its uncertainty. Both politically and industrially things are in a

most chaotic condition. I have conferred with Members of the Government, politicians outside the Government, manufacturers, workmen's representatives and professors from whom I have received the most contradictory views on the situation. There are those who take a hopeful view and express the opinion that the position is improving though very slowly. Others take exactly the opposite view and incline strongly to the opinion that not only are things very bad indeed but that they must be worse before any permanent improvement is to be expected. Those holding the latter view, when pressed to state a remedy, agree that what is needed is firm government, which they strongly hold cannot be obtained from the present Ministry and they want to see a Government made up entirely of Socialists. When this opinion was submitted I naturally became curious to know its real inwardness and, on pressing, found that the suggestion was only prompted because an opinion as to its absolute failure was firmly held. They frankly admitted that a short Socialist regime would prove so great a disaster that it would be like a whip to the Russians who would rise and demand some form of resolute and stable Government. I cannot accept this opinion and have everywhere advised that the position can only be improved gradually and that as a means to this end everything should be done to extend confidence in the present Government. I think the risks of the experiment to which I have referred are so great that not only might it not prove a disaster to Russia but to the Allied cause. It would have been a tremendous undertaking to have carried through either the war or the revolution, but to have both in hand at the same time is almost beyond the powers of any nation, much less a nation that has suffered from oppression for centuries.

He then turned to the industrial situation:

Looking at the position from the industrial standpoint, matters are almost more hopeless here than they are politically. A form of intoxication appears to have taken possession of such as the men's leaders as there are. Unfortunately there are no steadying influences akin to our Trade Unions and the demands that are put forward to the employers are so outrageous that it is obvious that they are not prompted with a desire for economic improvement as much as with a view to obtaining complete control of the industry. Some of these demands have represented far more than the entire capital of the company. They do not ask that they should come into operation from a prospective date but that they should be made retrospective from the first day of the war. All sorts of efforts are being made to take the control out of the hands of the Directors and Managers and in many cases the Managers are throwing up their positions. Unfortunately the last thing that many of them think about is getting on with the war and this idea appears to have largely permeated the Armies in addition to the civil population. What exactly will be the result I do not know, though I have not lost hope and to the best of my ability am assisting the Government to cope with the more serious aspects of the problem.[108]

On the same day he wrote to R.W. Raine on war-weariness and anti-Allied feeling in Petrograd:

I am afraid it has to be admitted that in civil life and in the army there is not only a great amount of war-weariness but a large percentage of the population have been bitten by pacifist theories. This is not surprising for, with the newly-won freedom newspapers and parties have sprung up like mushrooms and the teaching in the cheap press and the meeting that you can find at almost every street corner are calculated not only to disturb but to poison the mind. The Allies are attacked without reserve. The most slanderous statements are freely publicised against Great Britain whilst on the other hand Germany is scarcely ever mentioned. Indications are not lacking that much of this irresponsible propaganda has its inception, inspiration and support in German sources. I am in great hope that if this Government can remain in office they will gradually but surely overcome many of the difficulties and bring about a saner condition of public opinion.[109]

To T.W. Dowson he attempted to explain the beliefs of the rural peasantry after the Revolution:

The peasant, enjoying his new-won liberty, seems to have the idea from what has been told him, that the working classes at home know nothing of the liberty they are now enjoying here and that we have been left in the black darkness of the experience through which they have just come.[110]

Provisional Government group (*The Sphere*, 21 May 1917)

Writing two days later to George Roberts,[111] he relayed a prescient warning:

> The position here is uncertain politically and industrially. I had a report from Moscow on Monday which said:
>
> 'We are again drawing near to another crisis – this time to the most serious crisis of all. Every day the relations between the extremists and all those socialists who support the temporary Government are becoming more strained. In a few weeks we shall have two groups, the 'pro-Kerenskyites' and the 'pro-Leninites' and it remains to be seen which of these groups will prevail. At any rate before the 15th July the moderate socialists and the Coalition Government will have triumphed or we shall all be hanging from the nearest lamp posts. If the extremists triumph we shall have a few months of anarchy and then a strong reaction and the socialist cause in Russia will receive a check from which it will take years to recover.'
>
> This is the view of an active but moderate socialist and it is not far wide of the mark.[112]

Other socialists who were sympathetic to the Provisional Government were expressing similar forebodings. Alex Thompson wrote in *The Clarion* on 8 June 1917:

> The position in Petrograd ominously resembles that which existed in Paris forty-six years ago on the eve of Bloody Week when thirty thousand men, women and children were killed behind the barricades and in the gutters of the city.
>
> In Petrograd now, as in Paris then, the populace, intoxicated by a sudden rise to power, foolishly assumes functions for which they are not qualified by training or experience. The National Guard of the Commune spent precious time in holding meetings, discussing grievances, and electing officers when their hard-pressed fighting comrades were anxiously waiting for relief. The natural result was a disaster and grievous waste of life. The same thing is happening in Russia: the Workmen's and Soldiers' Delegates, like the Communists of 1871, are taking into their hands the selection and control of the experts responsible for their defence and safety. The natural result is that, as in 1871, the capable and self-respecting men are throwing up their jobs. Others are being killed or disappear. At least seven hundred naval officers, and no-one knows how many military, are said to have been killed when the Revolution broke out. Their successors were chosen by election. Now I understand that the troops exercise the right to choose their officers, subject to a veto by the higher officials of the War Office. All this means that discipline has been thrown to the winds. The national services are plunged into chaos. The power of the Russian Army is sapped. And the effect is not only one of grave peril to the Russian Revolution, but also of terribly increased losses to the Allied Democracies in France and Belgium, who now have to withstand the pressure of increased German forces withdrawn from the Russian front.[113]

'Out of the fiery chaos'

ALL-RUSSIA CONFERENCE OF THE COUNCILS
OF WORKERS' AND SOLDIERS' DELEGATES

The First All-Russia Conference of the Councils of Workers' and Soldiers' Delegates was held between 16 June and 7 July. There were 1,090 delegates, of whom 822 – each of whom represented at least 25,000 people – had the right to vote. The largest party was the Socialist Revolutionaries with 285 voting delegates, and they were followed by the Mensheviks with 248 and the Bolsheviks with 105. Overall, the Conference was dominated by parties that were generally supportive of the Provisional Government.

Julius West, a member of the Fabian Society, attended the Conference and later reported on what he termed 'The Triumph of the Jawbone' at this and the myriad other conferences and public meetings that were being held throughout Russia:

> The occasion of all this verbiage ... is that Russia has contracted a new habit. She holds Conferences, several at once, and all the time. They last sometimes from 9 am to 5 am, and then they start again. They go on for weeks. There have been Labour conferences, Socialist conferences, Professional conferences and the usual Party conferences. Thousands of them. They have not all been on the beaten track. By no means. A month or two ago there was the Conference of the Criminal Classes, held in Odessa, and more recently a sort of rash broke out over the map of Russia of Children's Conferences. The latter seem to have been a source of deep annoyance to the older generation. The infants of several towns demanded the return of the Romanovs, and in one or two places they discussed the Future of the Family.
>
> The explanation of this orgy of shemazzling is obvious. Before March you could not, for all practical purposes, make a speech in Russia ... The Revolution removed the gag. Everybody began to talk at once and is still at it. The importance of it all lies in the fact that the task of governing Russia has got mixed up with the very natural desire to address the meeting.

Soldiers at the Duma for the Conference of the Councils of Workers' and Soldiers' Delegates, held 16 June–7 July 1917

Talk, in fact, is the really important thing out here. It is in every mouth as the saying goes. And the craze for it shows no sign of abatement. ...

A member of the Executive Committee of the C.W.S.D. told me that the Conference wasted most of the time because they had not yet mastered the technique of holding such assemblies. Nobody as yet bothers about sending out agenda and reports some weeks before the Conference meets. There is no time-table and no time-limit. Conferences go on until it occurs to people that it is time to go home, when they reluctantly separate. 'We may go on for weeks and weeks before we get to your point', said my Executive friend, referring to something on the agenda in which I was specially interested. Well, it is not to be wondered at. The gag has been removed, and speech-making is no longer the luxury of a few. But one fears that cackling, though it saved Rome, will not save Russia.[114]

The opening speeches at the Conference were made by the Mensheviks, but then, as Morgan Philips Price, the *Manchester Guardian* correspondent, remembered,

> There … arose from an obscure corner of the room a thick-set little man with a round bald head and small Tartar eyes. He was leading a small group of delegates who had set themselves down on the extreme left and at the back of the hall. Nobody seemed to pay much attention to the corner where they sat, for there was a general impression that here had congregated the extremists, irreconcilables and faddists of all types who were forming a little 'cave of Adullam'. But as soon as this short, thick-set little man rose and strode with a firm step, and even firmer look upon his countenance, up the gangway, where sat the serried ranks of 'Revolutionary Democracy', a hush came upon the whole assembly. For it was Lenin, the leader of that small, insignificant Bolshevik minority at this first All-Russia Soviet Congress. No uncertain words came from his lips. Straight to the point he went from the first moment of his speech and pursued his opponents with merciless logic. 'Where are we?' he began, stretching out his short arms and looking questioningly at his audience. 'What is this Council of Workers' and Soldiers' Delegates? Is there anything like it in the world? No, of course not, because nothing so absurd as this exists in any country today except in Russia. Then let us have either one of two things: either a bourgeois Government with its plans of so-called social reforms on paper, such as exists in every other country now, or let us have that Government which you (pointing at Tseretelli)[115] seem to long for, but which you apparently have not the courage to bring into existence, a Government of the proletariat which has its historic parallel in 1792 in France.'

Lenin was then attacked by Kerensky who pointed out that the French Revolution had 'turned into a base Imperialism':

> 'You tell us that you fear reaction', he almost screamed, 'and yet you propose to lead us the way of France in 1792. Instead of appealing for reconstruction you clamour for destruction. Out of the fiery chaos that you wish to make will arise, like a Phoenix, a dictator'. He paused and walked slowly across the platform, till he was opposite the corner where the group surrounding Lenin was seated. Not a sound was heard in the hall, as we waited breathlessly for the next sentence. 'I will not be the dictator you are trying to create', and so saying he turned his back upon Lenin. The latter was

calmly stroking his chin, apparently wondering whether the words of Kerensky would come true, and on whose shoulders the cloak of dictatorship, if it came, would rest.[116]

Finding themselves in a minority, the Bolsheviks attempted to put pressure on the Conference by means of an 'armed demonstration', planned for 23 June. The aim of the demonstration was, as Trotsky put it, 'to tell the Socialist Revolutionaries and Mensheviks who had come from all parts of the country: "Spurn the bourgeoisie! Have done with the idea of coalition, and take the reins of power into your own hands!"' 'We were quite certain', he went on, 'that if the Social Revolutionaries and Mensheviks broke with the Liberal bourgeoisie, they would be compelled to seek support from the most energetic and most advanced elements of the proletariat, which would thus obtain the leading role in the Revolution.'[117] In the event, this demonstration 'miscarried'. Julius West saw what happened (or rather what failed to happen):

This afternoon it appeared it was going to be really serious, and that we were going to see what a revolution looked like 'in the nood' as the waiter described the potatoes. The Leninites had said that at 2 pm they were going to march down upon a Conference where they had been sat upon, and throw it out. All Petrograd was posted up with appeals to them to do nothing of the sort. Rumours spoke of Cossacks, machine-guns and other paraphernalia of a respectable revolution. At 2 pm, or a little later, I was on the spot. There were about six soldiers present with fixed bayonets. A boy was selling lemonade, another was profiteering, selling gherkins at 50 copecks each (normally one shilling). A few workers were mending the road, with all the thoughtful deliberation of the Russian navvy, apparently in order to give the Leninites a surer foundation when they arrived. They did not arrive. I went to meet them but could not find them. That is the worst of revolutions – they never do keep to the timetable.

Now, what on earth is one to make of a situation which is always putting off its appointments like that? People assure me that there are signs of returning sanity. A week or two ago, they allege, everybody who demonstrated wanted the whole earth. Now they are beginning to feel that if only the supply of food was improved a trifle that could be something to go on with. Last night I listened for a few minutes to an open-air meeting, addressed simultaneously by about fifty soldiers. One of the men with the loudest voices yelled, 'You've had three months of your ——— liberty, and look at the way prices have gone up!' It appears that the sentiment is a pretty general one. Prices are distinctly uppish. A pair of boots costs the equivalent of about £6. A friend, staying at a hotel, in a moment of rash extravagance, asked for an apple. It was forthcoming, and he ate it. Then the bill came along; the fruit was priced at 3s 6d. I came along with a tin of condensed meat lozenges, each guaranteed to contain a meal in itself, and tasting like a concentrated petrol tank. . . .

Now you know all about the situation. It's a rummy business. Revolutions are by no means all that they are cracked up to be.[118]

'A sudden rain of bullets'

THE JULY DAYS

By the middle of July 1917 it was clear that the latest offensive by the Russian Army in Galicia, led by General Lavr Kornilov, among others, had failed at the cost of some 200,000 casualties, and this intensified the anti-war feelings among the population in Petrograd. On 16 July spontaneous demonstrations broke out in the city. They were started by soldiers of the 1st Depot Machine Gun Regiment – a 'bad unit', according to British Military Attaché General Knox – who on the preceding day had held a meeting which, reported the Bolshevik organ *Pravda*, was 'remarkable for the exceptional enthusiasm of the ripening revolutionary movement'. As they marched through the centre of the city, they were joined by soldiers from other regiments and by large crowds of workmen. Military forces loyal to the Provisional Government responded and on 17 July more than 700 people were killed and wounded in armed clashes in the city. Influenced by revelations that the Bolsheviks had been receiving funding from Germany, neither the Mensheviks nor the Social Revolutionaries supported the uprising, which by 20 July had been crushed; the headquarters of the Bolshevik Party and the offices and printing press of *Pravda* were destroyed, and Lenin was forced to go into hiding.

British antiques dealer Bertie Stopford was in Petrograd throughout the period of the insurrection and recorded his experiences in his diary:

1 JULY 1917 (Sun)
At 9.20 a procession began to pass down the Nevski. The sailors' band headed it; everything was very quiet; but there was no panic in our street. The supporters of the Government stayed away.

3 JULY 1917 (Tues)
At 3 this morning the Cossacks took away the Anarchist prisoners from the Preobrajenski Barracks. I feel a state of general tension.

13 JULY 1917 (Fri)
Wake up at 11 am. No one answered my bell. Found hotel servants on strike, except cooks. Dressed, made my own bed, cleaned my bath, swept my room. I did the same for a rheumatic old lady on my corridor who was much upset by the strike.

16 JULY 1917 (Mon)
[In the evening he walked through the streets.] When I got to the Liteiny – the main artery from the popular quarter across the Neva – I found it all in effervescence. No trams – always a bad sign. Nobody seemed to know if anything had happened or was going to happen – many people spoke to me. Everybody was asking everybody else what was going on.

I walked down the Mochovaia, and a motor car full of students and Grenadier soldiers passed me and stopped at no. 28, where I saw rifles being brought out, put in the automobile, which turned round and left at full speed....

The Nevski was emptying fast, though there were still some strollers and some sightseers. Armoured cars and motor-lorries with armed men were tearing up and down. Three tiny children were dancing round together, excitedly singing out, 'Revoluzion, Revoluzion!' I left the Nevski to go down the Moika, which was quite calm. A good many diners were coming out of the restaurants.

[Later in the Sadovia he] ran up against a demonstration of workpeople and soldiers.

[At 1.15 am he visited the Anglo-Russian Hospital.] A lot of wounded from the fighting in the Nevski had been brought in, and we went straight up to the wards to see them ... The fighting in

the Nevski was between Bolshevik soldiers and Cossacks, who had
been drawn up across the street at the corner of Vladimir Prospekt.
The soldiers lay flat in the roadway and fired on the Cossacks. No
sooner did the Cossacks reply than the cowards crept to the side
and bolted into the nearest houses. Thank God, some of the brutes
were killed.

After I had had some tea I left the hospital and walked down
the Nevski to the Hotel de l'Europe. I saw only one shop window
broken – a cigar shop. I met many stretchers with wounded people
on them, and there was a great crowd on the Sadovia – the Nevski
was empty. I got back to the hotel and went to bed.

17 JULY 1917 (Tues)
Whilst walking about in the morning, heard fierce shooting but
did not get under fire. During luncheon at the hotel a battle took
place in the Sadovia close by; the bullets rattled down on the roof
opposite. Hand-grenades were being used by the Bolsheviks all over
Petrograd.

18 JULY 1917 (Weds)
Violent rain all night, which swept the Bolsheviks off the streets. No
trams and only an occasional *izvoschik* ... Dined at the Polovtsovs,
and heard that the Bolsheviks were to be 'polished off' tonight. This
would have been done last night but for the violent rain.

19 JULY 1917 (Thurs)
[On the way to the Embassy.] As I crossed the Champ de Mars a
number of soldiers at the Pavlovsk Barracks, sitting in the windows
with rifles, fired from time to time over my head into the Summer
Garden. I was not going to turn back for them. I pulled myself
together and walked across the Champ de Mars and entered the
Embassy. ...

About half past eleven a message came to say that the house of
the dancer, Kchessinskaia, which had been looted and taken over
by the Bolsheviks at the beginning of the Revolution, had been
captured by Government troops, and at ten minutes past one an
officer came to say that the Peter–Paul Fortress, which was being
held by the Soldiers and Workmen against the Government forces,
had capitulated ... In the evening I saw Cossacks on white horses
escorting Kerenski back from the station to the Winter Palace on his
return from Stavka.

Kerensky attending the public funeral for Cossacks who lost their lives during the 'July Days' uprisings (*The Sphere*, 1 September 1917)

20 JULY 1917 (Fri)
Severe fighting around the Nicolai railway station. Changes in the Cabinet. At midnight someone telephoned to say a battle was going on by the Palace Bridge, opposite the Winter Palace. Opened my windows, but could hear nothing; too tired to dress again.

21 JULY 1917 (Sat)
In last night's battle the Bolsheviki, who had collected at the end of Palace Bridge, were surrounded by Cossacks and cut into small pieces. I had a little piece of Bolshevik brought me later! The bad news from the Front, which I have known since Thursday, is now published.

23 JULY 1917 (Mon)
To the Polovtsovs after dinner. The General came in and told us Lenin had not yet been found. I suggested to search the Vladimir Palace, which I know has been a nest of revolutionaries for the last three months.[119]

In fact, Lenin was able to evade capture and went into hiding.

At the British Embassy Meriel Buchanan, daughter of the British Ambassador, had a ringside view of much of the fighting. She remembered that on 16 July,

> Already during the earlier part of the day the first signs of a coming trouble had shown themselves, so faint, so small, that at the time one did not notice them or take heed, and it was only afterwards, looking back, that one remembered. The Cadet members of the Government had resigned, and a few people shook their heads and looked grave. In the morning a long, slow procession of the soldiers over forty, who were asking to go back to their villages for the summer, marched through the town – dreary, slouching, hopeless-looking men with sullen faces. During the afternoon I went to see a friend who lived almost opposite the Military Arsenal. Before the doors a big crowd of workmen were collected listening to a man in a dirty yellow shirt who was making a speech. It was such a very common sight that I paid no attention to it at the moment, but when I came out nearly an hour later and found the crowd still there and even grown larger, I wondered vaguely what they were doing. The speaker in the yellow shirt had gone now, and the men just stood about, talking in excited voices, shouting, gesticulating. They looked so angry that I did not quite like to stay too long to try and listen to what they were saying. A woman standing in a dark doorway shook her head as I passed. 'There will be trouble again', I heard her mutter, half to herself.

In the evening, after dinner,

> [T]he crowd in front of the Embassy grew ever denser, all the trams had stopped, the bridge was a seething mass of people, and several private motors that passed were held up by soldiers who turned out the occupants without any ceremony and took possession of the cars themselves, swarming into them like a lot of insects, five or six inside, two on either step, two or three on the box, two more lying along the mudguards. And presently two fully-armed regiments came marching across the bridge, carrying banners inscribed in flaring white letters with 'Down with a Capitalist War – Down with the Upper Classes. Long live Anarchy. Bread, Peace, Freedom.' ...
>
> Armed motor-cars were buzzing in all directions now, and as slowly the sunset faded into a soft, gray dusk the crowd grew

denser and denser. General Knox arriving with one or two other English officers tried to telephone to the General Staff, but could get no information. Nobody knew what was the matter. Oh, yes, something was evidently wrong, but what it was, or why, nobody could tell. At last, at about eleven o'clock, General Knox went round to the Staff himself to try and gather a little more definite news. A little later one of the correspondents telephoned to say that they were fighting on the Nevsky, and at about half-past eleven a sudden volley of firing came up from somewhere on the Champ de Mars; and the Square in front of the Embassy, that had been a black mass of people, was cleared as if by magic as the crowd scattered in all directions, some of them taking shelter behind the Marble Palace just opposite, others hiding behind the Embassy itself, others again flying across the bridge. The firing, however, died away as suddenly as it had begun, and General Knox, coming back from the Staff, said that General Polovtzoff was quite calm and did not consider the trouble serious. The Cossacks were ready to come out if there were any very grave riots, but as yet it was thought there was no definite need and the Government had given no orders.

And meanwhile on the Nevsky some fierce fighting took place, the soldiers turning their machine-guns on the crowd without any reason or excuse, driving up and down the street, firing wildly and indiscriminately as they went. And later during the evening a crowd of armed workmen and soldiers surrounded the house of Prince Lvoff, where Monsieur Tereschenko and some of the other Ministers were having dinner. 'We have come to arrest the members of the Government who are here,' so ran the message the crowd sent in. The Ministers sent back word inviting them to enter and discuss with them, but though the house was unguarded and unprotected the crowd feared that a trap was being laid for them, and melted away, merely requisitioning the Ministers' motors that stood at the door.

On the morning of the following day (the 17th),

the town appeared almost peaceful. There were very few people in the streets, the trams made an attempt to run as usual, a few carts lumbered across the bridge as if nothing had happened. But presently the trams stopped running altogether, armed motors began to tear about again, any private car that dared show itself in the street was immediately stopped and taken possession of, and, in spite of an order from the Government forbidding any kind of demonstration or procession, huge bands of workmen with rifles and fixed bayonets kept on coming across the bridge. And a little after twelve three thousand of the Kronstadt sailors marched past the Embassy, an endless stream of evil-looking men, armed with every kind of weapon, cheered by the soldiers in the Fortress, though the ordinary public in the streets shrank away at sight of them.

Looking at them, one wondered what the fate of Petrograd would be if these ruffians with their unshaven faces, their slouching walk, their utter brutality were to have the town at their mercy. ...

Early in the afternoon there was again some heavy fighting on the Nevsky. Somebody had fired at the sailors from a window, with the result that they traversed the street with their machine-guns, and over a hundred people were killed. A little later, while I was sitting with my mother, bands of armed workmen came down the Quay, and aiming their rifles at all the houses, commanded in a threatening manner that every window be closed. Still a little later a crowd of soldiers surrounded the Embassy, and a Russian friend of mine who came to see me at that moment and had had some difficulty in getting through them told us that they were saying they had come to demand the publication of all the Secret Treaties, and that their intention was to attack the Embassy. However, presently the whole crowd of them melted away, something having evidently changed their mind, and about half an hour later the first Cossacks rode past: great, bronzed men, riding through the crowd of soldiers and motor-lorries full of armed workmen and sailors as carelessly as if there were not over a hundred rifles ready to fire on them at any moment. Several of the workmen shook their fists at them as they passed, muttering curses under their breath, but nobody stirred and not a shot was fired, and one began to feel that after all there was perhaps still a Government and a power in the country.

In the evening, whilst having dinner,

[W]e had just reached the pudding when the chasseur – rather white and agitated – appeared in the doorway. 'Excellency, the Cossacks are charging across the Square,' he announced.

Leaving our pudding untasted we made a slightly undignified rush to my father's study, from where a good view of the Square could be obtained, but only arrived at the windows in time to see one or two sailors hastily disappearing round the corner of the

Marble Palace, while line upon line of Cossacks swept up from the Champ de Mars, and turning the corner by the Embassy rode on down the Quay towards the Summer Gardens. They had as a matter of fact driven a crowd of Kronstadt sailors full tilt before them up from the Nevsky, forcing some of them to take refuge in the Marble Palace, while others scattered across the bridge. One of our house-maids declared that she had seen a Cossack cut a sailor's head clean off with one sweep of his sword, but I cannot vouch for the truth of this story, and I saw no signs of a headless body on the Quay.

We stayed for a minute or two to watch the remaining Cossacks ride past, clouds of dust sweeping up under their horses' hoofs, the points of their long lances standing out against the angry sky. Then we returned to the dining-room to finish our pudding, but we had hardly done so when a sharp volley of firing brought us again to our feet, and once more we hurried back to my father's room.

The firing seemed to be coming from the direction of the Summer Gardens, and for a few minutes it continued with unabated violence, but on the Quay itself there was nothing to be seen, only a little group of loitering soldiers by the corner of the bridge, all looking in the direction of that turmoil that we could not see. Then suddenly above the crack of the rifles came the report of a field-gun, and the soldiers scattered in all directions, two of them flinging themselves flat on their faces in the road. And hardly a minute later, with a wild scurry of flying hoofs, two riderless Cossack horses dashed past, knocking down a man who tried to stop them, disappearing down the Quay in a cloud of dust.

The firing had died down to an almost startling silence, broken only by a low rumble of distant thunder and the patter of one or two heavy drops of rain. Presently one of the English officers, who had gone out to try and gather news of what had happened, came back to say that the Cossacks had fallen into a Bolshevik ambush in the Summer Gardens, and that several of them had been killed. They were supposed to be fighting again in the Litenia, though which side was gaining the upper hand nobody knew.

Unable to tear ourselves from the windows we wandered aimlessly from room to room, while rapidly the thunder-clouds darkened behind the Fortress and the wind-driven dust whirled across the bridge. The crowd of loitering soldiers at the corner had thickened. Arguing angrily together they stood gathered in little groups, and now and then a word or two drifted up to us through the heavy stillness – 'the Government – Freedom – the Soviet – the

Capitalists – the Germans – the Allies.' Evidently their conversation turned on the same eternal subjects that had been discussed for so long and yet remained always undecided.

Suddenly, however, they stopped arguing, drew back a little, all staring down the Quay, and presently a huge Cossack appeared leading by the arm a ragged, disreputable looking soldier. In a silence that was curiously tense the crowd by the bridge watched them come, and, unarmed, save for the sword that clattered on the pavement, the Cossack faced them, and dragged the cringing soldier after him. Then – when they had almost passed – the soldier made a frantic effort to free himself from the restraining hand. 'Tavarische (comrades),' he cried, his voice rising to a hysterical scream, 'Tavarische!'

The silent little crowd of watching soldiers surged forward, hastily the Cossack tried to draw his sword, but before he could do so one of the surrounding soldiers wrenched it away from him and dealt him a terrific blow on the head. For a second as he fell to the ground we caught our breath thinking we were going to see him cut to pieces, but with a surprising agility he got to his feet again, and charging head-foremost into the surrounding crowd got clear, and made off down the Quay pursued by screams of rage and two or three bullets which apparently, however, none of them hit him.

Providentially, too, at that moment the rain came down in a sudden blinding sheet, and the soldiers, their collars turned up, made off in various directions, and peace and silence fell over the town.

The night passed quietly, but on the morning of the 18th

two or three armoured-cars suddenly appeared and stationed themselves on the Quay, and while we watched them with a certain anxiety motor after motor full of soldiers drove up and halted by the bridge, while the soldiers, getting out, lined up in front of the Embassy. Nobody seemed quite to know to which side they belonged or for what purpose they had come, but presently our little Russian officer bustled in to tell us that they were loyal troops and that the Government had decided to take up all the bridges and try and isolate the rebels and prevent them passing to and fro. At the same time he warned us that the Bolshevik troops quartered in the Fortress might try and prevent this measure being taken, might even use their big guns, in which case he begged us to go at once to the back of the house. ...

However, the Bolsheviks offered no resistance whatever. The big arch of the bridge was slowly swung open, guards were stationed along the Quay, and climbing back into their motors the rest of the soldiers drove off, and a dead calm seemed to settle down on everything.

Occasionally an armoured-car showed itself on the opposite shore, on the walls of the Fortress soldiers could be seen looking across the river, but nothing happened. A cloudless sky shone above the town, the spires and domes flashed with unbearable brilliance in the sunshine, the river lay as smooth and still as a sheet of deepest aquamarine.

The stand-off continued for the rest of the day, but at 6 a.m. on the morning of the 19th Buchanan was woken by

a violent report just outside, and getting up hastily saw that the whole Square was a mass of soldiers and sailors, who were all drawn up to attention and all seemed in some state of excitement. Quite who it was or what it was who had fired I could not make out, but I saw that the bridge had been swung back into position and one or two officers stood on it, looking anxiously across it. Evidently something was going to happen, and probably whatever it was it had to do with the mysterious action the Government intended taking against the Bolsheviks. Hearing at the same time a certain amount of movement going on in the house, I put on a dressing-gown and opened my door and ran straight into one of the English officers with an overcoat on over his pyjamas.

'Oh!' I was a little taken aback. 'Were you coming to call me? Is anything the matter?'

'Yes,' he answered briefly. 'Will you please go up and call your people and tell them they must go down to the coach-house at once. The Government are attacking the Fortress and the Bolsheviks will probably use their big guns.' ...

Coming downstairs again I met General Knox in a beautiful red dressing-gown. He met my cheerful smile with a frown. 'You oughtn't to be here at all,' he told me severely, and then said he was looking for my father, as the officer in command of the Government troops who were attacking the Fortress wished to speak to him.

In the bright morning sunshine we must have looked a somewhat dissipated and motley assembly, arrayed as we were in an odd assortment of dressing-gowns and coats; but the officer in command of the operations behaved as if there was nothing unusual in the circumstances, and as if it was the most natural thing in the world to be received on the Embassy staircase at six o'clock in the morning by an Ambassador with a greatcoat on over his pyjamas and a pair of bedroom slippers on his bare feet.

He told us that he was confident of being able to take the Fortress, but that the Embassy being in the direct line of fire it would be wiser for us to go to the back of the house and – in the eventuality of very severe fighting – be prepared to leave altogether at a moment's notice. ...

All down the Quay soldiers were kneeling behind the low stone wall with their rifles resting on the top and their eyes fixed on the opposite shore. A little way farther down several machine-guns were hidden in a big stack of wood, and the whole Square was packed with a dense mass of soldiers and sailors of the Naval Cadet School.

Now and then companies of soldiers preceded by armoured-cars advanced cautiously across the bridge, but the guns of the Fortress remained silent, and the red flag fluttered unconcernedly against the sky.

Once an armoured-car from the opposite shore began to advance across the bridge to meet the troops from our side, and the soldiers in the Square put their rifles to their shoulders – then after a second's breathless tension the Bolshevik motor turned and scuttled off in the opposite direction, and a little ripple of amusement ran down the lines of troops along the Quay. ...

More and more troops were advancing across the bridge, and now and then the crack of rifles or the rattle of machine-guns could be heard from the opposite shore, but still the guns of the Fortress remained silent, and presently we all went to dress.

At about half-past ten M. Tereschenko telephoned to my father begging him to come at once with my mother and myself to the Foreign Office, as he did not consider the Embassy to be safe. My father absolutely refused to leave, and mother would not go without him. They wanted, of course, to turn me out, and General Knox told me that I was more trouble than all the Russian army, but while they were still arguing about my fate a message was brought us that Lenin's palace had been taken by the Government troops and

Food shortages in the aftermath of the February Revolution (*The Sphere*, 24 March 1917)

that the Fortress was expected to yield very shortly, and I hastily seized on this to assure them that now it really was not worth my leaving the Embassy.

Occasional bodies of troops could still be seen advancing across the bridge, and now and then a certain amount of shooting could be heard, and it was not till nearly one that the Fortress actually surrendered, without having used those much-threatened big guns, or put up really any very great resistance.

Almost immediately a dead calm settled over Petrograd. Soldiers still guarded the bridge, but the trams started running again, the usual traffic was resumed, and the town began to wear its ordinary aspect. The Government had won the day and the force of the Bolshevik insurrection was broken, so everybody said; and yet the very next night machine-guns hidden in barges down the river, and under the bridges, suddenly opened fire on the Quay, while many of the streets were likewise swept by a sudden rain of bullets that came nobody quite knew from where or for what reason. Government troops were hastily summoned, and after about an hour or two the shooting died away as suddenly as it had begun.[120]

Two days after the defeat of the Bolsheviks, Bertie Stopford summed the week up in a letter to a friend:

We have had five days' hell. Tuesday was worse than any day in the Revolution, but it is not over yet. We must wade through a sea of blood before it can be ended....

For the moment all is quiet here, but there may yet be a pitched battle between those who want to maintain order and carry on the war, and those who don't want to do either....

[During the first revolution] the people were out for an ideal, this week it is pure anarchy, combined with nothing to eat.[121]

Edward Heald was absent from Petrograd on a trip to Finland during the July days, but on his return heard all about the abortive uprising from his colleague on the YMCA prisoner-of-war relief programme, a Mr Burri:

We got back at twilight last evening [22 July] to find the revolution over, but the streets still barricaded, and the cab driver took us on a long detour as the region around the Winter Palace is still unsafe.

Burri has been telling us about their experiences during the days just past. For two or three days a wild mob held control of the center of the city. The Bolsheviki started the affair by suddenly turning their armored cars and machine guns into the peaceful men and women walking along the Nevsky near the Sadovaya, and many were killed.

For three days it was unsafe for any person to appear in a uniform or a white collar. Burri was out with Sam Harper along the Nevsky when no other respectable persons were to be seen, and they said it was exciting enough.

Cossacks were called in from the front and saved the day. Things seem to be adjusting themselves again, but as Zemmer says, the experience that Russia seems to be going through is that of winding up and running down, and each time the winding up is a harder process and the running down comes quicker, and pretty soon the clock will stop running for good.

On the way back from Finland yesterday afternoon, we had for our seatmates a fat, jolly Russian merchant, a Russian officer, a little student, and a cripple. They all engaged in a ceaseless discussion of this last revolution and expressed themselves as hopeless about Russia's future unless Lenin and Trotsky can be disposed of.[122]

A week after the defeat of the attempted insurrection, Alex Thompson summed up the situation in Petrograd at the end of July under the headline 'The German Plot in Russia':

If I had not seen the insurrection of last week with my own eyes no correspondent's account could have persuaded me of its actual aimlessness, hopelessness and imbecility.

On Monday at noon Petrograd was as quiet and peaceful as Slocum Pogis. Within a couple of hours the city looked like Paris in the time of the Commune. Bolshevik troops with rifles occupied the main streets. Motor cars dashed about with armed men standing up in picturesque poster attitudes, others stretched out on steps and wings with fingers on triggers of rifles pointed at imaginary enemies ahead, machine-guns peeping out behind ready to blow the universe to smithereens. That night I saw a battalion of the 180th Regiment marching into the crowded Nevsky Prospekt, which is the one great street and promenade of Petrograd, and a few minutes later heard sustained machine-gun fire; the incomers had been mistaken for enemies by other rioters in the street, who opened fire on them, and from this characteristically idiotic mistake more than a hundred casualties resulted. That night the rebels held the bridges across the Neva and all the main streets; as I returned home at three in the morning a band of them, who had evidently included the law against vodka drinking amongst the objects of their revolt, held up my drosky, made me pay the driver in full, and then compelled me to walk.

On the next day there were fights between Cossacks and rioters, in which the former are said to have suffered severely. On Wednesday the Government at long last took a hand in the game, cut all but one of the bridges across the Neva, ordered peaceful citizens to stay at home, and proceeded to disarm the insurrectionists. But still the fortress of Peter and Paul and the ballet dancer's villa, which the Leninists had held for a month, remained in possession of the rebels. I went to see them on Wednesday night and found swarms of Cronstadt sailors and mutinous soldiers with rifles and machine-guns apparently determined to do or die. But they didn't. By noon next day both positions had been surrendered without the firing of a shot.

There never were in all the world's history such casual daredevils as these mutineers. At carrying red banners with defiant and blood-thirsty inscriptions they beat all the desperadoes that ever were. At crowding tramcars on which they are privileged to ride free – apparently with a view to provide them with employment and work off their martial energy – they take the skull and crossbones. But when it comes to fighting they are the smartest brigade the world has seen in the matter of discretion.

The fact is that none of them knew why they had been called out, nor what cause they were supposed to be fighting for.

The soldiers of the garrison of Petrograd who were concerned in the recent street troubles (700 people, mostly civilians, were killed or wounded) have held a meeting to express their regret and wonder at their own actions. These very casual revolutionaries explain that they were called to the streets by lying telephone messages from unknown persons. They now apologise, declare their allegiance to the Council of Soldiers' and Workmen's Delegates, assure them that it was only a slight misunderstanding and express their readiness to go to the Front. But the people who were killed by their almost incredible folly still remain dead.

The footling futility of the whole business puzzled me sore until we were informed of the documents incriminating Messrs.

Lenin, Trotsky and Co. in the great German conspiracy, and of the vast sums received and paid out by the Kaiser's old friend Madame Sumenson. There was one Bolshevik who really knew for whose profit and at whose bidding the inoffensive citizens of Petrograd were terrorised and killed: William Hohenzollern, Emperor of Sneaks and Spies, fruitfully understood.

For the present I think the mad, sad business is over. There was some machine-gun fighting on the quays the night before last and an affray outside the People's Palace near by, in which five soldiers were killed and thirteen civilian passers-by killed or injured. But today (Sunday) the citizens are out in thousands enjoying the fine weather and except for the everlasting clusters of chatty debaters at the street corners enjoying their new-born privilege and chronic faculty of free speech, the city is as tamely quiet as the Scottish Sabbath.

The Council of Soldiers' and Workmen's Delegates have held a meeting, at which Kerensky was present, and at which the enigmatic Oriental Cheidze declared that 'the Government will find in us help and support and we shall stop at no sacrifice to save the revolution and the country'. He then kissed Kerensky. But the rot in the army which caused the tragic retreat in Galicia and the massacre of thousands of helplessly fleeing brave men, was due to Lenin, Zinoviev and Kamenievo, who are accused of high treason; the unspeakable Trotsky, Posern, Moissieiv, Grinberg (all members of the Council), who openly or overtly encouraged mutiny. Unhappily even Cheidze's kiss will not stay the German invasion of Ukraine nor restore the slaughtered legions.

Ukrania, which wrenched its autonomy practically at the pistol's mouth from the reluctant consent of distracted Ministers, is now desperately anxious about the safety of its capital, Kiev, and about the fate of its rich harvests, threatened by the victorious German advance. The Ukraninans [sic] are feverishly arming to save their new-won independence, and, what is even more important, Russia. But is there time now, in the face of the German guns, to repair the disorganisation produced by their madly untimely revolt?

The bourgeois Liberals are still sulking in their tents, unwilling to help in saving the country, because the Socialist Ministers, who entreatingly hold out the hand of Coalition, have proposed to allay the restlessness of the peasants by temporary measures which smack somewhat of Socialism. As if Ministers had any alternative!

Heroic Kerensky spends himself unsparingly in titanic efforts to pull the storm-tossed ship of state straight, and he is helped devotedly by his fellow-Socialists, especially Tsereteli and Skobelev.[123] But the whirlpool of troubles is such, I think, as never before faced any men in all the records of history.

Yet nobody seems to worry, and though many households must have been brought to grief and mourning the people in the streets seem as unconcerned as though the week's reign of terror, the reverses at the Front, the Ministerial crisis, and the growing shortage of food, were nothing more than one might reasonably expect. They are wonderfully impassive, these Russians. 'What is to be, will be', seems to be the universal motto, and so what's the use of worrying?

The war, the revolution, the last week's insurrection, have changed nothing in the city's aspect since my visit of fourteen years ago. It is the same city of splendid possibilities and shabby semi-realisation – which, when I came to think of it, is probably the reason the main streets are called 'Prospects'. The people – women, soldiers, officers, 'nuts' – still cross themselves with mechanical devoutness when passing churches and sacred ikons, which latter are to be found not only in the streets but in all restaurants, and even in the Socialist Ministers' offices. The beggars are as numerous as ever. The izvoshtchiks, in their monstrously padded petticoats, still take their precarious slumbers on the box seats of their cabs, and still grow excessively wide-awake when the guileless foreign victim looms into view. Since I was here fourteen years ago their stunted top hats have perhaps grown a little older but, naturally, not more shabby. Their droskys have accumulated a few more layers of the dust of ages, and the string by which their axles are secured may in some cases show further signs of wear, their horses are, if possible, thinner, the holes in the cobblestone pavements are steeper and more soul-stirring to the unaccustomed passenger, and the fares have obeyed the scriptural injunction to increase and multiply. But otherwise Petrograd's chief means of locomotion is beautifully unchanged.

No coins of any sort are now in circulation, but only notes. The ancient regime issued paper currency to the amount of 9,950,000,000 roubles. The total actually exceeds 12 milliards, and the printing of papers continues wholesale, with the natural result that the rouble, whose exchange value in English was formerly 2s 1d, is now exchanged for less than a shilling. For small change stamps are used, and also notes of five, three, two and one kopecks, the latter denomination being worth, at present rate of exchange, one hundredth part of a shilling. The prices of all commodities, thanks largely to our cosmopolitan friend, the profiteer, have risen enormously; and wages – or at least the demands of the workers – have unsuccessfully tried to keep pace with them. When employers have professed inability to pay, the workers have in some cases demanded three to six years' drafts on the capital and assets of the company. The increase in wages demanded for all Russia has been estimated at five to six milliards of roubles. The output has at the same time declined enormously; in one of the biggest works in Petrograd the production in January was 150,000 poods and the wages were 500,000 roubles. The production in April had shrunk to 57,000 poods, and the wages had increased to a million roubles. You will not be surprised to know, under the circumstances, that employers show great eagerness to hand over the concern to State control, nor will you be surprised, bearing in mind the State's financial pinch, that this eagerness is not reciprocated.

The well-dressed and well-fed appearance of the people proves that there is little poverty. But there is obviously much inconvenience. Women stand in street queues for bread, for flour, for sugar, for meat, for butter, for lamp oil, and even for their husbands' tobacco. In some cases, as in the case of meat, they will take their stand in the evening to be in time for the morning supply. When they find time to do other household work was to me a puzzling mystery until I asked Ransome of the 'Daily News'. 'They don't do any', he answered airily, 'they just push things under the bed'. This confirms my view that the Russian people think more deeply than ours, and justifies the London Tommy who casually observed to me: 'I can't think why they call it Russia; I've never seen the beggars rush.'

Bread, very black and glutinous, is served every two days, the ration being ¾ lb per person per day; the price was formerly 1½ kopecks per pound; in the early days of the war people thought famine was come when the price rose to 3, then 4, then 5 kopecks per lb; it is now 10½ kopecks. The meat allowance is ½ lb a head per week; before the war the poor could buy meat for 15 kopecks; the lowest price is now 80, and the well-to-do pay for fillet as much as 3 roubles 75 kopecks a pound. Flour is unobtainable. The sugar ration is 2 lb a month. One may buy two dozen new potatoes for 70 kopecks, and cherries are 2 roubles a pound. Clothes are ruinously dear. An Englishman who recently went home sold his old garments before starting; he obtained 180 roubles for each of his two best suits and 150 for a third. I have paid 2½ roubles for socks, whose heels were gaping holes in two days. Being unable to get my washing back from the laundry I tried to buy a suit of pyjamas, but when I was asked 75 roubles I concluded to curb my appetite for midnight ostentation.

The likeness of this people to our own strikes me more than ever. There is a difference in dress; some of the working men still wear top boots and the embroidered Russian cotton shirt with stiffened collarpiece; and some of the women – or rather the girls – happily retain the picturesque white or yellow kerchief on the head and the gaudy cashmere shawl or splash of loud elementary colour in silk blouse or skirt. But this slight superficial difference apart, the crowd in the streets, the tramcars, and the restaurants, look very like the English. ...

Miracles, they say, always happen when they are badly wanted in Russia. This is another way of saying that the Russians are people of extraordinary, quick changes of mood and temper, and that, as the vulgar say, it is never safe to bet on them.[124]

Once the insurrection had been suppressed, things returned to normal, at least on the surface. On 29 July the forester Edward Stebbing noted in his diary:

On the surface the capital has much the same appearance it presented in the days of the Czar before the war. The same cosmo-politan crowd, intent on its own pleasure and amusement, fills the Nevski, but though the bulk of the soldiery have a loafing, brazen or furtive look about them, there is still a residue who salute their officers in the streets of the capital. That much is to the good, at any rate, and might easily prove significant of a change for the better. The one change for the bad is in the food and prices. The latter are preposterous, and the former of poor quality and small in quantity. At the Hôtel Europe, where they did you *en prince* in the old days, in this respect there is a great change. The waiters have imbibed the revolutionary spirit and their service for a first-class hotel, as this used to be, is beneath contempt.

Stebbing also witnessed the funeral of the five Cossack soldiers who had died during the uprising. It was attended by numerous dignitaries:

It was intended as a rebuke, I was told, to the Red Socialist groups who had organised the funeral of the victims of the Revolution. These latter were buried in the centre of the Champ de Mars, and the graves are now covered with grass. The bodies were enclosed in red coffins and were escorted to the burial-place by a giant multitude waving thousands of red banners; but no clergy were permitted to officiate, and there was no religious ceremony whatsoever. It is said that several of the relatives engaged priests to conduct private services over the graves subsequently. It is also an open secret that others carried off the bodies of their dead before the funeral took place, rather than have them buried in this sacrilegious fashion. And that in consequence many of the coffins carried to the grave with such revolutionary fervour were filled with bricks in default of bodies. Perhaps the day will dawn, however, when the last resting-place of those who gave their lives in the birth throes of the Revolution will be marked with a monument which will represent to generations yet unborn the event which will bring real freedom to the country.

But yesterday's ceremony presented a very marked contrast to the 'red burial.'[125]

Yet the defeat of the Bolsheviks, real as it seemed in the immediate aftermath of the uprising, proved to be a false dawn for the supporters of the Provisional Government. Meriel Buchanan wrote:

And now that they had the power in their hands, Kerensky and the Government let the propitious moment pass. The Kronstadt sailors, taken prisoners in the Fortress, were set at liberty instead of being shot as traitors. Lenin, having been given ample warning that the troops were coming to arrest him, had walked out of his back door and disappeared nobody quite knew where, and several of the other Bolshevik leaders were set free.

'We must shed no blood!' so Kerensky preached, the idealist in him once more overcoming the statesman and ruler, hesitating to strike a crushing blow at the insidious evil of Bolshevism that was spreading like a disease through the ranks of the army. And the Cossacks burying their dead in the wonderful cemetery of the Alexander Nevsky, marched with surly faces in the long procession – these, their comrades who had fallen were given a wonderful burial – with flowers and music and much pomp. But what good was that going to do them now? They had given their lives to save

Leon Trotsky

a Government that had been overthrown by a horde of rebels, and the Government accepted the sacrifice and did nothing to punish the rebels. You must not shed the blood of your brothers! But had not their brothers' blood been shed, and was it to go unavenged? It was a question that remained unanswered, but was not forgotten.[126]

As for the Bolsheviks themselves, their version of events was that the disturbances had begun 'spontaneously', after which the Bolshevik Central Committee felt obliged to take over the leadership of what they claimed was a mass revolt in Petrograd. This view was neatly expressed by Maxim Litvinov, who wrote in his 1918 history of the Revolution that 'the masses of Petrograd again rose in revolt – this time against the Provisional Government as a whole and the coalition principle in particular – without any lead from the Bolshevik Party, but no doubt under the influence of its propaganda'. Litvinov added that, 'in spite of its promising beginning', the uprising had failed because 'it had not been organised', but also because 'a mass of forged documents had been secretly set in circulation among the Petrograd troops, 'with the connivance of the Government', showing that Lenin, Trotsky and other Bolsheviks were in the pay of Germany'.[127]

Trotsky's verdict was somewhat similar:

The workers and soldiers were exerting pressure from below giving violent expression to their discontent with the official policy of the Soviet, and demanded from our party more drastic action. We considered that in view of the still backward condition of the provinces the hour for such action had not yet struck; but at the same time we feared lest the events at the front might produce an immense confusion in the ranks of the revolutionary workers and create despair amongst them.

He added that 'the party propagandists in the lower ranks went hand in hand with the masses and carried on an uncompromising agitation.'[128]

'Down with war!'

BOLSHEVIK PROPAGANDA AND
DEMORALIZATION AT THE FRONT

Despite the failure of the 'July Days' uprising, and Lenin's having to go into hiding, the Bolsheviks were able to continue their work of preaching 'Peace and Liberty' at the front more or less unhindered. Nurse Florence Farmborough witnessed one such occasion in August 1917:

SATURDAY, 26th AUGUST
We have been told that a meeting is to be held in the neighbourhood. Although meetings organised by the rank and file are strictly prohibited unless sanctioned by the Commanding Officer, there is no doubt that they are taking place.

Strange-looking men – some in uniform, others in civilian clothes – have been seen combing the Russian Fronts, section by section, and organising informal meetings with the troops. So now that such a personage is due to visit our Front, we Sisters are extremely anxious to hear for ourselves the 'message of good-will' which he is supposed to deliver.

SUNDAY, 27th AUGUST
It was a most extraordinary meeting! Never, in our wildest dreams did we imagine that we should listen to such an outpouring of treachery. We sat in a group among the trees, surrounded on all sides by soldiers. Some of our hospital Brothers were there and I caught sight of several of our transport drivers.

The man who had come to speak to the soldiers had an ordinary face and was dressed in ordinary Russian clothes: dark trousers and a dark shirt, buttoned on the left and worn outside his trousers, with a black belt round the waist. His face was serious and pale, but he smiled and nodded once or twice to one or another of the audience, as though he recognised friends. He spoke for a time about Russia, her vast territory, her wealth and the many overlords who, possessing enormous estates and resources, were revered on account of their riches throughout the western world. Then he described the impoverished peasantry who, unschooled, uncared-for and half-starved, were eking out a miserable existence by tilling and cultivating the land belonging to those same overlords. War had burst upon Russia and enemies had invaded her territory, and who were the men who had sacrificed themselves to fight the ruthless invaders and drive them off Russian soil? Not the wealthy overlords, not the despotic land-owners; no! – they were safely installed in their fortress-homes. It was those downtrodden countrymen who had been roped in in their thousands, in their millions, to stem the tide of invasion; when they had been killed, others had been quickly collected and sent to replace them. There had been no end to the slaughter and sacrifice of the Russian peasant. Enemy guns had devoured them daily, hourly; every minute of the day and night, the heavy guns had feasted on them and every minute new recruits were being seized and thrust like fodder into the voracious jaws of the enemy's cannon. But now a miraculous event had taken place! The Tsar – that arch-potentate, that arch-tyrant – had been dethroned and dismissed. Russia had been pronounced a free country! – the Russian citizens a free people! Freedom had come at last to the downtrodden people of Russia.

Our doctors were moving restlessly. They were, as always, in officers' uniform. I wondered if they were thinking it was high time to leave, but they stayed. Undoubtedly, it was the wisest thing to do. I glanced around. Most of the soldiers were young and raw, inexperienced and impressionable; all of them drawn from far-off corners of what, until recently, had been known as the Russian Empire. What easy prey they would be for seditious guile! New ideas could so readily take hold of their gullible minds and a cunning speaker would soon be aware that he could sway them this way and that with his oratory.

The speaker was still harping on the theme of freedom. Freedom, he declared, was a possession so great, so precious, one dared not treat it lightly. But war was an enemy of freedom, because it destroyed peace, and without peace there could be no freedom. It was up to the Russian soldier to do all in his power to procure peace. And the best and quickest way to bring about a guaranteed peace was to *refuse to fight*. War could not be fought if there were no soldiers to fight! War was never a one-sided operation! Then, when peace had at last come to Russia, freedom could be enjoyed. The free men of Free Russia would own their own land. The great tracts of privately-owned territory would be split up and divided fairly among the peasantry. There would be common ownership of all properties and possessions. Once the Russian soldier had established peace in his homeland, he would reap benefits undreamt of. Peace above all else! Down with war!

The soldiers were all astir; they were whispering, coughing, muttering. But they were all in full accord with the orator; he held them in his hand! Their stolid faces were animated and jubilant. 'Tovarishchi! [Comrades!]' he was calling them. 'Tovarishchi! You free men of Free Russia! You will demand peace!' 'We will!' they shouted in reply. 'You will assert your rights as free Russian citizens!' 'We will assert our rights,' they echoed with one voice. 'You will never allow yourselves to be pushed into the trenches to sacrifice your lives in vain!' 'Never!' they roared in unison.

There swept through my mind the memory of another meeting, where the enthusiasm of thousands of loyal soldiers had been kindled by the patriotic words of Kerensky. That was only some three short months ago.[129]

The effects were soon to be seen. In November 1917 Petty Officer Jack Pincott, an Australian who was attached to the Armoured Car Division of the Royal Navy's Flying Corps and who had been fighting in Russia since 1915, returned home on leave and gave a graphic account of the retreat on the South-Western Front after the failure of Kerensky's offensive in the summer. Here he describes General Lavr Kornilov, who had become unpopular in Petrograd after restoring order following the February Revolution but had nevertheless been appointed Commander in Chief of the Russian Army by Kerensky on 1 August:

Korniloff did everything possible in the attempt to keep the Russians at it, but it was of no avail. Meetings were held in the trenches, and many of the Russians became half-hearted. We were distributed among them to try and add backbone, and the Cossacks were all solid. The bombardment, prior to the advance, was begun. There was plenty of ammunition, plenty of rations, and everything was favorable – everything except one thing, the spirit of some but not all of the Russians. After our bombardment of the Austro-Germans had gone on for three days the order came to advance. Many of the Russians went on all conquering, but others simply would not leave the trenches. Their officers cried for shame. Yes, some of those Russian officers proved themselves if ever men did. They went out and beseeched their men to follow, but too often

Women soldiers fighting in the 'Battalion of Death' led by Marie Bochkareva (bottom left) (The Sphere, 18 August 1914)

there was no response. While one regiment would be ultra loyal and dash forward, sometimes to a three miles depth in the enemy lines, others funked it absolutely.

The officers stood on the trenches, and, pulling the epaulets from their uniform, waited till an Austro-German shell or bullet sent them out forever. They showed the men who would not fight that they at least knew how to die. There could not have been anything more tragically thrilling in the war than the self-sacrifice of these Russian officers. Some of the rank and file would not on any account leave the safety of the trenches. It riled us. One of our men – a chap from New Zealand – got hold of some of them and literally threw them out. We lost several of our best men in this engagement. Our cars went ahead in the hope that the Russians would regain courage, but it was no use. A lull in the attack became necessary, and then the source of the desire not to fight became exposed. The German spies in the ranks sent the cry broadcast, 'The German cavalry has surrounded us'. Two Russian regiments had previously left the trenches with their officers powerless to stop them, and the revolt spread. It developed into a panic.

'Nemelski Cavalaire' was the one mad cry. Retreat was necessary. Not hundreds, not thousands, but millions of men on the run. The Russians went back 100 miles in a few days. Still with the same mad cry, they kept on running, running, running – to they didn't know where. Anything in the way was cast aside. Cars and carts got mixed up in the crush and the rush down the narrow streets … and when 50 miles behind we were forced to come after them we saw signs of a debacle everywhere. It was absolute chaos. The Cossacks attempted to quell the fears, but without result. We were fighting rearguard actions all the time. The Austro-Germans had been practically invited to come on, and the spectacle was seen of them fighting hand to hand with the Russian artillery.

It had to stop somewhere, but nobody knows where that mad run would have stopped only for a British officer. Loyal Russian regiments and the Cossacks had sought to round them up, and it was the manoeuvre of this British officer, Colonel Valentine, that saved the situation, for a while at any rate. The road of retreat was through hills with a railway intersecting, and he contrived to get a stationmaster to send trains along and block up the road. He held up the mob for a while, though many scrambled through and on again. But with the hold-up came opportunity for thought and some reason at length prevailed. The runaways were prevailed upon to make another stand, and showing how feeble was the force against them, they, as far as I know, still hold the line there. Whole regiments have, however, disappeared, either into the heart of Russia, or taken prisoner by the Germans. We lost 12 cars in the retreat.

And, perhaps thinking ahead to the events of September, Pincott added this comment on Kornilov:

> The situation is full of possibilities, but my own opinion is that Korniloff is the one man who may save Russia. He is a Cossack and it is the Cossacks who are the better class and absolutely loyal to Russia and the Allies. Of fine physique and outstanding personality, Korniloff has proved himself a tremendously brave man, and the Cossacks swear by him and will do anything for him. He has been wounded three times, and was once when wounded taken prisoner by the Austrians. His own strategy and the loyalty and bravery of the Cossacks resulted in his rescue.[130]

Kornilov himself was soon to come to the same conclusion.

'Object lessons for Democrats'

THE DISILLUSIONMENT OF A SOCIAL DEMOCRAT

As the army became increasingly ineffective and the Provisional Government lurched from one ministerial crisis to another, some British Social Democrats began to lose heart. When news of the February Revolution first reached Britain, it was greeted rapturously by Alex Thompson of The Clarion:

> Best of all is the great and blessed wonder of the Russian Revolution.
>
> Do not let us invite future disappointment by excessive present hopes. The prospect as revealed to us in the reports from Petrograd looks too good to be true. A Russian Republic at one swoop and without shot or blow? An end to the knout and the pogrom,

the Bastille of Peter and Paul and the Siberian prisons, Finland's servitude and Poland's oppression, and end of all the 'dark forces' of ignorance, superstition, and tyranny which have so long stifled the enlightened aspirations of the freedom-loving, idealistic Russian people? It cannot be that so vast a victory for Humanity's cause has been definitely won at so small a cost!

There must be a reactionary party. There must still be some power behind the deposed Tsar. The dark forces will not, they cannot, 'take it lying down'. We must expect some attempt at counter-revolution.

Again, it cannot be that the mixed elements which have combined in the making of this glorious world-surprise will exactly agree as to the bases of resettlement and rebuilding. There is a bourgeois commercial element which will demand nothing more revolutionary than an increase of votes. There is an ultra-Communistic agricultural element which will expect an immediate redistribution of land and property. There is a vast ill-informed industrial element which is said to have tried already to turn the military rank and file against its officers. Between these various elements conflict is almost sure to arise in the establishment of the New Order ...

But when all the potential troubles have been recognised, there is still a tremendous and positive gain. Something has been accomplished which can never be undone. Down-trodden Russia stands erect. A vast nation of slaves has broken its shackles. Free Russia has entered the United States of free democratic peoples ...

If the war brings the human race no other boon than the Russian Revolution, it will have achieved a stupendous triumph for mankind.

But it is now certain that it will bring even more than this victory. The thunderclap of the Russian Revolution will, like the upheaval of the great French Revolution of 1789, re-echo through all the corridors of the surviving royal and imperial courts. The fall of the Romanoffs will shake all the thrones and dynasties of Europe. ...

The Russian revolution is the greatest and most decisive victory of the war.[131]

Contrast this with his assessment of the state of the Revolution, and of Russia in general, written shortly after the July Days:

The Russian revolution, which fired the democracies of the world with enthusiasm and high hopes five months ago, stands in grave peril of breakdown and defeat, and it is important that the causes jeopardising its success should be clearly understood by Socialists in all countries lest they should be tempted to defend that which is neither Socialistic nor defensible, thereby discrediting their cause.

The plain truth is that whilst many Socialists helped in making the Revolution, the great mass of the revolutionaries are blind and incoherent rebels, full of wants but utterly empty of knowledge, experience or governing faculties. The despotism whose barbarous repressions goaded them to revolt had cunningly shaped its policy to the deliberate end of making Revolution, if it ever came, a mere whirl and clash of incompatible and undirected forces doomed by their own vague aimlessness to impotence and mutual destruction. That deliberate purpose of Imperial rule has up to the present achieved its devilish purpose, and the result is that the Revolution has produced phenomena not Socialistic at all, but on the contrary anarchistic, and the new Republic stands now, after five months' perilous quick-whirling struggle, the precarious 'waste chaos of a dream'.

The reactionary parties are quite right in contending that the great majority of the Russian people are not, and never have been, Socialists. Three fourths of the people – one hundred and twenty of the country's one hundred and sixty million – are engaged in agriculture, and, like the peasantry in most countries, they are much more eager to acquire property rights than to destroy them. When I asked Tsereteli, the Socialist Minister, what proportion of the Russian peasantry could be counted as Socialists, he answered with a cynical but convincing frankness: 'You may count all those who have nothing, but when they have anything you cannot count them any longer'. As probably eighty per cent of them are wholly illiterate, and as no man can be truly accounted a Socialist or a Democrat without some study of economics or political learning, Tsereteli's rough assessment of the Russian peasantry's political enlightenment and social altruism may not be disputed.

Those of them who have any learning at all have been crammed with superstition to the fatty degeneration of their brains as meticu-lously as geese are crammed at Strasburg to the fatty degeneration of their livers. ...

The fact is that the people have been as firmly rooted in this soil of drunkenness, debauchery, superstition and ignorance, as in the land which they tilled and whose ownership they coveted. The Revolution, with its boast of freedom and its challenge of established authority, has given them the opportunity of appeasing their earth-hunger, but certainly it has not made them Socialists. Their method of asserting their new rights is indeed the reverse of Socialistic, for the Socialist Minister, Chernov, the pet abomination of the reactionaries, has been driven to resign because, as he explained to me, he has been trying by Socialistic measures to prevent the anarchistic scramble for the best slices of land in which, in some cases, entire village communities have been killed or wounded.

The industrial classes in the towns are, as their wild, chaotic, purposeless insurrections of last month showed, equally ignorant and anarchistic. Their claim to an improved standard of life is manifestly just, but their impossible demands are simply paralysing industry and ruining Russia ... The Socialist Minister of Labour, Skobelev, whom I found very sympathetic and understanding, is doing his utmost to divert the industrial tumult into Socialistic order, but he also finds his task terribly hindered by the anarchistic tendencies of the workers.

But the worst trouble of all is, of course, the anarchism of the army, and here, I must insist, the fault lies chiefly in that vague pacifist sentimentalism with which well-meaning idealists of our own party has infected socialism....

Longuet, the French Pacifist Socialist, recognises and proclaims the fact that 'Lenin has been the most formidable enemy of the Revolution, that his doctrinaire fanaticism can only result in catastrophe for Russia and service for German imperialism'....

If all the dreamers in Russia could repair the mischief they have done as quickly and completely as those with practical responsibility have repented it, there might still be time to save the Revolution of Russia.[132]

Faced with an ever-deteriorating situation, in August Kerensky once again reshuffled the government and created a new 'patriotic national' ministry made up of four Cadets, two Radical Democrats and eight Socialists. Thompson commented:

Most people agree that this is the last possible attempt at Coalition. If it fails the reactionaries, in order finally to discredit Socialism, will probably ask the Sowiet [sic] to undertake sole responsibility, but it may be safely assumed that the Sowiet will decline.

... it is generally believed that if the present Coalition fails it will be succeeded by neither Sowiet nor Cadets but by military dictatorship, or perhaps a joint dictatorship of General Kornilov with the indispensable Kerensky. If that fails, then ————?

But if, as now seems likely, the military rot can be stayed, and if the still more formidable danger of food shortage can be staved off, there is reason to hope that the new Ministry may live at least till the elections for the Constituent Assembly give definite mandate to a more regular Government. The last month's events have certainly had a quietening effect. The failure of the Bolshevik insurrection in Petrograd, followed by the prosecution of the chief Leninites on clear evidence that their Pacifist agitation was inspired and financed by the Kaiser's agents, has been a great eye-opener...

It is true that the Bolsheviks have nevertheless ventured on a stealthy conference in a suburb of Petrograd, but the Government have announced their resolve to stop such manifestations of their activity in future, and though still strong at Moscow and in the Donetz mining region, the once formidable Bolsheviks appear to have no sympathisers with pluck and power to protest.

Their downfall has necessarily involved a considerable weakening of the influence of the Sowiet, and consequently of Socialist prestige, and even of revolutionary enthusiasm. The vastly prevalent desire, so far as I am able to judge, is for strong Government, ruthless suppression of disorder, a return to iron discipline in the army, and perhaps even some form of industrial coercion to arrest the steady drop in output and ruinous rise in wages.

This was perilously close to advocating a dictatorship by a 'strong man', but as Thompson also noted in the same article, it was psychologically impossible for Kerensky to 'deliberately flout the wishes of the Sowiet, which has given him his pedestal'.[133]

Reflecting on these events a year later, Thompson succinctly summarized Kerensky's dilemma, and compared it to that Gambetta had faced in 1871:

I was a close observer of Kerensky's titanic struggle to restore discipline and order in Russia between June and October of last year ... It was a pitiful business. Before Kerensky had assumed power the Sowiets had established what they called 'democratic control' in the army. The effect was suggested to me by a private soldier in the camp at Moscow. 'There are fifty thousand of us here', he said, 'but we are not allowed to obey any order of Korniloff until it has been debated by the local Sowiet.' War under such conditions was, of course, impossible....

[Kerensky was] in the position of a circus rider with one foot on each of two untamed, erratic and steadily divergent horses....

The growling force of Bolshevism, steadily growing on war-weariness and hunger, had defeated him. He had played the part against Prussianism that Gambetta played in 1871, but his struggle was even more desperate and hopeless than Gambetta's.[134]

'Denounced as a traitor'

THE KORNILOV AFFAIR

At the front, too, things continued to deteriorate as Bolshevik propaganda, skilfully aided by the Germans, continued to have its effect on the already war-weary Russian troops. On the Northern Front, following the battle of Jugla, the Russian 12th Army retreated and German troops entered Riga on 3 September, directly threatening Petrograd itself. As The Clarion's reporter in the city, V.K. Vitrine, noted, the news did little for morale in the city, but merely increased the feelings of despondency and defeatism, whilst the politicians continued to prefer talk to action:

PETROGRAD, 7 SEPTEMBER 1917
This week has been more eventful than usual, even for Petrograd, in the midst of the Revolution. The serious defeat of the Russians in the Riga region, with the consequent rout of the army and direct threat to the capital, must have helped the Germans to digest their 'Kriegsbrod'. The effect on Petrograd has been extraordinary. Outwardly complete calm reigns, a stranger arriving in the city would not be aware that anything untoward had happened.

The Russians have been politically starved for hundreds of years. No paper, periodical, pamphlet or book could be printed until it had been microscopically examined by the censor. No lecture, performance or public meeting could be held without wearying and numerous restrictions. Now they are fed on the rich food of liberty, which often is pure license, their weakened digestions have rebelled against the stuff served out to them. They are now like a patient convalescing; extremely apathetic and inert. They do not care; entirely despondent, they are gradually sinking into despair. ...

Today Petrograd is full of people who glibly use all the terminology of Western Socialism, understanding it as well as the Kharkov policeman.[135]

The people have had education denied them. Every effort in the direction of political advancement was immediately quenched in a fortress cell or Siberian exile. These very people, continuously denied every vestige of citizenship, are now called upon to rule themselves. They have neither tradition, nor administrative experience, nor cohesion, nor, for the matter of that, any quality for the purpose.

The result we see in the complete breakdown of discipline, for no army, and certainly not one faced by the most determined foe yet known to history, can be run by political committees and public meetings held within range of the enemy's rifle fire. The Russians have tried what the more enlightened and experienced Western peoples have never dared. In consequence the army is a rabble. For months it fraternised with the Germans, who made use of the opportunity to find out all the secrets of the defence. When the moment came for striking every heavy gun on the Russian side was ranged and silenced within a few minutes of the artillery opening fire. The men, physically softened by refusal to exercise or keep themselves fit and busy, crumpled before the German attack. Their *morale* had gone under the constant influence of political agitation.

I hear now that, with the exception of comparatively few units, the rest are 'simply retreating'. As I write the wildest rumours are circulating. The Provisional Government, whose honesty of purpose is beyond question, are attempting to stem the torrent. But the people have no cohesion, whilst the Government is the object of attack from 'Right' and 'Left'. It has no solid foundation to stand on; if it is to hold on to its job it must placate all loud-voiced criticism or use force. It does not possess the latter nor can it resort to persuasion with success at a time when men's ideas are in a state of flux and change as often as there are hours in a day. For three days now the population of Petrograd has known that their homes are directly threatened by the enemy. What has it done? It has remained depressed, cowed, apathetic and despairing. No authoritative voice has rung out a clear call to duty, for duty it is a still-born child of the Revolution. It merely groans. The numerous Soviets, Dumas, Committees have met, they all have sat in solemn session from 9 am to 6 am the following morning, recommenced the next day, and gone on till the same hour. What have they done? Talked, talked, jabbered, jabbered. Whilst the enemy piles success upon success.

The only burst of feeling after the fall of Riga was known was a disgraceful procession of a few people shouting 'Hurrah' in the Nevski in honour of the defeat. When one soldier was asked why he shouted 'Hurrah', he replied, 'every victory on any side brings us nearer to peace. What does it matter which side wins'.

The Germans have been clever, as they are always clever, when they calculate on human frailty and weakness. They have used idealists run amok to sow madness among the people. They are reaping a record harvest. Is it too late for Russia to wake up even whilst the enemy knock at the gate? There is just time. Possibly there are just two men who can save the situation. Will they be able to do so? The next two or three weeks will answer the question.[136]

The two men Vitrine had in mind were Kerensky and General Kornilov. Both were touted as 'strong men' who could act as Bonaparte did in the French Revolution and restore some kind of order to the country, but one problem was that each distrusted the other. In order to establish some kind of common ground the government invited representatives of all parties (except the Bolsheviks) to a conference in Moscow in early August. Alex Thompson reported in The Clarion the contrast between the two protagonists when they attended the conference:

Kerensky will not have improved his standing in the love and favour of the respectabilities by his sudden divorce from his wife and his hasty marriage with his wife's relative in the ex-Tsar's apartments in the Winter Palace. That kind of thing is regarded as romantic in the history of Kings and Emperors but it is not generally approved in persons not specially brought up to it.

But he does so many things which are not exactly nice. Even I, who have watched his feverish progress with fascinated awe, found my belief in the man staggered when I saw him attended at the Moscow Conference by a military and naval aide-de-camp, who stood behind his chair through the long hours of the Conference like the bodyguard of some vain and pompous potentate. But, on the other hand, I marvelled as much as ever at his prompt peremptory management of the clashing elements assembled there. Before the Conference actually started the bourgeois parties held several preparatory sittings, at which the champions of military dictatorship talked in the boldest fighting strain of their resolve to clear out the Government, including Kerensky.

General Kornilov, when he came to Moscow on the Sunday, made a State pageant of his arrival, driving through the ancient capital with a retinue of officers of high degree from all parts of the Empire and making a special halt at a shrine invariably visited by the ex-Tsar on his visits to Moscow. On the next day the Conference should have started at eleven, but it was adjourned till nearly two in order that Kerensky might have a preliminary interview with Kornilov. What happened during those two hours I, of course, do not know, but I do know that the great military revolt which had been so briefly heralded somehow fizzled out.

Kornilov spoke, and Kerensky led the applause which greeted him, but he did not deliver the expected attack on the Government. Miliukov, the Cadet leader, who had been vitriolic in his indictment of the Government at the preliminary Conference, concluded a mild criticism at the public sitting with the statement that his party felt bound to support the Ministry. There was a stormy scene when a party of Cossack officers, who had evidently been dining, shouted insulting remarks from Kornilov's box to a Cossack soldier who was speaking in defence of the Sowiet; Kerensky turned to the box with masterful gesture and declared that to attack a man from the dark recesses of that fastness was the act of a coward. The heated officers immediately rushed on to the stage, clearly bent on personal violence, and, being turned back, stood for the rest of the proceedings in front of the box defiantly twirling fierce and bellicose moustachios.

Thompson concluded that 'the net effect of the Conference was Kerensky's signal victory over the projected counter-revolution', but he also noted that after he left Petrograd 'Kornilov has tried it again with an armed rebellious force, but again he appears to have been defeated'.[137] This refers to the so-called 'Kornilov Affair' when the general announced his intention of marching his troops into Petrograd, arresting the Bolsheviks and dissolving the Soviet. Kerensky resisted this move and called on the Soviet for help, even going so far as to arm them from military supplies provided by the Allies. The Soviet forces were successful in their defence of the capital, and as a result a good number of army officers were lynched for their support, real or supposed, of the plot. But of even greater significance was the fact that the weakness of the government was laid bare for all to see.

Both at the time and since, a degree of mystery has hung over the exact details of the Kornilov Affair. Kerensky himself described it as a right-wing conspiracy, whereas some historians have argued that the two men had agreed on the need for the military to restore order in Russia only for Kerensky to renege on the deal for fear of losing power, and others have suggested that the plot was in fact engineered by Kerensky so that he could dismiss the general and become dictator of Russia himself. And, of course, there is also the theory that it was all a terrible mix-up and mistake, caused in large part by the Procurator of the Holy Synod, Vladimir Lvov,[138] who acted as an intermediary in the negotiations. Writing shortly after the event, Meriel Buchanan seems to have subscribed to this view:

> So intricate and contradictory are the workings of the whole plot that it is almost impossible to know what really happened or what is the exact truth. Already for some time past there had been vague talk of a counter-Revolutionary party who intended to overthrow the Government and dissolve the Soviet, but whether Korniloff had any sympathy with them is very much to be doubted.
>
> What seems, however, certain is that, fearing a Bolshevik rising, the Government negotiated with Korniloff to send troops up to Petrograd to quell the insurrection under the command of General Krimoff. Then M. Vladimir Lvoff, former Procurator of the Holy Synod, arrived at headquarters, authorised by his own account to discuss the situation with General Korniloff and come to an agreement as to the formation of a stronger Government. Did he wilfully exceed his powers? Or only inadvertently make the mistake that brought about such a disaster? According to the statement made by Monsieur Savinkoff[139] he was authorised to lay three propositions before General Korniloff. The first being that he should form a Government with Kerensky as Minister of Justice and Savinkoff as Minister of War. The second that he should declare himself Dictator. The third that he, Kerensky, and Savinkoff

should form a Triumvirate having equal powers of government. General Korniloff adopted the third proposition, and Monsieur Lvoff returned to Petrograd charged with his answer. But, whether intentionally or by mistake, he informed Kerensky that Korniloff had chosen the second proposition. Doubting the possibility of such an answer, Kerensky connected himself by wireless with the Stavka and asked General Korniloff whether he confirmed the message Monsieur Lvoff had delivered. Believing the question to refer to the proposed Triumvirate General Korniloff replied in the affirmative, but Kerensky did not at once break with him, and it was only under pressure from M. Nekrassoff,[140] Minister of Ways and Communications, that he eventually decided to treat Korniloff as a traitor and demand his instant resignation. This sudden distrust and change decided General Korniloff to act alone, and he ordered his troops to advance on Petrograd. Had he led them in person, the ultimate result might have been very different, but he remained at headquarters to direct operations, and unfortunately did not take the troops into his confidence. The soldiers believed they were going to quell a Bolshevik insurrection, and when they came near the capital and found that they were to fight against the Government declared that they had been ordered to advance under false pretences. Bolshevik propaganda spread its insidious reports among them – Korniloff was a traitor and a spy; he had committed suicide; he was plotting against the Revolution. Swayed this way and that, the troops wavered, and at last, turning against their officers, refused to advance.[141]

Bertie Stopford, too, subscribed to this analysis of what had happened. In a letter of 17 September he wrote:

There is still a mystery about [Kornilov's] failure, but there is no doubt that Kerenski was in the complot with Kornilov, and that through Lvov's treachery – or madness – Kerenski left Kornilov in the lurch.

To which he later added a note that

Lvov – Cousin of the former President of the Council – was sent from Moscow by Kerenski to see how the land lay at Moghilev and report to him. Apparently he was taken into Kornilov's confidence, and is said to have given the game away to Kerenski – possibly in a fit of insanity.[142]

Nurse Florence Farmborough recorded how the news of the rift between Kerensky and Kornilov was received at the front:

MONDAY, 28th AUGUST [10 September NS]
Today, something has happened which has spread dismay and consternation in our unit. Two official telegrams have reached our medical staff, containing instructions which have completely mystified us. One was from Alexander Kerensky, Prime Minister of the Coalition Government; the other from General Kornilov, Commander-in-Chief of the Russian Armies. Some dissension must have flared up between these two great men, for – sad to relate – each has denounced the other as a *traitor*. It seems incredible, but alas! it lies before us in black and white. What could have happened to cause these two famous Russians to fly at each other's throats and condemn each other publicly? In the despatch signed by Kerensky there were strict injunctions not to obey any orders issued by Kornilov, who had proved himself a traitor to his country, had been deprived of his military rank and dismissed from the Army.

It directed that all military telegraph and telephone services should be supervised by special delegates, to prevent any suspicious communication from being distributed among Russian troops. The second telegram, signed by Kornilov, denounced Kerensky as a traitor and accused him of being in league with the enemies of Russia. What irony that these telegrams should arrive at the same time! To us it all seemed quite inexplicable; but there were the telegrams, lying side by side on the table, for all the members of our *Letuchka* to read!

Very soon it was confirmed that Kornilov, on account of dif-ferences between himself and Kerensky, had been charged with treacherous conspiracy against the Government and dismissed. 'Conspiracy' was a hard word; perhaps it had been coined by Kerensky himself, for it was known that the General, embittered by the demoralisation of the forces, had attributed this to the reforms instituted by Kerensky: moreover, he had accused the Prime Minister of being responsible for the desertions which had brought about the fall of Riga. Kornilov was supported by Milyukov, former Minister for Foreign Affairs and Leader of the Constitutional Democrats: he, too, was vehement in his denunciation of the Kerensky reforms. It must have been a bitter pill for Kerensky to swallow. He was an idealist; but was there room in Russia, in the present harrowing days, for idealists? ...

When the news of Kornilov's fall had spread, many soldiers were bewildered and vowed that they were ready to man the trenches if only they had *someone* in whom they could put their trust. 'Whom can we believe?' they asked. And the uncertainty fostered despair. The Divisional Commander was called in. He met his soldiers face to face, answered all their questions as best he could and, after much hesitation, accompanied by many a 'hem' and a 'ha', finally told the men that he sided with Kerensky. So a telegram was drawn up and sent from our division to the Prime Minister, indicating that the soldiers were ready to support the Government. It was, we were assured, the right thing to do; nevertheless a sense of disloyalty towards our valiant General caused us much uneasiness.[143]

In England, too, there was much uneasiness, and there seems little doubt that the British government, through its embassy in Petrograd, was prepared to support Kornilov, as the last hope of retaining the Russian army as a fighting force in the war. Sir Hugh Thornton recorded some of the diplomatic traffic in his diary:

10 SEPTEMBER 1917
Despatch to Russia decided on during past few days which in effect backs up Korniloff in his attempt to restore discipline in the Russian Army.

13 SEPTEMBER 1917
Very pessimistic telegrams from Buchanan (Petrograd). He says that if Korniloff does not succeed practically all hope of Russia continuing in the war must be given up.[144]

Bertie Stopford appears to have had advance knowledge of the attempted coup, and may even have played a small part in encouraging Kornilov in his plans, for like Buchanan he felt that a military dictatorship was the only way both to avoid anarchy and to keep Russia on the side of the Allies in the war. His letters and diaries reveal his hopes and anxieties surrounding the affair:

LETTER, 19 AUGUST 1917
The Government gets weaker every day; they missed the psychological moment for gaining complete control after the Bolshevik Revolution (July 18) which, by the way, was a most unpleasant experience. Kornilov is a very strong little man, and we may yet see

him at the head of a military dictatorship. I foresee much trouble ahead and much bloodshed.

LETTER, 7 SEPTEMBER 1917

I have means of knowing that we are on the eve of great events, but we shall have to wade in blood before the liberation of Russia is attained.

At Raoult, the wine-merchant's, I saw a militia-man make a scene with a soldier who had a permit for wine. He was a Bolshevik pretending to be a police-agent, in order to confiscate the wine for his own benefit, but the soldier got away.

DIARY, 11 SEPTEMBER 1917

Bread – only one slice! Fête-day, but very few people at the Kasan [sic] Sobor (cathedral in the Nevski) – sure sign of general unrest. Myriads of candles burning before the Kasan icon. In the afternoon to the Ismailovski Barracks and saw four lorries delivering cartridges at the barracks. Some officers told me they had met the Grand Duke Michael in a guarded car. He had been brought up from Gatchina to the État-Major. My windows open all day in order to hear the first signs of the Cossacks' arrival. As the afternoon advanced and I heard no firing, my heart sank, with a presentiment that the *coup d'état* had failed.

DIARY, 12 SEPTEMBER 1917

The last few days have seemed like a life-time. Yesterday I went through more conflicting emotions than at any time since the murder of the 'Unmentionable'. The announcement of Kornilov's submission, though published by all the newspapers, comes only from the Provisional Government ... For my own part, I am still not quite sure; it requires time to verify Provisional Government 'news'. Meanwhile there is nothing heard from Kornilov.

LETTER, 13 SEPTEMBER 1917

Ill all to-day from overstrung nerves after the intense excitement of yesterday. People of all classes profoundly disappointed at the tragedy of Kornilov's miscalculation. On Kornilov's approach sixty thousand workmen were armed by the Provisional Government. They keep their arms so we are now completely in their power ...

It is all over! Kornilov has failed. ...

As the Kornilov attempt to bring order has failed, I will tell you what I foresee now, for the cards are shuffled again. Kerenski is already in the hands of the Soviet. The Soviet now have virtually full power, and the Bolsheviks will become more daring and try to turn out the Government; then would come anarchy, with 70,000 workmen fully armed. The failure of Kornilov has completely knocked me over, and yesterday I could not walk. I still foresee an ocean of blood before order comes.[145]

Meriel Buchanan wrote of the aftermath that

it seemed with Kornilov's downfall the glory of the Russian army was gone for ever, that nothing was left of it but a rabble of dirty, disorderly soldiers who spent their days slouching forlornly about the streets, taking free rides in the trams, stealing and drinking whenever the opportunity offered.[146]

Stopford began to consider the consequences of Kornilov's failure. On 14 September he wrote in his diary:

How long he [Kerensky] can retain [power] remains to be seen. An undiluted Soviet Government could mean massacres and a separate peace with Germany.[147]

He determined that there was nothing more he could do in Petrograd, and he left for home on 26 September, arriving in Aberdeen, where he was 'delighted to see policemen again' on 6 October.[148] He was carrying with him, secreted in two Gladstone bags, a considerable quantity of the Romanov jewels, entrusted to him by his friend the Grand Duchess Vladimir.[149]

Nor was Stopford the only Briton to leave Russia at this time. Following the failure of Kornilov's attempted coup, the British Embassy announced that it could no longer be responsible for dependent women and children in Petrograd. As Meriel Buchanan remembered, 'Nearly all the women and children of the British Colony were being sent away, though several wives refused to leave their husbands and preferred to stay, braving the discomforts and hardships of daily life in Petrograd.'[150] One of those to leave was Mabel King, who, a few years later, wrote a detailed account of her experiences during the long journey back to England:

The hoped-for turn of events in Russia did not come; on the contrary, as summer succeeded spring in the year 1917 things went steadily from bad to worse. The capital grew to look more unkempt and uncared for, disorders were more frequent, food scarcer, and more difficult to obtain. The long queues that during the preceding winter had waited for hours in the bitter cold – the first-comers taking up their station at 4 o'clock in the morning, and waiting till 10 or 11 for a small portion of unpalatable, badly cooked black bread, thankful to get that, and sometimes turned away without it – did not diminish in number or in length, but became more and more a feature of the city. There were queues now for each of the few articles of food or clothing still obtainable, and it became the most urgent task of the day, and one occupying nearly the whole of it, to obtain the barest necessities of life.

It may be asked why we stayed so long in this country of anarchy and famine, but it must be remembered that, apart from a natural unwillingness to leave our friends, both English and Russian, who were unable to get away, the difficulties of travelling were enormous. The German submarine campaign was at its height, ships were being sunk at a terrific rate, and only the most urgent necessity could justify the request for an escorted passage to England.

The day came, however, towards the end of the summer, when the British Consul in Petrograd announced that he could no longer be responsible for British women and children in Petrograd. A crisis might arise in which their presence in the city would hamper swiftness of action on the part of the British authorities, and all who could do so were asked to leave the country under the auspices of the British Government, all possible facilities and protection to be granted for the purpose. There was no resource, therefore, but to begin preparations for departure, and these were arduous and painful enough. Heavy baggage was limited to one trunk a piece, which meant parting with practically all our effects and the treasures of many years' collection. Books and printed matter of all descriptions were absolutely taboo, and only one small package of photos, strictly censored, and sealed with the official Russian seal, could be taken on the journey, not to be opened until we reached England. Two weeks of unremitting and exhausting work were necessary to get our passports in order; the Russian official methods, always dilatory, were now ten-fold more so, besides which four foreign visas must be obtained, another difficult matter in the prevailing disorder.

We left Petrograd finally in the late evening of September 18, after bidding a sorrowful farewell to those of our English friends whose duties still held them to their posts; and to our poor broken-hearted Russian friends, who already foresaw the awful abyss towards which the relentless tide of anarchy and bloodshed was hurling them. For the Provisional Government had proved a dismal failure; no leader of moderate views had arisen to take the place which Kerensky was powerless to hold; Lenin, the sworn enemy of the aristocracy and the bourgeoisie, with his promises of bread and land, was fast becoming the demi-god of the proletariat, that inarticulate mass of the peasantry held so long in bondage, but now breaking free from all control, and capable of deeds of inexpressible horror.

Our route was to be a long and circuitous one; northward through Finland as far as Tornea and Happaranda, the frontier towns of Finland and Sweden respectively; southward through-out nearly the length of Sweden to Stockholm, passing a night there; thence to Christiania, where again the journey would be broken; leaving the following day for Bergen, where we hoped to find the Admiralty-escorted boat, which should convoy us across the submarine-infested North Sea to 'somewhere in Britain.'

The first part of our journey was accomplished without extreme discomfort. Certainly it was annoying to be aroused at all hours of the night to have passports inspected by peremptory officials, and to be kept waiting for hours and hours at the various frontiers while searching examinations of all kinds were made, any suspected cases being most rigorously dealt with. It was strange, too, to be practically prisoners throughout the journey, and never allowed to go beyond the platform of any station, however long the halt. In Sweden the feeling of hostility towards the English was very marked, food was scarce, and had been rationed from the early days of the war; no porters were available, and, in changing trains at dead of night, we had on one occasion to get our baggage some distance along the line as best we could in total darkness. One redeeming feature of this part of the journey, however, was the hospitable look of the little station restaurants, invitingly open at some unearthly hour of the night, where one helped oneself to tea or coffee and sandwiches during the few minutes' stay, hastily paying the attendant at the door as one made a hurried dash for the train again.

Our minds were not detached enough to fully appreciate the beauties of Stockholm and Christiania, but I have a vivid recollection of the wonderful journey across Norway, during which the train passes through 70 tunnels (some so short that they are more like archways on the mountain side), climbs up above the snowline at Myndal, and descends again to sea level at Bergen. The scenery is gorgeous, and the rail-way carriages so arranged that a full view could be enjoyed.

In Norway we were received with the utmost cordiality and on reaching the little hamlet of Bolken, about 20 miles from Bergen, we were told we must await our turn for the boat, Bergen being already overflowing with refugees. We experienced a quite primitive feeling of delight at the sight of the well-supplied supper table – we had not seen such abundance for years! It was quite a joy, too, during the three weeks that followed to see the children of the party visibly growing fatter on the good fare provided, and, indeed we all benefited by our stay in this lovely spot, with its pure mountain air and glorious walks, and the kindly hospitality of our Norwegian host and hostess, whose three beautiful daughters, dressed in the quaint and pretty native costume, waited so deftly at table, and lent an additional charm to this unpremeditated holiday.

The news came at last that we were sailing the next day – longer notice could not be given, as sailing dates must be kept a profound secret. Our immediate party consisted of about 30 British residents from Petrograd, but under the same escort were travelling the last of the recruits from Russia, many of whom, though British subjects, had never left Russia before, and whose wives and children, in many cases, could not speak a word of English. It was more than possible that the Germans would have wind of this, and the U boats, if possible, would be more vigilant than usual. We left Bergen at 5 o'clock the next evening, and for four hours steamed quietly through the fiords.

At 9 o'clock we emerged into the open sea to find a heavy storm raging, and our progress would be necessarily very slow, as the two destroyers accompanying us on either side were constantly being submerged. Our vessel, carrying 500 passengers, was an old cattle boat, the only transport available, and when we were shown our accommodation in the hold we vowed that nothing would induce us to go below. On embarking we were given cards, with a number indicating our respective places on lifeboat or raft or buoy in case of a torpedo. But when, in spite of our vows to the contrary, as the sea grew more tempestuous, and I, an impossibly bad sailor, quite unable to keep up, we were obliged to take refuge in the cattle hold, we knew that if the worst happened we could only go quietly to the bottom; for it was impossible, ill as we were, and with such a terrific sea, to think of climbing the steep notched plank to the lower deck, and the perpendicular ladder to the upper deck, before we could even begin the search for our raft. As the storm increased in intensity, men, women, and children crowded down into this inferno, the atmosphere of which became more and more appalling. The old boat groaned and creaked, and from time to time tremendous crashes were heard, my friend murmuring to my almost unconscious ear, 'There goes the mast!' or 'That must be the funnel!' But still we ploughed our way through the angry sea, saved from the inevitable submarine attack, as we learned afterwards, by the violence of the storm. The crossing, which should have taken 18 hours, lasted 40, 20 of which (and they seemed like years) were spent under these awful conditions in the hold. But the worst experiences come to an end. Word came at last that we were nearing Aberdeen; in spite of the pitchy darkness – not a light was visible – the captain, who had practically never left the bridge for three nights and days, succeeded in getting safe anchorage within the harbour. Then followed a less terrible night, stretched on the engine room table, sleep out of the question; the landing next morning at Aberdeen; the five hours' wait amid much confusion before getting free of the Customs; and, at last, just a month from the time we left Petrograd, we stood free once more on British soil.[151]

Others, however, were unable or unwilling as yet to leave. At the front Florence Farmborough also pondered the future:

4 [17] SEPTEMBER 1917
We hear that Kornilov has been arrested, and do not know whether to be sad or glad; our loyalties are so evenly divided. Kerensky has been our hero since the political revolution in March 1917, but it was thanks to Kornilov that our Armies ... achieved such success in Galicia during the recent summer campaigns.

Alongside the demoralization of the troops, which she could see going on all around her, her own morale was also beginning to fail. The following day she wrote:

I did not go near the hospital in the afternoon: I was feeling far
from well. But I knew what was wrong with me. It was that my
love for my Red Cross work was slowly fading; I was becoming sick
of wounds, illness, dirt and filth. That was the dreadful truth, and I
had to face it. The daily fears about Russia; her ghastly predicament;
the wholesale desertion by her soldiers; the hatred and insolence of
the deserters; the unfriendliness of the Roumanians; the absence of
news from home – all had combined to unnerve me. I felt deeply
ashamed to think that I was growing tired of my work; where had
my passionate enthusiasm gone? And my vows? Sick at heart, I sat
for many long minutes a prey to dejection and grievous reflection.[152]

The only winners from the Kornilov affair were the Bolsheviks.
As Trotsky wrote:

The growth of the influence and strength of the Bolsheviks was
undoubted, and it had now received an irresistible impetus. The
Bolsheviks had warned against the Coalition, against the July
offensive, and had foretold the Korniloff rebellion. The popular
masses could now see that we had been right. At the most anxious
moments of the Korniloff plot, when the Caucasian 'Savage'
Division was marching on Petrograd, the Petrograd Soviet, with the
unwilling connivance of the Government, had armed the workers.
The regiments which had been summoned against us had long ago
become transformed in the hot atmosphere of Petrograd, and were
now entirely on our side. The Korniloff attempt was bound finally
to open the eyes of the army to the inadmissibility of any further
understanding with the bourgeois counter-revolutionaries. ...
[T]he winding up of the Korniloff adventure ... had fundamentally
altered the correlation of forces in our favour.[153]

'How I saw the Red Dawn'

THE BOLSHEVIK UPRISING

Following the defeat of Kornilov, there was a general feeling that the Provisional Government was too weak to survive for very much longer. Many factors contributed to this. The breakdown in trade which can be seen as one of the triggers for the February revolution had worsened, exacerbating the shortage of food, fuel and raw materials in the country. Industrial output was cut and conflict between workers and employers intensified, with the result that prices soared and employment prospects shrank. The number of strikes grew. By May, peasant unrest had become critical. Furthermore, the Provisional Government's unpopular decision to continue the war with Germany and its 'dual power' with the Petrograd Soviet made it impossible to pass many of its reforms. It increasingly seemed that the Bolsheviks would make a second attempt to overthrow it and they themselves did not seek to conceal that this was their aim. Maxim Litvinov wrote that

> the Bolsheviks actively began organising the masses for a new rising, and openly proclaimed in their papers and at innumerable public meetings their intention to lead the people in an effort to overthrow the Government and the 'parliament.' Never in previous history had a rising been prepared so openly, so publicly, under the eyes of all the world, as this second, the Bolshevik, revolution. It was a public challenge, as it were, to the Kerenskys, the Tseretellis, the Tchernoffs, and the entire bourgeoisie to defend themselves against the coming onslaught. The challenge was laughed at or denounced as criminal, and measures were taken to meet it should it really, by chance, be carried out. But when the night of November 6–7, fixed for the commencement of the operations, came, the whole edifice reared up by the coalition-mongers and their Government and precious bourgeoisie collapsed like a house of cards. Workmen organised in Red Guards and troops commanded by leaders appointed by a Military Revolutionary Committee quietly went round the various Government establishments, such as the central telephone station, the military staff

quarters, etc., and took possession of them, and in the course of the following day the Government was arrested, all Petrograd (and then Moscow) was in the hands of the Bolsheviks, a new Government under the title of Council of People's Commissaries was formed, and the great revolution was accomplished without any bloodshed.[154]

So well signalled was the uprising that on 1 November British Military Attaché General Knox recorded in his diary that 'the Bolshevik trial of strength is expected for Wednesday, 7th November.'[155]

One Englishman who was able to observe at close quarters both the demoralization and the impotence of the authorities and the work of the Bolsheviks in radicalizing the workers in the factories was a Corporal Miller, who was based in the Anglo-Russian Commission, a body whose task was ostensibly to speed the flow of British aid (principally war material) to Russia. Miller's task, as a serving British soldier, and moreover an NCO rather than an officer, was also to try to raise the morale of the Russian troops on the front line, encouraging them to resist the German advance with news of support for Russia among their British comrades on the Western Front. He was a fluent Russian speaker, and was almost certainly also a secret agent, as his report to his boss, Lt.-Colonel George Crosfield,[156] on 'Conditions prevailing in the Russian capital' eventually made its way into the papers of the British War Cabinet. This is dated 29 September 1917, and reads as follows:

> Petrograd with population of over three millions is in a state of chaos. There is no real authority of law. There is no strong hand of Government. It is really a 'free' city. Everyone can do as h[i]s stupefied by pangs of hunger, or anguish of despair brain dictates him. Ignorant masses freed by cruel circumstances from the iron grip of despotical rule, found themselves at the mercy of their fate. Every individual is a complete stranger to all human impulses known in the west under the name of moral obligations and duties of citizenship. Full absence of any organised efforts towards regularisation of that chaotical state of life facilitates domination of animal instinct. Ruthless disregard to everything individual animal wants, disregard to order, absolute indifference even to laws of decency – strength – a brutal animal strength is the order of the

day. Streets are full of beggars, crippled men and destitute women with infants in arms. Destitution beyond all imagination – men, women and children sleeping in the streets at this time of year.

At least half of the population spends almost the whole of its time in endless queues in all streets, waiting for almost every article of the first life's necessity. Such queues are chronic – they can be seen everywhere, and at all times of the day and night. Shortage of food and clothing as great as it is now, threatens to become even greater during the winter months. It is impossible to survey the prospects of the coming winter without dread and apprehension. Reign of terror and lawlessness establishes itself firmer with every day. Murders, robbery and violence are being perpetrated in astonishing extent. The city militia at its best is powerless, and in a great many instances proved to be infected with the general disease of corruption. Crime unpunished by a powerless hand of Law encourages imposition upon the Law itself. Most of the crimes are being done in broad daylight by uniformed villains gaining entrance into dwellings of their victims under pretence of authority – under the name of the Law.

The present Provisional Government is powerless. It may hide the real cause of its impotence, blaming the party antagonism as factor preventing them from carrying out their duties, but in reality this is not the case. I tried to work for the Political Department of the War Ministry, and soon found out that they will not do anything for the following reasons – firstly, because they have no notions of doing anything, and secondly they are not free from party influences themselves. The Provisional Government badly suffers from lack of initiative, creative thought and energy, and even it is wanting in honesty, and disinterestedness of purpose free from the dictates of personal ambition. The truth of Korniloff affair, if it will ever be disclosed, shall prove that last conclusion of mine.

The Council of Workers and Soldiers Delegates is nothing less than an exhibition of national stupidity and ignorance. The majority of its members are half illiterate men, who got there by means that are openly doubted. In short, they are dodging the trenches. All affairs of the C.W.S.D. seem to be directed to prevention of forming really Coalitionary Government embodying all living power of the nation. Other parties are too far blinded by class prejudices to be able to see anything in a light of reason and common sense. While Cadets are being kept aloft by consciousness of self-importance, Bolsheviks (Leninists) are doing their deadly work of ruin and treachery. Social democrats, Mensheviks (Plekhanoff's party) are powerless to prevent them by themselves. Social Revolutionaries could have been dominating strength in the country embodying the very spirit of revolution, but unfortunately they too, being subjected to general mania for arguments, cannot agree amongst themselves over some trifles, and let their chances go by. Other organisations, about thirty in number to my knowledge, are either too weak or too strictly subjective. Thus the masses of the population are being left on the mercy of their fate – unorganised, undisciplined, sinking in the habit of laziness and its consequences – poverty and want. The State Treasury is empty. The country is flooded with paper currency, which already amounts to 15 thousands millions roubles in legal issues. How much there is of a counterfeit kind, God only knows. Peasantry alone keeps over half that amount, and having abundance of paper money with which it does not part, it also refuses to sell for money its products. From today's press I see that the Petrograd City Duma is pawning its valuables in order to raise money to pay its officials with.

Bolsheviks (Leninists) are exploiting prevailing circumstances to their advantage. Their work never ceases. Their propaganda is being energetically kept up all the time and everywhere, not only in Petrograd, but throughout Russia. They have abundance of means and men, while other well meaning organisations are practically inactive through want of either. Thus, thanking to efforts of Leninists, labour production has fallen to one quarter of its normal output. Many works of importance have been ruined and closed. Many are about to close. General unemployment is imminent. Besides that, several of the largest Munition works were burnt in Petrograd and Kasan [sic], so that the Army again is facing prospects of munition famine. To find out the real situation on Munition works, I visited the Putilops [sic] works on several occasions. In spite of warnings not to speak, I took the risk, and after a few minutes was fairly thrown out. However, I did not give in. Disguised as a working man, I spent several days within the works. From all I have seen there, I came to the conclusion that all 30,000 men employed there are being bullied by a few hundreds of armed villains – Bolsheviks, who neither would work themselves, not let others work. They argue with knife, revolver or stone in their hands. The bulk of the working mass consists of good, well disposed men who feel the criminal folly of their policy, and would gladly work providing they had a protecting hand of Law and authority to depend upon against villainous assaults, threats and insults of the bullies. A strong

21 Illustration of Lenin arriving in Petrograd after his journey through Germany by sealed train, April 1917

22 Provisional Government poster with the caption 'Subscribe to the freedom loan!'

23 Cover of Henry Keeling's book *Bolshevism: Mr. Keeling's Five Years in Russia*, 1919

Second Edition.

Office and Editorial Rooms	Advertising Rates.
PETROGRAD	Before text:
8, Gogol St.	R. 3,00 per line nonpareil.
Tel. 434-78.	After text:
	R. 1,25 per line nonpareil.
	Subscriptions:
	Yearly R. 50. Monthly R. 5.

RUSSIAN DAILY NEWS

OFFICE: 8 GOGOL STREET, PETROGRAD

№ 735. SATURDAY, 28 (10) NOVEMBER, 1917.   PETROGRAD.   20 COPECKS.

FIGHTING APPROACHES CITY

Slight Panic in Petrograd Streets
Government Troops Advancing
Artillery Battle at Gatchina

Troops are said to be on their way to Petrograd from Gatchina under command of Kerensky.

The Izmailoff and Semenoff Regiments as well as armoured car men, with the exception of three machines in the Smolny Institute, declined further to support the Military Revolutionary Committee.

A delegate of the City Duma, member of the Social Revolutionary Party, visited the cruiser "Aurora" and other ships in the Neva. The sailors stated that they had further misled and would not further fire on the city.

It is stated that seven ministers have been released from the fortress, including Masloff, and Maliantovich. Kerensky has issued an order to the effect, that he, Minister President of the Provisional Government and Commander-in-Chief of all the armed forces of the Russian Republic, arrived here to-day at the head of troops from the front loyal to the country. All Petrograd troops who through mistakes have joined the band of traitors to the country and to the revolution to return immediately to their duty. Dated Gatchina, Oct 27.

On the Petrograd-Gatchina road an artillery duel is in progress. All along the route are armoured cars and other military automobiles.

The Pavlovsky regiment, which sided with the Military Revolutionary Committee, is reported badly beaten by the Provisional Government troops, and in full retreat towards Petrograd. The casualties on both sides are said to be considerable.

The statement that the Committee of Safety has been arrested is denied.

In consequence of the battle, many fires are reported to have broken out in the town of Gatchina itself.

At 2 p.m. it was reported that sounds of firing could be heard in Petrograd from the direction of the river Neva.

This morning bands of armed workmen were observed on the Nevsky, proceeding towards the Kammennostrovski. It was reported that they were to assemble at the Bolshaia Monetnaia.

Soldiers and workmen were marching in the direction of the Moskovskaia Zastava leading towards Tsarskoe Selo to oppose the Provisional Government's troops.

At 2.45 p.m. there was heavy rifle shooting at the Nikolai Station.

At 1.50 p.m. a young officer was killed by the insurgent guard at an open-air meeting on the corner of Mikhailovsky and Nevsky. He was remonstrating with the guards when they opened fire five shots took effect and he fell mortally wounded. The guard continued to fire and there were several casualties among the crowd.

The report that Prince Tumanoff was lynched and his body thrown into the Moika is denied. He has been arrested.

The Ukraine refuses to support the Petrograd Soviet. This means that no food or other supplies will reach Petrograd from that district.

Officers of the Petrograd Staff who refused to take orders from the Military Revolutionary Committee have been placed in confinement.

CADETS' STORY OF WINTER PALACE DEFENCE.

The final surrender of the Ministers took place in the Council Chamber of the Winter Palace, after all the forces defending the Palace, except a dozen cadets, had surrendered and given up their arms.

We learned the full story of the event from one of the defenders.

"At 3,30 on Thursday morning, after an eight hours' attack," says this cadet, "our group gathered in the small corridor outside the Council Chamber. Suddenly groups of soldiers, sailors and Red Guards rushed upon us from all sides. We tried to stop them and to arrest them, but they said that it was no use, as they were in great force, and that our other men had surrendered. Nevertheless we resisted and tried to drive them back down the corridor.

As we had been ordered not to fire, we were slowly pressed back towards the Council Chamber. After a brief struggle there, we withdrew one by one into the Ministers' Chamber. Then the Lieutenant in command of the Soviet troops calmly said to the Ministers, some of whom were seated round the table, others standing. We represent the Revolutionary Committee. There is no use in resisting, as even Kerensky has been arrested. What more do you want. The Ministers submitted quietly. We cadets were then disarmed, put out of the room, and told to leave the Palace. The Ministers were later taken to the Fortress.

According to the Military Revolutionary Committee there were no casualties among the defenders of the Winter Palace. The besiegers report six killed and many wounded.

The City Duma, at a special session, protested against the violation of the freedom of the press and of speech.

The Duma protested strenuously against the closing of the "City Council Gazette."

The Revolutionary Committee has dissolved the "Centroflot". It will be remembered that the "Centroflot" refused to recognise the new authority.

Alarming news has been received from Siberia, where, it is reported, dissension has broken out among the soldiers.

The following report has been received of events in Moscow. "It is reported that part of the Moscow garrison, with the Commanding General at its head, has remained true to the Provisional Government. A battle is reported to have taken place between these troops and the supporters of the Revolutionary Committee. The latter were obliged to retreat to the Kremlin, which it is rumoured is being besieged.

The City Duma has resolved to send special commissaries to all governments, which have grain supplies, whose duty it will be to increase the transport of corn for Petrograd.

The employees of the Ministries of Labour, Food, Railways, and Education passed resolutions declaring that they would work only with a government recognised by the entire Russian people.

The employees of the Petrograd City Duma have been ordered not to obey instructions from the Military Committee.

FROM THE BRITISH EMBASSY.

It has been brought to the notice of the British Embassy that the following statement has appeared in the Russian press.

"A conference of the Diplomatic Corps took place on October 26. At the conference, so it is reported, it was decided not to enter into any relations with Smolny, and to find out whether there were any troops on the side of the Provisional Government. If all the armies go over to the side of the Soviet, the ambassadors will immediately leave Russia."

The British Embassy desires to state that there is no truth in this assertion, and that the only questions discussed were the necessary measures for the protection of the foreign colonies in Petrograd.

The following is the peace programme adopted by the Congress of Soviets last night:
1) All nations now at war are to be requested to consider immediate peace.
2) A three months truce is to be declared on all Russian fronts.
3) The formula, no annexations and no contributions is to be applied to all nations.
4) Any country which has been annexed may free itself by a plebiscite.
5) The new Russian Government is ready to enter into peace discussions with any nation.
6) Lenin believes that the workers and soldiers of all nations would now arise and demand peace.

KALUGA, Oct. 25.

All citizens of Kaluga are instructed by the local authorities to hand in to the Military Governor all arms and lock their gates for the night at 8.30 p.m.   (Pravda)

Office and
Editorial Rooms
PETROGRAD
8, Gogol St.
Tel. 434-78.

RUSSIAN
DAILY NEWS

№ 741. FRIDAY, 3 (16) NOVEMBER, 1917.   PETROGRAD.   30 COPECKS.

Advertising Rates.
Before text:
R. 3.00 per line nonpareil.
After text:
R. 1.25 per line nonpareil.
Subscriptions:
Yearly R. 50. Monthly R. 5.

CABINET NOT YET FORMED

Revolutionary Troops Oppose Separate Peace
Kaiser Said to Have Rejected Peace Offers
Regiments Demand Disarming of Workmen
Moscow in Dire Distress

Some detachments of troops, who had returned from the Revolutionary front, paraded the town yesterday, bearing banners with the inscription: "Down with a Separate Peace!"

The well-known Bolshevik member of the Military Revolutionary Committee, Volodarsky, has resigned his post as member of the City Duma.

The temper at Smolny according to our correspondents, is warlike and victorious. The Bolsheviks consider themselves the victors. They are agreeable to a coalition, but are against the proposed Council, saying: "We made the revolution. We have conquered. And now they want to place us in the minority".

Yesterday about 3.30 p.m., a large crowd marched along the Litany and Vladimirsky in the direction of the Tsarskoe Selo station, composed of about one hundred of the Red guard, and many men and women workers from the arsenal— about 2,000 in all — with flags and banners, many of which were used on May 1 last. Others, however, were inscribed "Immediate peace", "Arm all Russian workmen rather than allow slavery", and "Workers should control all production". Spectators looked on with indifference.

It may be worth noting that one of the young men at the head of a group of the Red Guard was dressed in the uniform of the Page Corps.

At the corner of the Nevsky and Litany the procession was met by one of the regiments of Guards. No greetings were exchanged between them; on the contrary the attitude of the Red Guard was evidently distrustful and even frightened.

The Committee at the City Duma for the sale of railway tickets has been temporarily closed. The sale of railway tickets is now concentrated at the Nicholas railway, in the Znamensky Hotel.

It is not difficult to receive tickets in exchange for coupons issued by the Commissary of the City Committee. The number of passengers by the Nicholas railway has considerably decreased, probably caused by the indefinite position existing throughout Russia. The absence of carters, porters, and other railway employees makes it impossible to forward a large amount of luggage.   (Narod)

At the present time, the question of the guarding of the foreign embassies, missions, and consulates, from possible excesses of the mob, has been satisfactorily arranged. On the day of the Bolshevik uprising, the majority of the diplomatic representatives applied to various institutions requesting that guards should be sent for their defence.

Until October 29, this duty was performed by Junkers. In particular the American Embassy was guarded by the Junkers of the Nicholas Cavalry School.

At present, the majority of the embassies are guarded by the Polish Company of the Petrograd Garrison, who are entirely excluded from any participation in the conflict between Provisional Government and the Revolutionary Committee.

Some missions, such as the Swedish, Belgian, Serbian, have placed no special guard over their premises.   (Narod)

The rumour that Mr. A. F. Kerensky has committed suicide has received no confirmation.

The rumour that Leon Trotsky received a reply from the German Government to the effect that no peace with Russia is possible until the Monarchy is restored or the Constituent Assembly meets, was not denied at midnight last night.

With regard to the reports which have been spread throughout the city, concerning a visit of the representatives of the Social Revolutionary party and the Mensheviks to the Allied Ambassadors, and alleged conversations on the present state of affairs, as well as about a statement made by the Ambassadors, that in case the former government is retained, an Allied Conference would be convened in Petrograd to discuss the aims of the war, the French Embassy states that no parties' representatives have visited the Embassies. The Allied Embassies, in general, for reasons easily understood, are refraining from expressing any opinions whatever about the present state of affairs in Russia.

The Committee, which is endeavouring to form a new coalition ministry as a solution to the present desperate situation, is in constant session, but up to the present no settlement has been reached.

It is reported that the cruiser "Respublica," which the Bolsheviks demanded should be sent from Kronshadt, has gone ashore in the Marine Canal, closing up the fairway and preventing the return of the other ships.   (Narod)

It is rumoured at Smolny that the Ukraine has despatched 150,000 troops against Gen. Kaledin, who is operating in the Donetz Basin.

COAL SHORTAGE SERIOUS.

The railroads are experiencing great difficulties with respect to coal. The entire Russian railroad system requires fifty-two million poods a month. However, in September the railroads obtained thirty-five million poods, and for October still less. It is difficult to say how much they will get for November, but anyhow the speeding up of general disruption, consequent upon the Bolshevik rising, permits of no hopes of an improvement. The railroads are now working on their reserves. Normally these are sufficient for twelve days, but on several lines the reserves are only enough for two or three days, or less.

The output of coal in the Donetz Basin is low, and falls continuously. The statistics of the Ministry of Ways of Communication show that before the war a miner turned out 1200 poods per month on an average; in November 1916 this had fallen to 750 poods, and at the present moment the average is 420 poods. As a result 58,000,000 poods were produced in September of this year, against 116,000,000 poods in September 1916. Under this state of affairs the entire railroad traffic in Russia must come to a standstill by the end of November. As such a stoppage would be a catastrophe terrible in its consequences, the Ministry of Ways of Communication has resolved to reduce the supply of coal for industrial purposes. For this reason the Ministry of Trade and Industry is shutting down twenty blast furnaces in the Donetz Basin. But for all that, twenty passenger trains have been taken off the southern railroads from November 1, owing to lack of coal.

THE WAR.

French Front.
        October 31.

To the North-East and West of Rheims the Germans, under cover of increased artillery fire, unsuccessfully attempted several attacks. The night was quiet everywhere else.

October 31. The German artillery, which was heavily bombarded by our own, rained fire into the French front lines in the Champagne near Monts and at several points on the Argonne front.

In yesterday's session of the City Duma Mayor Schreider, announced having received a telegram from Moscow, stating that fighting there still continues. The central part of the city is ruined, The Ouspensky Cathedral, and the Vassili Blajenny Church, are destroyed. The City Hall and Nikitsky Street are much damaged. Vandalism is prevalent in the entire city.

The City Duma of Moscow asked Petrograd for help, whereupon the Petrograd City Duma decided to send five commissaries, who left for Moscow yesterday afternoon.

The Military Revolutionary Committee have sent 1,100 Red Guards to help the Revolutionary troops in Moscow.

JEWISH STATE TO BE ESTABLISHED IN PALESTINE.

An official declaration was issued by the British Government with regard to the re-establishing of a Jewish State in Palestine.

25 Front page of the *Russian Daily News* on 16 November 1917

29th, September 1917

Petrograd.

To Lieut. Colonel
    G. Crosfield D.S.O.

Sir,

I wrote four letters to Mr Jarrite and one to yourself
with addressed envelopes enclosed, but had no reply as yet.   It
is possible that my letters were held up though in my opinion,
I did not write anything that would have been objected by the
War Censor.   A month before the end of my leave, I saw the
British Military Attache in Petrograd with paper from a non-party
organisation — "The Battalions of Freedom" — certifying the need
for extension of my leave.   The Attache expressed his confidence
that such shall be granted.   It has been duly wired for by the
Anglo-Russian Commission in Petrograd.   In the future, I am
expecting to be sent by that Commission to the front.

In the meantime, I am taking the opportunity of
forwarding to you in the Diplomatic bag this report.   It is
general account of all I have learned during my stay in Petrograd.
I cannot go to the front without uniform, and generally my work
in the Army is greatly hindered by the same reason.

I shall generalise my report under the following
two headings :—

        (1)   Conditions prevailing in the Russian Capital.

        (2)   The Russian Army.

For the future, should extension of my leave be granted
my permanent address shall be:—

        The ANGLO-RUSSIAN COMMISSION,

                Fontanka 15,
                  Petrograd.

I am, Sir, having the honour of being your obedient
and well wishing servant,

                Corpl. A. Miller.

26 Letter and report sent by Corporal Miller to Lt-Colonel Crosfield
on 29 September 1917

CONDITIONS PREVAILING IN THE RUSSIAN CAPITAL

Petrograd with population of over three millions is in a state
of chaos.   There is no real authority of law.   There is no
strong hand of Government.   It is really a "free" city.   Everyone
can do as h s stupified by pangs of hunger, or anguish of despair
brain dictates him.   Ignorant masses freed by cruel circumstances
from the iron grip of despotical rule, found themselves at the mercy
of their fate.   Every individual is a complete stranger to all
human impulses known in the west under the name of moral obligations
and duties of citizenship.   Full absence of any organised efforts
towards regularisation of that chaotical state of life facilitates
domination of animal instinct.   Ruthless disregard to everything
individual animal wants, disregard to order, absolute indifference
even to laws of decency - strength - a brutal animal strength, is
the order of the day.   Streets are full of beggars , crippled
men and destitute women with infants in arms.   Destitution beyond
all imagination - men, women and children sleeping in streets at
this time of the year.

At the least, half of the whole population spends almost the whole
of its time in endless queues in all streets, waiting for almost
every article of the first life's necessity.   Such queues are
chronic - they can be seen everywhere, and at all times of the day and
night.   Shortage of food and clothing as great as it is now,
threatens to become even greater during the winter months.   It is
impossible to survey the prospects of the coming winter without
dread and apprehension.   Reign of terror and lawlessness establishes
itself firmer with every day.   Murders, robbery and violence are being perpetrated in astonishing extent.   The city militia at its
best is powerless, and in a great many instances proved to be infected
with the general disease of corruption.   Crime unpunished by a
powerless hand of Law encourages imposition upon the Law itself.
Most of the crimes are being done in broad daylight by uniformed
villains gaining entrance into dwellings of their victims under
pretence of authority - in the name of the Law.

        The pres/ent Provisional Government is powerless. It

27 Janet Jeffery fleeing Russia, illustration by Sydney Seymour Lucas
from *The Sphere*, 3 January 1920

28 Poster for Eisenstein's film *October*

29 'Illiterate man is a blind man: failures and misfortunes await him everywhere.' Soviet poster promoting literacy, by Alexei Radokov, 1920

30 'Cossack, with whom are you? With us or with them?' Soviet poster questioning Cossacks' loyalty, by Dmitry Moor, 1920

31 'In order to have more, it is necessary to produce more. In order to produce more, it is necessary to know more.' Soviet poster encouraging productivity, by Alexander Zelensky, 1920

32 Postcard of Lenin, 1924

33 Soviet poster calling for the proletarians of all countries to unite, 1921

34 Soviet poster welcoming the Third Comintern, 1918–20

35 Poster of Lenin with the slogan 'Peace to the People; Land to the Peasants; Power to the Soviets'

36 The Nevsky Prospekt in 1919

authority able to remove all harmful elements would soon bring the work to its normal levels. In other works the things can be mended even easier than at Putiloffs.

Everywhere men are tired of disorder and anarchy and pray for a strong Administrative hand. People are fed up with words and tempting, never realising promises. He who will succeed to give the masses results instead of words shall win unanimous support. No one shall examine his political views. This is the truth of the situation. There is the opportunity for the Provisional Government if it is wise enough to take it, and there is the danger of realisation of counter revolution also.

There is food in the country, and even in the city itself. He who can afford to pay 260 roubles for a sack of flour need not stand in the street best part of the day waiting for his ½ lb of bread. About 1,000 yards away from where I am writing – at the Nicolaevsky Station, 30 wagons of foodstuffs are rotting away, while population cannot always get sufficient food even at the fabulous prices. They stood there for the last two months. The Government knew about it. Why is it being kept there, and wasted away is more than I can tell. Transport disorganisation is being shouted about at every street corner; and in every paper, yet at the same time I know of 2,000 Poles – boiler makers specialised in repairs of railway engines, who tried to get on the job, but in vain.

Miller, like so many other observers, saw the hand of Germany behind the Bolsheviks, reporting that

There can be only one explanation of all this mysterious phenomenon in life of Petrograd – German intrigues.

Who are the men standing at the head of social movement in Russia, such as Lenin & Company – traitors who have sold themselves to the enemy, or merely irresponsible fools and fanatical idiots is an open question. The fact is that whatever Lenin's intentions may be, he, by his propaganda, committed a most inconsistent act of foolery (not saying treachery) – unification of all the dark and criminal forces in the country under the banner of Socialism. In the name of 'Brotherhood' and 'Socialism' a strong governing power is being opposed with an equal zeal by a fanatical socialist whose morbid imagination sees in it return to the old regime, a murderer and a thief apprehending and [sic] end to the carriers [sic – careers], a traitor fearing the just punishment which he deserved, and a

Отъ Военно-Революціоннаго Комитета при Петроградскомъ Совѣтѣ Рабочихъ и Солдатскихъ Депутатовъ.

Къ Гоажданамъ Россіи.

Временное Правительство низложено. Государственная власть перешла въ руки органа Петроградскаго Совѣта Рабочихъ и Солдатскихъ Депутатовъ Военно-Революціоннаго Комитета, стоящаго во главѣ Петроградскаго пролетаріата и гарнизона.

Дѣло, за которое боролся народъ: немедленное предложеніе демократическаго мира, отмѣна помѣщичьей собственности на землю, рабочій контроль надъ производствомъ, созданіе Совѣтскаго Правительства — это дѣло обезпечено.

ДА ЗДРАВСТВУЕТЪ РЕВОЛЮЦІЯ РАБОЧИХЪ, СОЛДАТЪ И КРЕСТЬЯНЪ!

Военно-Революціонн[...]
при Петроградс[...]
Рабочихъ и Солдатс[...]

25 октября 1917 г. 10 ч. утра.

Reproduction of a Bolshevik poster announcing the end of the Provisional Government and the transferral of power to the Petrograd Soviet, 7 November 1917

From the War-Revolutionary Committee of the Petrograd Soviet of Workmen and Soldiers Deputies.

To the Citizens of Russia:

The Provisional Government is deposed. The State power has passed into the hands of the organ of the Petrograd Soviet of Workers' and Soldiers' Deputies, the Military Revolutionary Committee, which stands at the head of the Petrograd proletariat and garrison.

The aims for which the people were fighting—immediate proposal of a democratic peace, abolition of landlord property-rights in the land, labor control over production, creation of a Soviet Government, —these aims have been achieved.

LONG LIVE THE REVOLUTION OF WORKMEN, SOLDIERS AND PEASANTS!

Military-Revolutionary Committee of the Petrograd Soviet of Workers and Soldier's Deputies.

NOVEMBER 7, 1917

German spy wishing to carry on his dirty work uninterrupted. To what extent it favours German work in Russia can be judged from the following facts which were established by a private person by his own initiative, and at his own expense. This is the scheme:– There exists a German organisation with a foreign capital of several thousands millions roubles with Headquarters in Finland (Helsingforce [sic]). At the head of it stands some Count Severs. His staff consists of 30,000 agents paid on an average 1,000 roubles man monthly. Running accounts of that organisation in various banks in Petrograd amount to 400,000 roubles. Petrograd is divided into 30 districts, Russia in five. It aims at re-establishment of monarchy with one of several Romanoffs known for their pro-German sympathies, which would lead to a Russia–German entente. Its methods of work are disorganisation of the country, which would lead to economical collapse. It works in the army, deepening the hatred and mistrust of soldiers towards their officers as well as amongst the working classes preventing any attempt at an increase in production and amongst the population at large, creating panic. Burning the Munition works in Petrograd and Cason [sic] was this work, and they were the authors of Vyborg's drama. Also it is established by the same person where, when, and for what price were bought Members of the Finnish Council, and what they were told to say. All these facts with documentary proofs were duly handed to the authorities, and it is hoped that necessary steps are being taken now to avert the disaster. Personally, I have seen and heard of many instances of almost incredible audacity and impudence of that organisation.[157]

At the same time Kerensky's government was losing the support of the one body which could have prevented the Revolution taking place, the Cossack Regiments stationed in and around the capital. On the evening on 6 November a meeting of the 1st, 4th and 14th Don Cossack Cavalry was held to determine their course of action. General Knox wrote:

The men expressed their unwillingness to support Kerenski, who had called them 'counter-revolutionaries' and their chosen leader, Kornilov, a 'traitor.' Further, they pointed out that an attempt to put down a Bolshevik uprising, unsupported as they were by infantry, would result in bloodshed and would probably fail. Later a deputation visited Kerenski, and his refusal to declare the Bolshevik organisation illegal confirmed the Cossacks in their resolution to remain neutral.[158]

Of the many eyewitness accounts of the Bolshevik uprising, John Reed's *Ten Days That Shook the World* is justly famous, but he was by no means the only foreign observer to be at the centre of affairs on the critical days of 6 and 7 November. The account by journalist Morgan Philips Price, written a couple of years later, captures the drama of the scene at the Smolny Institute, as well as Lenin's commanding presence:

It was the evening of November 6th, and I repaired to the Smolny Institute, where the Executive of the old Menshevik Soviet had their offices. Roars of cheers were coming from the great hall. The Petrograd Soviet was sitting and Trotsky was making a rousing speech to the delegates arriving for the Second All-Russian Soviet Congress. All was bustle and hurry, and a look of confidence was on everyone's face. 'Demos' was arising from the depth, crude and defiant. Representatives of 'revolutionary-democracy', sitting in the old Menshevik Executive upstairs, seemed strangely isolated from realities.

Trotsky was in the chair, and on the tribune rose a short, bald-headed little man, whom I had seen six months before, leading the tiny insignificant Bolshevik group in the First Soviet Congress. It was Lenin, without his moustache, which he had shaved off in order to change his appearance during the period of his forced concealment, now drawing to a close. He spoke of the coming Soviet Congress as the only guarantee for bringing peace, land and workers' control to Russia. Then someone whispered into my ear that news had just arrived that the Revolutionary Military Committee, with the aid of Red Guards from the factories and a part of the garrison who had occupied the Winter Palace, had arrested all the Ministers, with the exception of Kerensky, who had escaped in a motor car. I went to the Bolshevik Party Bureau on the lower floor. Here I found a sort of improvised revolution-ary intelligence department, from which delegates to all parts of the city were being despatched. Upstairs in the bureau of the old Menshevik and Social Revolutionary Executive the silence of the grave reigned. A few girl typists were sorting papers, and the editor of the Menshevik 'Izvestia', Rozanoff, was still trying to keep a steady countenance.

On the following day (November 7th) the great hall of the Smolny was filled with delegates from every part of North and Central Russia – from those parts, in fact, where the poor

РАЙОННЫМЪ
Совѣтамъ Рабочихъ Депутатовъ
Фабрично-Заводскимъ Комитетамъ

ПРИКАЗЪ.

Корниловскія банды Керенскаго угрожаютъ подступамъ къ столицѣ. Отданы всѣ необходимыя распоряженія для того, чтобы безпощадно раздавить контръ-революціонное покушеніе противъ народа и его завоеваній.

Армія и Красная Гвардія революціи нуждаются въ немедленной поддержкѣ рабочихъ.

Приказываемъ районнымъ Совѣтамъ и фабр.-зав. комитетамъ:

1) выдвинуть наибольшее количество рабочихъ для рытья окоповъ, воздвиганія баррикадъ и укрѣпленія проволочныхъ загражденій;

2) гдѣ для этого потребуется **прекращеніе работъ** на фабрикахъ и заводахъ, **немедленно исполнить**;

3) собрать всю имѣющуюся въ запасѣ колючую и простую проволоку, а равно всѣ орудія, **необходимыя для рытья окоповъ и возведенія баррикадъ**;

4) все имѣющееся оружіе имѣть при себѣ;

5) соблюдать строжайшую дисциплину и быть готовыми поддержать армію революціи всѣми средствами.

Предсѣдатель Петроградскаго Совѣта Раб. и Солд. Депутатовъ
Народный Комиссаръ ЛЕВЪ ТРОЦКІЙ.

Предсѣдатель Военно-Революціоннаго Ком
Главнокомандующій [

Reproduction of a proclamation issued by the Petrograd Soviet, November 1917

TO THE DISTRICT
SOVIETS OF WORKER'S DEPUTIES AND SHOP-FACTORY COMMITTEES

ORDER

THE KORNILOV BANDS OF KERENSKY ARE THREATENING THE OUTSKIRTS OF OUR CAPITAL. ALL NECESSARY ORDERS HAVE BEEN GIVEN TO CRUSH MERCILESSLY EVERY COUNTER-REVOLUTIONARY ATTEMPT AGAINST THE PEOPLE AND ITS CONQUESTS.

THE ARMY AND THE RED GUARD OF THE REVOLUTION ARE IN NEED OF IMMEDIATE SUPPORT OF THE WORKERS.

THE DISTRICT SOVIETS AND SHOP-FACTORY COMMITTEES ARE ORDERED:

1) To bring forward the largest possible number of workers to dig trenches, erect barricades and set up wire defenses;

2) Wherever necessary for this purpose to **SUSPEND WORK** in shops and factories, it must be done **IMMEDIATELY**.

3) To collect all available plain and barbed wire, as well as all tools **FOR DIGGING TRENCHES AND ERECTING BARRICADES;**

4) **ALL AVAILABLE ARMS TO BE CARRIED ON PERSONS;**

5) **Strictest discipline must be preserved and all must be ready to support the Army of the Revolution to the utmost.**

President of the Petrograd Soviet of Workers & Soldiers Deputies
People's Commissar LEV TROTSKY.

President of the Military-Revolutionary Committee
Chief Commander PODVOISKY.

half-proletarian peasants, land-hungry soldier-deserters dominated the village and skilled artisans the urban Soviets. Up on the platform rose Lenin. His voice was weak, apparently from excitement, and he spoke with some slight indecision. He seemed to feel that the issue was still doubtful and that it was difficult to put forward a programme right here and now. A Council of People's Commissars, he said, was being set up and the list of names would be submitted to the Congress. The Council would propose to the Congress resolutions dealing with an immediate armistice at the front, with the rights of the Peasant Land Committees in the temporary possession of the landlords' latifundias, and with the control by Factory Workers' Committees over all operations of employers and managers. 'We appeal to our comrades in England, France and Germany to follow our example', he concluded, 'and we believe the people, who gave Karl Marx to the world, will not be deaf to our appeal. We believe that our words will be heard by the descendants of the Paris Communards and that the British workers will not forget their inheritance from the Chartists.'

About 10 o'clock at night I passed out of the Smolny Institute. In the street outside a group of workmen and Baltic sailors were discussing the Congress over a log fire. I passed along the banks of the Neva, already beginning to freeze in the shallows near the wharfs. A raw November fog was blowing up from the Finnish Gulf. Opposite the Vassily Ostroff lay the light cruiser 'Aurora' and a destroyer with guns trained on the Winter Palace. 'Stop!' shouted a voice, and I recognised a cordon of Red Guards across the road. I was standing near the Winter Palace, which was now the seat of the Revolutionary Military Committee. 'Where are the Ministers of Kerensky?' I asked one of the guards. 'Safe across the river in the Petropavlovsk Fortress', came the laconic reply. 'You can't pass along here', said another.

I crossed the great Neva Bridge and approached the Petropavlovsk. The Red Guards were standing round the gates and the Red Flag was flying from the tower of the 'bastille' of Tsarism. Yesterday Kerensky's Government of doubting Thomases in the Winter Palace was directing the fortunes of crumbling social order. On this night its members were in this fortress, where they had but yesterday kept the Bolshevik leaders. The wheel of fortune had gone round and the Caliphs of the hour had passed. With their passage the Russian Revolution had entered a new phase. The Soviets of workmen, peasants and soldiers had at last come into their own.[159]

Something of the excitement, as well as the sense of uncertainty and apprehension, of those days can also be found in the account of J.S. Goode, an Australian who later became a lecturer in Russian at the University of Melbourne. He recounted his experiences and impressions of the Revolution in an article written in 1932 which describes spontaneous speeches and arguments on the streets of Petrograd:

People of all ranks and ages flooded the streets and moved from one meeting to another.

'Should we end the war? Should the Soviets rule? Should the land be immediately divided up between the peasants? Should the workers control the factories?'

These were a few of the burning questions that were passionately discussed and debated everywhere. Wandering among the crowds I came to a public square where a mass of many thousand[s] of people listened eagerly to a speech made by a slim, frail student with flashing eyes.

'The whole powers of the nation must be vested with the Constituent Assembly, the only rightful authority to represent the whole nation.' The clear penetrating voice with the sincerity of youth raising to the heights of pathos seemed to appeal to the audience. Watching the assembly I noticed that many of the working men present were looking at the student with sympathy and admiration. ...

Suddenly a storm broke out. All eyes were now fixed upon a solidly built man in a well tailored suit who approached the tribune with sure and brisk steps.

'Never, never and never, comrades ...' came the ringing, metallic words of the newcomer, and such was the persuasive power in the man's voice and demeanor that the words were echoed in the multitude of his listeners who involuntarily repeated them.

Tapping the table forcibly with his open hand and using his powerful voice to its full advantage, the man was viciously attacking the previous speaker. It was not a speech. It was rather a cannonade, each word being a deadly bullet from the human machine gun, each utterance coming home and striking its man. The student was smashed, torn into pieces, outwitted and outpointed.

The newcomer was Trotzky [sic].

He then describes how he returned to his lodgings and discussed events with the residents there:

> Haunted by ominous whispers and by the ghost-like shadows of the lurking passers-by I felt a strange sensation of losing the sense of reality, the sense of time and place. I hurried home and knocked twice at the iron gates of the house where I lived. ...
>
> On the eve of November 7 we held a meeting of our house committee. 'Are we going to do something in the form of co-operation with organisations working against the Bolsheviks?' I asked the chairman, a staunch conservative member of the Duma.
>
> 'Kerensky is doomed. We cannot help him,' said the chairman dryly. 'And, after all,' added he, 'I think that Lenin is no worse than Kerensky.'
>
> 'I agree with our chairman,' said another tenant, a well known musician. 'Our young friend is too radically minded to view facts in their true proportions. The Bolshies cannot stay for more than six weeks. All we can do now is "to wait and see" as the Englishmen say.'

On the night of 7 November, the conflict escalated:

> I was awakened by a terrific cannonade. I went to the gates and looked at the street. A man dashed across.
>
> 'They are trying to get the Central Exchange,' he shouted. 'The cadets are giving them a hot time.'
>
> Up we dashed, to the telephone.
>
> 'Still working,' came a whisper from the musician, when he gave the number of his friend, a journalist, to the telephone girl. 'Hallo! What's the latest?'
>
> As the musician was listening 20 pairs of eager eyes tried to read his thoughts. Suddenly he dropped the receiver. 'Finished. They have got the Central. The Petrograd garrison has surrendered. The Government is abandoned. The cadets are fighting desperately.'

Goode and his companions could hear a 'dull roaring noise' coming from afar. They turned the lights off and watched from the windows facing the street as an 'avalanche' of men and women rushed down it:

The crack of the discharged guns, the bang of broken windows, the cries of the wounded, all these sounds blended into one infernal cacophony of destruction and chaos. And then, hovering in the air, hideous and ghastly, repulsive and revolting, came the howling of the mob. That howling of the looting mob! There were no shrill notes or shoutings in the howling, but it crept into our bodies and made them paralysed. The demarkation line between the man and the beast ceased to exist and we heard the voice of the cave man in his lust to kill.

A motor lorry full of armed men stopped, at the front of the house opposite ours. A tall sailor in a leather jacket, evidently the leader of the party, alightened and asked to open the gates. Two men similarly dressed, with hand grenades and revolvers, accompanied him. The gates were open without delay, and the three men entered the house. ...

Soon a whistle was heard, and 10 more armed men followed their comrades. The party returned back in about an hour's time with a dozen prisoners. They were thrown on the lorry and driven away. I knew the most of them. They belonged to the Socialist Revolutionary Party and University students and school teachers. ...

We awoke in a new world, and felt like travellers coming to an unknown country equipped with a map, but without a compass.[160]

At the British Embassy, Meriel Buchanan noted that by Thursday, 8 November 'the fighting seemed to be over', and went on to report that

The Ministers were prisoners in the Fortress, the Bolsheviks, for the moment at any rate, were complete masters of the situation, and the whole town was in their hands.

The normal life of the town continued as if nothing much had changed, though most faces wore an anxious, hunted expression, and soldiers and armed workmen filled all the streets. It was rumoured that Lenin had made himself head of the new Government, and that Trotsky was to be made Commissary of the Foreign Office. Very often we had half-jestingly spoken of such a possibility, but now that we were faced with it as almost a fact it seemed beyond belief. It could not possibly last. Petrograd itself might perhaps be forced to submit to such a rule for a short time, but that the whole of Russia should be governed by such men was not credible.[161]

In Moscow there was more fighting than in Petrograd. British businessman Arthur Marshall, who had travelled from the capital to Moscow just as the Revolution broke out, later published in his newspaper, the *Russian Daily News*, an account by a 'well-known foreign resident of Petrograd' (almost certainly himself) of what he had witnessed in Moscow:

The trouble became bad on Friday last. It was apparent for several days that an outburst between the government troops and the civilian guards was inevitable; and there was a good deal of rifle fire about the city, and armed patrols were constantly in collision. On Saturday the artillery was brought into play and the fighting was very severe. I spent the whole of Saturday in Moscow. The fighting seemed to be centering around the Kremlin and in the business sections of the city, while in the outskirts everything was fairly quiet. I assumed from what I observed that the Englishmen and the Americans at the National Hotel had taken ample precautions for their safety, inasmuch as they had plenty of notice, and perhaps were all well concentrated at the English Club, so that anybody could have information as to the situation. The nearest I got to the National Hotel was about a half-mile away. There was very lively shooting going on at the bottom of this street near the great square.

It was possible to move around through the zone of action. When you were told to halt you had to halt. Then after you explained who you were, you would be passed along from post to post. I got into the hands of the Red Guard and this is my experience:

They would say, 'We will shoot you if you haven't permission', but after you got their permission to advance, you could do so.

On Sunday there was very heavy shooting. The artillery sounded very plainly at Metishe where I was twelve versts away. Then on Monday came a lull. A truce was declared on that day during which each side excused each other. There had been heavy rifle fighting, artillery fighting, and hand to hand fighting around the Kremlin, and each side had been in possession two or three times.

Efforts during this truce were made to form a government. A government was formed, and then the truce was broken on Tuesday, and the shooting began again. On Tuesday I tried to get to the National Hotel, but was unable to do so. The fighting was still confined to the centre of the city. The civilian guards, Maximalists, were being reinforced from outlying districts, and it was reported that the government troops were approaching Moscow from Kiev, and had arrived within twenty versts of the city.

I have heard rumours of a terrific destruction of property in Moscow, and of frightful loss of life. There is no doubt a heavy loss of life, and I have heard it estimated at as much as from 500 to 5,000.

I do not think, however, that the higher figure is correct. I am also of the opinion that the loss of life among non-combatants is very slight.

If anyone was hurt in this affair, it was through his own rashness. When I left the government troops were in control of the central part of the city, and the Bolsheviks were in control outside of that section. It would seem that the artillery changed hands several times.

On Tuesday there was very heavy gun firing; there were no telephones in operation; no telegraph wires operating outside of Moscow; and strikes had been declared everywhere. I had been told on Sunday that a great many of the buildings in the central part of the city had been smashed into atoms. I investigated this on Monday, and it all proved to be without foundation. Naturally, some damage had been done; but it was much slighter than the mildest of the reports. It was also absurd to say that as many as 13,000 people had been killed or wounded.

The trouble in Moscow is not ended, or was not up til [sic] yesterday.

There has been no massacre of civilians, and my honest judgement is that there has been very little looting.[162]

On the critical day when the Revolution broke out, Nurse Florence Farmborough was travelling on a train from the front to Moscow:

WEDNESDAY, 8th NOVEMBER
Standing in the corridor were two officers, in greatcoats of civilian cut. I had heard that some officers disguised their rank in order not to clash with the Bolsheviki. Perhaps, in Kiyev, these men would feel safer in civilian garb. From them I heard that in Moscow the railways and stations were still in the hands of the Bolsheviki and that they and they only gave permission to travellers to enter the city. In the city itself, at night, no one dared leave his home. I was very anxious to hear what was happening in Petrograd, but when I broached the subject, nobody seemed inclined to discuss it. I

decided that either they knew nothing, or, knowing too much, they were loath to speak of it.

Two days later her train reached Moscow:

FRIDAY, 10th NOVEMBER. Moscow
We steamed slowly into Moscow about 4 in the afternoon. There was a rush to descend: the soldiers were shouting, pushing, jostling each other. The platform was full of people, military and civilian: bustling and hustling, colliding with each other, gesticulating excitedly. I had expected to see armed guards parading up and down but there was none to be seen until I reached the exit. There stood about twenty of them – the men whom they called *Bolsheviki*. I looked at them critically: to me they looked exactly like any other soldiers, only they were not lolling about, with drooping shoulders and bored expressions. They were erect, with determined faces and keen eyes always on the alert; they held guns in their hands and daggers, in leather pouches, were suspended from their belts. A broad, red band was attached to their left uniform-sleeve. They barred the way, demanding the permit or pass.

They treated the soldiers lightly, sometimes even with a friendly word. But the civilian travellers' tickets and passes were carefully scrutinised, their addresses noted, and certain information written into a large book. When it was my turn, I showed them my documents, ticket and permit. The guard took them to a uniformed man at a table. He examined them meticulously and noted down the particulars in his book. 'Was I returning to the Front?' 'Yes, in a week or ten days' time.' 'Where was I staying in Moscow?' I gave the name of my friends and the number of their house in the Plushchika Ulitsa. 'Of whom did the family consist?' I told them that it was a widowed lady with two daughters. The guards were civil enough; they returned my papers and told me that, on the morrow, I must be sure to register with the police. I was allowed to pass into the street: I found a white world, still and motionless.

Some days later she described the effects of the new regime on the city:

The war against intellectuals which began in Petrograd is now threatening to sweep over Moscow. Men and women of good families are being forced from their homes and compelled to do the most menial tasks, such as selling Bolshevist newspapers in the streets or pasting Bolshevist posters on to walls. As an old friend of the Usovs aptly put it: 'The Bolsheviki are trying to pull the cultured classes of Russia down to the level of the uncultured, but they will never succeed in raising the uncultured to the level of the cultured.' ...

Portraits of Lenin have begun to appear in public squares, adorned with red ribbons, while the Red Flag of Free Russia, bearing the words 'Svoboda! Ravenstvo! Bratstvo! [Liberty! Equality! Fraternity!]', has been erected on important buildings. The Bolsheviki are sending out innumerable manifestoes and pamphlets. A few have come into my possession, too long-winded to translate into my diary. Their message, always couched in most inflammatory language, urges the 'free men' of the New Proletarian State to assist in the destruction of capitalism, to uphold the peace negotiations and to safeguard the Revolution by taking up arms against all those 'bourgeois' forces which seek to destroy their lawful rights.

The Bolsheviki are forming councils, committees, sub-committees, courts, leagues, parties, societies; they are talented talkers and gifted orators. The masses of the people flock to their call. Already they have established the nucleus of the Proletarian Republic and drawn up their political programme; and, what is more surprising, they have successfully organised the Red Army – in great part drawn from the disloyal soldiers of the Imperial Army. One and all wage war against the 'intelligentsia' and the 'bourgeoisie' – nicknames given to the educated people and the middle-class or 'idle rich'. There is no doubt that Lenin and Trotsky are intent on exterminating the Russian intellectual classes.[163]

The Australian jockey 'Brownie' Carslake was also still in Moscow at the time of the Bolshevik Revolution, and he noted that 'it was a very uncomfortable time for us in many ways'. Perhaps most upsetting for anyone whose life was bound up with horses was the treatment meted out by the Bolsheviks to the 'aristocratic' horses in the city's racing stables. Under the heading 'Royal Horse Killed by Reds', Carslake told how he

was horrified ... to hear of the terrible fate that had overtaken many of the Russian racehorses. The powers that be must have been completely mad, for they decided that racehorses were aristocratic beings, and they got rid of them in the most ghastly manner you can conceive.

I heard that they were tied two and two together and petrol poured over them and set alight. That good horse of King Edward's, Minoru, who won the Derby for him and was later sold to Russia for breeding purposes, suffered death in this horrible way.

Unsurprisingly, Carslake and the 'two or three other English jockeys' still remaining in Moscow decided that it was time to leave, and eventually, after an adventurous journey, at first by land through Finland to Oslo and then by sea, when they were attacked by German submarines, they arrived back in England at the beginning of December, after which they 'went straight off to attend the December sales' and resumed their life in the saddle.[164]

Other Englishmen too decided that it was time to leave. Hugh Walpole, for example, who had only arrived back in Petrograd at the end of October, had already made the decision to leave when the Revolution broke out, and he was only narrowly able to escape the city and cross the border into Finland. His diary entries for the period are terse and to the point:

6 NOVEMBER 1917
Kahn tells me that this afternoon Kerensky asked for full authority against the Bolsheviks. He's shown such weakness, however, that there's not much to be hoped from him, I fear. Going home find the Nevski crowded in quite the old style. At home they beg me not to go out. However I get to the Embassy for dinner through crowded but quiet streets. There the latest news is that Kerensky has defied the Bolsheviks and arrested the Committee.

7 NOVEMBER 1917
Alarums and excursions once again. News in the morning that the Bolsheviks have the upper hand. Don't know whether to go or not … Firing in the evening. Shelling of Winter Palace. Learn as I go to bed that the whole town is in the hands of the Bolsheviks.

8 NOVEMBER 1917
Up at six. K. like an angel also up. Cab arrived, drove off in pitch blackness to Astoria, where I fetched Hicks. Putting up barricades in the streets. Saw the damage the shells had done at the Winter

Palace. Got to the station all right and finally started. Got through Bely Ostrov without trouble. Rest of the day as usual, swooned, thought much of K., and Russia, read Lord Jim. Too strange to feel that this time I'm not coming back.[165]

'Human life is very cheap'

LIVING UNDER BOLSHEVISM

Once they had seized control, the Bolsheviks moved quickly and purposefully to consolidate their power. They faced down a strike by the civil service, sacking the majority of the existing officials and replaced them with men of their own stamp; they harassed their political opponents without let-up; and they took a firm grip on the food supply in Petrograd and the other major cities. Most importantly, Lenin recognized that if the Revolution was to survive, the war with Germany had to be brought to an end, no matter how humiliating the terms. This would not only be popular with the soldiers but would provide a vital breathing space in which the new government could concentrate on gaining effective control of the whole country and fighting enemies at home instead of those abroad. Russia's participation in the First World War came to an end with the signing of the Brest-Litovsk treaty – between the Bolshevik government and the Central Powers – on 3 March 1918.

Although, as Meriel Buchanan noted, 'For the first few days of the Bolshevik rule food was more plentiful, and several wagons full of provisions intended for the front were handed out free to the crowd',[166] conditions for the majority of the population rapidly deteriorated. Arthur Marshall, still hoping to sign a new contract with the Russian government, and doing his best to continue to run his various businesses spread across the country from Kiev to Vladivostock, chronicled the situation in his letters to his wife, in which his natural optimism and very laudable desire to maintain morale among his workforce fail to disguise his increasing desperation:

16 NOVEMBER 1917 Petrograd

[T]he position remains here in the same uncertain state. We have no government that is a recognised government and I don't know when we shall have. There may or may not have to be a civil war to accomplish that much to be desired result. When we consider that there is no Government one can only wonder at the very remarkable peace that is reigning & the law & order.

The elections are going on but the result is still uncertain.

The works are also going on but slowly.

The rewriting of the Contract is also going on but also slowly.

I am wondering who is going to sign it when it is written. There is no council of ministers to do so, but perhaps the war office will do so themselves. At any rate that is what I am working to achieve. ...

All this trouble is most annoying and worrying and almost heart breaking, but the only thing to do is slog away at the difficulties until they disappear and then get home to you all. ...

If I did not keep quite calm & cheerful about it all I don't think I should have any staff left by now, they see me calm & so feel much happier & safer.

26 NOVEMBER 1917 Petrograd

I am once more back in Petrograd after a rather unpleasant journey from Moscow with a train of deserting soldiers. ...

Life here is full of interest despite the fact that most of the interest is based on intense wrong and unpleasantness and despite all this I feel that I would not have missed being out here and doing my little bit to help for anything. It is hard to do much but all that one can do is so urgently needed and I do not have one spare moment from morning till night.

Added to all this we do now & again have little excitements by way of rifle fire and revolver practice. ...

You really need not worry at all. I am not a young adventurer and always take quite good care of myself although I don't let anything interfere with duty & try to set the rest of them an example of keeping cool and going about one's duties in a perfectly normal fashion and above all in avoiding pessimism.

The new contract looks like coming to a definite head at last...

We are having our newspaper 'stopped' but I hope to get over that difficulty soon.

I have been in Petrograd all this week and a very worrying week I have had of it. They, the Bolsheviks, shut down our newspaper twice, but that is only one of the tiny little difficulties and I wish it was all.

The Bolsheviks have also stated their intention of seizing the works at Mitischi. That is a much more serious matter. Still more serious we have not yet got our contract settled...

The Government of this country is still a matter for conjecture. The present state of affairs cannot of course last, but the end of it is not yet in sight and troubles continue and disorders continue and one has to sit & think & scheme & plan and all the time without any solid ground under one's feet for doing the thinking, scheming & planning.

Where is this country drifting to & what can one do to help it? I can tell you it takes all my optimism to prevent my saying, 'I am tired of it all, let's chuck it & clear out'. But chuck it I won't & clear out I won't but I will get the matter cleared up instead & will continue to work so that the future may repay all the present trouble and to what little extent I can I will do my best to get the general mess over here cleared up. Every Englishman over here has a duty now, a hard & worrying unpleasant duty, but nonetheless a duty to perform. As I told my English staff at Mitischi it may not be nice to stay on & work over here, but it is necessary & we must all do our duty & try & defeat the German designs in this country....

It is so hard to get work done. One is not only short of staff, but the staff one has works rottenly. The Russian part of it spends its time on Committees in place of being at work and the English portion is correspondingly prevented from getting its work done....

You would be frightened at housekeeping here where it is necessary to pay about 15/- for a pound of butter and all sorts of absurd prices for everything and anything.

A cabman asked me last night £1.10.0 for a drive of 1½ miles. I walked. However at times I have spent in a day for cabs £7 or £8. Money here seems to have no value at all or at any rate its value gets less every day.

Boots have now reached £20 to £25 a pair and a suit of clothes costs £80. I was offered on the train £120 for the new suit I bought in London for £6 and before I leave I shall sell off any old clothes and shall get for each of my old suits not less than £15.

29 DECEMBER 1917 Petrograd

Add to all one's difficulties the political situation and the absolute
lack of knowledge as to what will take place even how we shall get
on through the winter & you can imagine that it takes quite a lot of
energy to cheer myself up & when you add to that the fact that the
job of cheering up another two dozen or so Englishmen who often
get frightfully down in the dumps & another two hundred or so
Russians who get their heads full of all sorts of fantastic ideas and
another 300 Russian workmen who are full of all sorts of socialistic
nonsense ... and who I have to lead carefully and diplomatically
in the way they should go and explain everything like a father to a
baby but with all the cunningness of a serpent to lead them the way
you want whilst giving way to their fantastic ideas in other things.

... the British may on no account desert Russia or lose any
chance of helping her. All this trouble is not her fault but her
misfortune & after all it should seem as a very firm lesson to our
own people & a warning as to what road not to take.

Russia has been led astray by the paid agitators and she has
begun to tire of him & not to believe in him & to see in him only
misery famine filth & disorder.

The electric light now only burns a few hours a day because we
are short of fuel, & this because we have bad management, no men,
only masters. No-one thinks it his job to work.... Bread could be
had for a shilling, now for days you can't get it. Streets were kept
clean in winter & now they are almost impassable. ...

Soldiers sell cigarettes in the streets and don't even clean their
own barracks. It's nobody's job to clean anything. At night they
rather like to wander about in place of sleeping for the barracks
are cold, it is nobody's job to heat them & so they look out for
someone's wine cellar to rob, or someone's overcoat to steal.

All the same if one can imagine Great Britain getting into a state
like this the streets would be 1000 times more unsafe & generally
the conditions 1000 times worse than here for here the great mass
of the people take no part in it but unfortunately do not appear to
have the gumption to take any part in putting it right.

It is a funny country and conversations I have had with some
of them would make one laugh were it not so serious & pitiable.
Even the ones who do dreadfully stupid socialistic things in the
bulk do them with the best of motives. It's really wonderful if you
can imagine the state of Great Britain were the power to be handed
over to all the mad socialistic cranks each having the right to work

out his own particular hobby to its bitter end, then perhaps you can imagine a little what this country is like. Can you imagine an election at home with not 2 or 3 parties to vote for but the choice of 23 parties.

30 DECEMBER 1917–2 JANUARY 1918 Petrograd
The latest news is that all the Banks have been seized by the Bolsheviks. What result this will have I don't yet know but it is not more comforting from a business point of view than it was before they did it.

... searches by the red guard on one pretext or another are a very frequent occurrence.

[The staff need bucking up:] At times it almost makes me angry to think that they require it. They seem to think that in war time they should be provided with feather beds and silk eiderdowns, peaches and puff pastry and feel hurt because they don't get it.

We are owed about one million roubles on general business and about 8,000,000 roubles on the Car Works contract but to get the money is like drawing blood out of a stone.

4 JANUARY 1918
I have had perforce to give up my breakfast of tea & bread & butter & taken to tea, a little cold meat & a very little bread & butter. I suppose some time or other all this will end & Russia will once more be a country flowing with milk and honey.[167]

A similar situation pertained in Moscow, where Florence Farmborough was still staying with friends. In January 1918 she wrote:

The food rations are, naturally, quite inadequate; many people have sought work with, or sanctioned by, the *Bolsheviki*, in order to supplement their meagre diet. Gradually, as foodstuffs become more and more scarce, there is no doubt that a large percentage of the Muscovite population is half-starved. Some restaurants are still open, but they can supply food only at a price. If one is hungry – as one always is – one does not enquire too closely into the kind, or quality, of the meat. Horse flesh provides the main meat supply; it can be cooked and served in a variety of ways in order to disguise both origin and taste. Twice I have eaten horse flesh with relish: the first time, it had no specific taste, rather like a well-spiced mince; the second time, there was no mistaking it; it was a steak, coarse and stringy with a slightly sweet flavour. At the first mouthful I knew what I was eating; but, as hunger is the best sauce, I had no qualms in demolishing every scrap. Horse flesh has, however, now become a real delicacy and can be compared favourably with the flesh of cats, dogs and rodents.[168]

In the immediate aftermath of the Revolution and the formation of the Bolshevik government, there were attempts by some of the other parties to persuade the Bolsheviks to enter into a new coalition, but as Arthur Marshall's paper, the *Russian Daily News*, reported, the Bolsheviks were in no mood to compromise:

> The temper at the Smolny according to our correspondents is warlike and victorious. The Bolsheviks consider themselves the victors. They are agreeable to a coalition, but are against the proposed Coalition, saying: 'We made the revolution. We have conquered. And now they want to place us in the minority.'[169]

It was also noted that the Bolsheviks were beginning to take their revenge on their ideological opponents, no matter how distinguished their revolutionary past:

> On Tuesday the Red Guards began searching private houses, demanding the handing over of all arms. At 4 pm some of the Red Guard came to Mr. Plekhanoff's house, where he was lying ill in bed.
>
> Under threat of being shot, he was forced to get up; arms were demanded although there were none in the house.
>
> The Red Guard asked Mr. Plekhanoff such questions as 'What class of society do you belong to; they say you are a minister or a member of the State Duma?' Mr. Plekhanoff replied that he had been a revolutionary who for forty years had devoted his life to the struggle for liberty.
>
> One of the Red Guards replied that he had now sold himself to the bourgeoisie. In the evening the Red Guard again appeared at Mr. Plekhanoff's and demanded arms; and on November 1st they paid him a third visit. These aimless searches, rude treatment, and the danger of excesses produced an exceedingly painful effect on Mr. Plekhanoff. Yesterday morning, after the third search, he began coughing up blood. His temperature rose to 79 degrees [sic], and his state in the opinion of the doctor is very critical.

Civilians queuing for soap in August 1917

On the same day, at the Alexandroff station, Red Guards also attacked a train carrying troops loyal to the former government:

> Eye witnesses state that the Bolsheviks had stationed a detachment on the railroad, and the soldiers were ordered to leave the waggons. While they were doing so a ruthless fire was opened. The Red Guard broke into the waggons and massacred the soldiers. All the waggons were filled with bodies.
>
> In the words of eye-witnesses, the soldiers present a fearful spectacle, many having been bayoneted in their sleep, and their faces mutilated.[170]

Meriel Buchanan noted that 'disorders and desultory street fighting increased day by day', culminating when bands of soldiers and sailors pillaged the wine cellars of the Winter Palace:

The Preobrajinsky regiment, whose barracks were next door and who were supposed to be on guard, tried at first to put up a feeble resistance, but very soon joined in the general plunder themselves. All during the night the orgy continued, and several encounters took place between drunken bands of soldiers and sailors, and from the Embassy we heard the constant sound of firing all down the Quay and the Millionaia.

Early the next morning, the news having rapidly spread through the town, crowds arrived on the scene to try and get a little booty. Soldiers in huge motor-lorries drove up to the Palace and went away, their motors full of cases of priceless wine. Women, their arms full of bottles, could be seen trying to sell them to passers-by in the streets. Even the children had their share of the plunder, and could be met carrying a bottle of champagne or perhaps some valuable old liqueur.

About midday an armed force of sailors and one or two armoured-cars arrived on the scene to try and restore order. The Palace was surrounded and nobody was allowed to pass anywhere near.

Thousands of bottles of wine were destroyed and thrown over into the ice, the sailors firing into the bottles the quicker to break them; but the horde of drunken soldiers was so immense that the orgy still continued without any abatement, and order only began to be restored on the arrival of a company of firemen, who flooded the cellars, and drowned a lot of soldiers who were too drunk to escape.

Even as far down the Quay as the Embassy the air was infected with the reek of spirits, and everywhere drunken soldiers lay about, broken bottles littered the streets, the snow was stained rose red and yellow where in many places the wine had been spilt. All through the town the drunken hordes spread themselves, firing indiscriminately at each other or anybody who molested them. Scenes of indescribable horror and disgust took place, the crowds in some instances scooping up the dirty, wine-stained snow, drinking it out of their hands, fighting with each other over the remains. And everywhere the soldiers were inciting the people to murder and pillage. It was so easy – you had only to take your rifle, and everybody had a firearm of some sort – to knock down a few shutters or break a few windows and take whatever you found.[171]

Nevertheless, there were some lighter moments:

A story was told at this time of a man who was stopped by a band of thieves and robbed of his watch and money and his coat. Shivering, he said to one of the robbers, 'You might at least give me your coat in exchange. Mine was new and yours is old, and you can't want two coats.' After some hesitation the thief eventually gave him his dirty old sheepskin coat and the man hurried home, thankful of at least some covering in the cold. Arrived at his lodgings, he took off the coat, and found in the pocket what was evidently the result of the robber's day: three or four diamond rings and a sum of money far exceeding that of which he had been robbed himself.[172]

In Moscow, Florence Farmborough's friends

impressed on me the need to dress shabbily when in the street. It is sufficient to wear a white collar, or even to have white hands, to be recognised as a *bourgeois* and dealt with accordingly. A fur coat is instantly seized; should the owner show any resistance, he is liable to be arrested, or shot immediately. Among the many new laws which have been instituted by the Bolshevist régime is one which is known as *samosud*, or *samoupravstvo*, which can be interpreted as 'self-judgment', whereby the Red Guards are entitled to take the law into their own hands and kill or torture as they deem it necessary. I saw an instance of this *samosud* only a day or two ago. I was walking towards Plushchika Street when, in a nearby house, rifle-shots were heard. A door in the wall suddenly opened and a *dvornik* [yard-porter] called to me hurriedly: 'Barishnya! Come inside, quickly!' I went in and he closed the door. 'What is happening?' I asked. 'They are all a lot of thieves,' he answered. 'Some went into the house to steal; others wanted to do the same. They met, and began killing each other. Set a thief to catch a thief!' he added with a chuckle. When I left the yard, I saw two men, with guns, running off down the street; a third lay prostrate on the road near the house.[173]

Meriel Buchanan and Florence Farmborough left Russia shortly after the Revolution, but other Englishwomen remained in the country for much longer. One, who was living in Petrograd, and whose name still remains unknown, only managed to return to England in June 1920. Later that year she provided a graphic account of conditions in the city after the formation of the Bolshevik government:

Petrograd is a dead city under the present regime. There is hardly any traffic, and children play in the middle of the principal streets; occasionally a large motor rushes past, generally filled with soldiers. There are very few horses to be seen, nearly all are eaten or have died of starvation and ill-usage. The shops are closed, and only the Government co-operative stores are open. There one gets a half-pound of black bread every day, and a pound of very moist sugar every few months. Sometimes one obtains a pound or two of cranberries, a little salt, quarter pound of coffee, a few herrings and potatoes, and a little piece of soap. The markets are also open, and all kinds of food can be bought there, but the prices are so extraordinarily high that most people can hardly afford to buy anything. Black bread is 400 roubles a pound, butter is about 3,000, sugar 3,600, and a pound of potatoes varies from 100 to 400 roubles. (The pre-war value of the rouble was about 2s. 1d.). Sometimes the markets are surrounded by soldiers, all the people who happen to be either buying or selling are arrested, the provisions are confiscated, and the market is closed for a couple of days. No one is surprised, and everyone looks on such an occurrence as perfectly natural. In a few days the market is reopened and everything goes on as usual, except that the prices are somewhat raised.

The air in Petrograd is beautifully clear, and the sky is a wondrous blue. Nearly all works and factories are closed and wood is at such a price that private individuals burn as little as possible. Smoke is seldom seen coming out of the chimneys. During the winter whole families, father, mother, and children, lived in one room, the others being closed in order to economise fuel. Some cooking had to be done at home, as the soup provided by the soup kitchens was generally of the worst possible quality – water, a little grain of some sort, a few cabbage leaves or frozen potatoes, a little herring. So all bought funny little stoves made of sheet-iron, with a long chimney that went into the fireplace. These little stoves while in use raised the temperature of the room about one to two degrees. Many people had two or three degrees of frost (Réaumur) in their rooms. When the cold became unbearable and there was nothing to cook with people chopped up their furniture for firewood. They began with kitchen stools, and common tables and cupboards. When these were gone they broke up the better furniture. Beautiful old mahogany, chairs and tables were burnt to cook a few potatoes. Most houses are very empty, as one is compelled either to sell one's belongings or simply to exchange them for food. For a pair of window curtains one gets two or three pounds of flour. For a table-cloth one receives a pound or so of butter; Curtains, tablecloths, furniture materials are all used for clothes, as no manufactured articles can be bought anywhere.

In private houses the electric light is turned on for a few hours a week at most unexpected moments – from 6 to 7 in the evening, sometimes, from 2 to 3 in the morning. It is nearly impossible to get kerosene or candles. But the Bolsheviks are thoughtful and try to improve matters. As the weather gets lighter they put the clocks on, so that life in Petrograd begins with the sun and ends with the sun. On 28th February a decree is issued that from 1st March the clocks must be put on an hour. For a day or two there was much confusion; everyone was late for their work and missed their trains, &c. About the middle of April the clocks were put on another hour or two, so that 8 o'clock in the morning was really 5 o'clock, and 11 o'clock bed-time was really only 8 o'clock. In the autumn the clocks are gradually put back.

Thanks to the cold, all the pipes burst in the winter, houses were flooded, and then the water was cut off. We had to go down to the basement to get water, and all the slops, refuse, &c., had to be emptied out into the yard. When the spring came and the ground began to thaw the sanitary condition of the town was dreadful. The Bolsheviks again managed things very cleverly. They issued a decree that the bourgeois population should clean out the yards, cesspools, and dustbins, and drag all the dirt in sledges or carts to the Nevsky and other streets down which tram lines are laid. Here the dirt was emptied out and in a day or two trams dragging open cars behind them came and took the mountains of filth away.

As the town is in such an insanitary condition and food is so scarce there are many infectious diseases. At one time there was an epidemic of the worst form of typhus. Notices appeared on all the walls telling people to beware of lice, as the infection is principally spread by these insects. Some of the notices ran as follows: 'We have conquered Judenitch, Kolchak, and the Allies! Is it possible that we shall not conquer this last enemy – the louse?' Then followed very excellent advice about the necessity of bathing often, of changing one's linen constantly, of washing one's hair in hot water. There is no fuel, there is no soap, there is very little hot water, and only two or three of the public bath-houses are opened, for one or two days a week. There are fewer than 1,000 medical men at present in Petrograd, and there are hardly any medicaments.

If medicine is ordered at the chemists it takes three or four days to prepare it, the patient must bring his own bottle, and he receives about one-quarter of the quantity proscribed, Very few people recover when they are ill. Death is even more complicated than life. The body cannot be buried at once; the coffin must be got by special permission; it is a glass-wooden shell, roughly knocked together out of boards. The dead must await their turn to be buried. If you die at home your relatives drag you to the cemetery on a little sledge in winter – horses are too expensive – or a hand-cart or wheelbarrow in summer. The gravedigger only consents to dig the grave if you give him many hundred roubles or several pounds of bread, flour, or butter. If you die at the hospital your naked body is put in the dead-house with a whole lot of other bodies. If your relations find your corpse they can bury you how and where they like; if not you are put into a cart with the others, covered over with matting, and buried in a general grave – men and women together – and no prayers are read.

As there is such a shortage of food, and no one is properly nourished, miserable little babies are born. Vice, especially among children, is on the increase, at the schools religion is not taught – nearly nothing is being done in the way of education, and punishment is strictly forbidden. Respect for parents and teachers, of old age and wisdom, does not exist. Some of the 'Commissars' are quite young boys. They have much energy, but no experience, and very little education. Freedom of speech is a thing of the past; for a careless word uttered in the streets or in the tram one is often arrested. One's house may be searched, one's property may be confiscated, that is, stolen, and one may be arrested at any moment – and there is no redress, no one to appeal to. One goes out to see friends, or to church, or to the cinema, or a concert. Soldiers come to make a search or to verify your papers. You are arrested and kept for weeks or months. Then the soldiers go to your house, search through all your things, read your letters, and often go and arrest the people who wrote the letters to you. You generally do not even know why you are arrested: the reason the Bolsheviks give is always the same – speculation or counter-revolution. After being arrested you are taken to the Gorokhovaia No. 2,[174] the seat of the Extraordinary Commission. You are kept here for a few days and then sent to one of the other prisons. Sometimes you are imprisoned for months without a single examination, sometimes you are examined many times. The judges are members of the Extraordinary Commission.

They are men of many, different types – former soldiers or sergeants, workmen, Jews, Letts [Latvians]. Some are quite young, the greater part of them are half educated and totally uncivilised. Some, though very few, are men of education. The examination is often a farce – with a tragic end.

Human life is very cheap, and thousands of people have been shot. According to the decree of January 1920, capital punishment was abolished in Petrograd. But on 26th January several hundred men and women were shot. Among these was Charles Davison, an English engineer.[175] Most of the people who were shot had been in prison for some time. On the night of 26th January they were taken from the Shpalernaia prison,[176] in motor lorries. The motor horns were going, and the motors were kept working the whole time, so that the shouts of the soldiers and the cries of the victims as they were being forced into the lorries were not heard. They were taken to Kovalevo[177] – about 7 miles from Petrograd, and there in an open field, in the middle of a wood they were shot. Some peasants were hiding in the wood, and saw the whole scene. Many of the women implored the soldiers to spare them for the sake of their children but all to no purpose. The shooting went on for many hours and then the bodies were covered up with snow. In the spring, when the ground became soft, six big graves were dug, each about six or seven yards long, into which the bodies were thrown. These graves are now covered with flowers and many little paths are trodden through the wood, for the peasants come here to pray for the souls of the dead. Pieces of skulls and bones still lie about, also broken glasses and cups and torn socks. As there were many people to be shot and the night was cold, big bonfires were lit and hot tea was prepared for the soldiers. The soldiers took the socks off their victims' feet and threw their own shabby ones away. ...

Whatever is spoilt or broken has to remain spoilt and broken. The different Government offices occupy some beautiful private houses, the owners of which have either run away or been arrested. In a short time the house is in a filthy mess, the furniture broken, torn, and stained, the drains and sanitary arrangements in an unspeakable condition. Then the said Government offices remove to some other beautiful private house, and stay until things are in the same dreadful state as in the previous house, and then they move on again.

The people in Petrograd are naturally dissatisfied with the present form of Government; they grumble a great deal, but seem too half-hearted and physically weak to do anything themselves.

Every winter they say that in the spring, when the navigation is open, there will be a change, that next year it will be better, that this state of affairs cannot continue. The spring comes and there is no change, things go from bad to worse, life gets more difficult, more and more human lives are lost, and only the strongest survive, or those who become members of the Communist party – some from sheer despair, and others to gain their own ends.[178]

British printer and photographer Henry Keeling also remained in Petrograd for much of this period. As a worker, and moreover one who appears to have known the new Soviet Commissar for Education, Lunacharsky, he was to a certain degree in a privileged position, but even so he soon began to become disillusioned with the Bolshevik regime. Through his contacts in the factories he was aware of the fact that, initially at least, the Bolsheviks were in a tiny minority, and he realized that one of the principal means by which they were able to consolidate their position in the cities was through the control of food:

> The trump card of all was the division of the people into the now famous four categories. Theoretically there was a good deal to be said for a rationing system based on work done, but it worked out as one of the greatest engines of oppression and injustice that was ever devised by the wit of man.
>
> I make no personal complaint, because I was always in the first category – although that did not save me from semi-starvation. The first category included at the commencement all manual workmen and peasants. The second comprised those engaged in clerical work but who did not have more than one employee. The third category was that of employers who had more than one employee, and the fourth consisted of those who lived on rent and interest.
>
> The super-categories to whom this division never applied were the Navy – which was troublesome; the Army, which fed itself; the railway servants, whose strong organisation enabled them to exact terms from the Bolsheviks, and, of course, the Commissar and his immediate friends. These latter were the best fed people in Russia, they had the power to commandeer anything and everything, and used it.
>
> Something might be said for the system if the lowest category could have secured sufficient food to enable them to live, but in

a short time the fourth class disappeared altogether. They either escaped from the country, rotted in prison, or quietly starved to death – when they were not shot outright.

Of the other categories little need be said because it soon became evident that only those in the first category could hope to survive and only then by the aid of illicit buying.

Insecurity was made a fine art, and although at first there was a feeling of hope that matters would soon improve, this gradually gave way to despair as regulation after regulation was added to the list, making everyone feel that it was impossible to do anything except by favour of the Bolsheviks. House to house searchings, constant arrests – I was arrested at least six times and sometimes kept prisoner for hours. If one asked to see the warrant, a revolver was promptly produced with the remark, 'Here is our warrant. That's quite enough for you'....

The position [in the towns] is dreadful beyond all description. I was in many of the towns at one time or another in 1918 and can testify that in every place the struggle to get food is the one thing that dominates all else. Home life is one everlasting struggle to obtain food.

The decrees would make people imagine that a very fair basis has been arranged, at least for first category workmen, but it had not for a long time been possible to secure even a small part of the allowance which appears on the ration card. It is only by illicit buying that one could hope to survive, and that hope is now gone owing to the refusal of those who possess food in the villages to part with it for paper money. I was given a post later on under the new Education Minister, Lunarcharsky, as chief photographer, and took it for the not unimportant reason that I thought that working directly under the Bolsheviks might enable me to get more food. I thought I might perhaps be fed like the Red Guards, but it was not so. We had quarters in the Winter Place, and delightful quarters they were, those which the late Tsar used to occupy overlooking the Neva; but somehow a hungry man is seldom much struck with the beauty of his surroundings or the nobleness of ideals. My salary was 1,500 roubles (£150) per month, but it might just as well have been 15s. for all the use it became later on....

We were allowed to exchange our food cards for a dinner once a day at a public restaurant. The dinner in December [1918] consisted of a basin of watery soup with a small onion as the only visible thing in it; this was followed by a second course of very salt fish and one-eighth of a pound of bread – black bread, of course.

In December last we were without bread for six consecutive days.

On one occasion some women were standing near me; hearing that I was an Englishman they called out, 'Oh, when are the Allies coming to save us from this terrible torture?' They added, 'We pray on our knees every day that an end may soon come to our starvation and terror.' Every day after this as long as I continued to go to this dining place they used to say, 'How long?' or 'How shall we endure all this?' 'Surely they will never leave us to starve to death.' One incident, which occurred frequently, but which I personally saw only once, was the sudden raid on the glass case.

In a glass case in the dining place I frequented a sample dinner was displayed each day. This is done to enable the diner to compare what is served to him with what he ought to have. One day standing quite close to me was a young fellow apparently looking intently for leavings of our dinners, but every now and then gazing anxiously at the displayed dinner in the middle of the room.

Suddenly I heard a crash and everybody in the place jumped up in alarm – nerves were always on edge in Petrograd. On looking up I saw that this poor starved creature had knocked over the glass case and before anyone could recover from their surprise he had crammed the food into his mouth with both hands and tried to get away.

The manager caught him and was evidently intending to give him to the first Red Guard he could find, and would have done so but for several of the women who offered to pay for the damage done, and one woman in a burst of pity gave him her food coupon for the day. How I grew to hate these public dining places; the long queue in which I had to wait for my ticket, then the queue for the dinner itself. Scores of times I have waited from thirty to fifty minutes before getting the only meal of the day.

What could one do? The dinners cost 3½ roubles (about 7s.) in December, and if you wanted to buy a piece of bread in the street it would cost 5 roubles for quite a tiny biscuit of black bread, and that very often composed of half potato flour. At one time they gave us oats instead of bread, but not being a horse they were useless to me.

Before you had the right to dine at one of these places it was first necessary to get a special ration card. This in itself was an endless and troublesome process. Having secured this card you had to go and get registered at one or the other of these dining-rooms for a certain period. You could only dine at one place and you had to get registered where you could.

In the first days of January there was a delay in the issue of these cards in our house, and it was not until the new year was three days gone that we obtained them. In consequence we were too late to register anywhere, so that even the small comfort of the public dinner was denied us. We had to depend on stealth for all we could get plus our bread ration of half a pound of bread for the first category men. My own wages, being the highest paid, enabled me to buy anything which could be got at first ... but for the bulk of work-people, especially those with families, it must have been too dreadful even to think about. To see the women hunting for food would break the heart of a stone. A horse falls in the street and one would see the women cutting the head from the body and others cutting pieces which could be conveniently carried home.[179]

Arthur Marshall too remained in Petrograd and, whilst attempting to retain his customary optimism, chronicled the increasingly desperate situation in which he found himself in his letters to his wife, which also illustrate how the peace signed between Bolshevik Russia and Imperial Germany at Brest-Litovsk on 3 March 1918 made matters for nationals of the Allied countries markedly more difficult:

11 JANUARY 1918
[Sitting in candlelight]: Very few candles to be had so I have to economise in the number and the cost is 2/- each. [formerly 2½ d]

27 JANUARY 1918
[O]ne more week & nothing accomplished that is worth having accomplished.
[Life is] Damned Rotten.
I get hopeless news from everywhere, from Vladi, from Omsk, from Ekaterinburg, from Arkhangel, from Nizni Novgorod, from Kieff, from Moscow, from Mititschi, from Petrograd, from the newspapers, from the Printing Business, from everywhere and about everything.
Things can't go on but when will the end come. That is what I want to know & what we all want to know. ...

I can't get money out of the bank. I can't get debts paid because people here have no money to pay them with. The Government owes me millions of roubles, the [?larger] works another million or so, I have another two millions of stock here, another two millions in the railways. I can't sell anything because no-one has any money. I can't buy anything because I haven't any. I have the printing works on strike because I can't pay their wages. I haven't printed the paper for four days now. ...

The contract is still much where it was, a little better perhaps but not much. I used to scheme, but my God, how I have to scheme & worry & scheme & worry again. It used to be pleasurable but now all the pleasure has gone out of it. It has got to be my job to look ahead & act before events, but how to forecast events? Anything may happen...

Lucky indeed are those people who go home to England & join the colours & serve in the trenches with no thought for tomorrow.

[More shooting] From all accounts however they only killed about 150 men during the whole business. Rotten shots they must be...

We are changing over to the new calendar next week and I am not at all sorry.

14 FEBRUARY 1918

Things out here seem to drift from one situation to another with bewildering speed & it is very hard to forecast the end and still harder to decide what to do to help it to be a good end for both countries. Not even those Russians who are supposed to be guiding the destinies of the place know how the thing is going to do ...
In some ways we are so Gilbert & Sullivanny that it reminds me of Siam. But Siam with all its little idiosyncracies was an ideally regulated state as compared with the present state of affairs here.

The irony of it all is that anything they want to do can easily be done lawfully & in order and in fact many of the things they want are things that we already have in England and I believe that they are anxious to do them lawfully & in order but to be able to do so they must have the cooperation of the nation especially the intelligent classes & the intelligent classes have gone on strike & in place of doing normal work are sweeping up snow at £1.12.0 per day. This sounds a lot but over here means nothing at the present living rates. I saw a man pay 16/- to a cabman for driving him ½ mile today, and pay it without discussion... They say that in a fortnight we shall have no bread here. ...

At the present moment the Bolsheviks who say they want peace are fighting little civil wars all over the country, Finland, Siberia, Archangel, Ukrainy, Cossacks, etc and are talking about wars with Roumania & perhaps Sweden & last but not least with Germany. It is said that Austria is at peace with the Ukrainy. Perhaps, but we don't believe it. Austria is supposed to have attacked us and Turkey too, but we don't believe either without some real confirmation from London.

22 FEBRUARY 1918

The absurd sort of peace that the Bolsheviks declared, the peace that was on one side only, had the result that was to be expected and the Germans started to advance into the country and the Bolsheviks held up their hands in horror & said if that is what you will do we will sign the peace you wanted us to sign.

Then the Germans kept up a masterly silence & still advanced. What the result will be Heaven alone knows. ... General mobilisation has been ordered although what they have to mobilise & what they will get as the result is something that only those who have lived out here during the last year will know in reality.

Will the Germans come to Petrograd is the question that everyone is asking & that no-one is in a position to answer.

Perhaps they will, perhaps not. I personally rather think they will, but also think that if they do it will be as a peaceful penetration with the purpose of restoring order or at any rate of attempting to restore order to this benighted country rather than attempt to conquer and take possession of it.

Peaceful penetration or otherwise however we cannot afford to stay on here & run the risk of being interned and therefore I have had to make all our plans for leaving despite the fact that I do not believe it will be necessary.

I shall certainly send home part of the staff through Kola unless things clear up during the next few days and shall probably leave myself for Moscow to clear up matters in Mititischi & Moscow and see what really happens in Petrograd before leaving this country.

After that if necessary I shall probably leave via Siberia and Vladivostock & clear up matters on the way.

It is a rotten business altogether and under present conditions very difficult to clear matters up at all but we must do it somehow.

I have shut down the Russian Daily News after a series of strikes & troubles with the workmen & now have to go through a whole lot of trouble in order to liquidate it. I wish it had not been necessary but it was absolutely impossible to go on as we were losing money right and left. ...

Oh this country, it out nightmares anything that was ever dreamt by the maddest of madmen after a hot supper on the cheesiest of cheeses.

17 MARCH 1918
I have taken every precaution to enable me to get away at once should any danger arise and have already sent off the majority of the staff.

We know now that peace has been signed but we do not know yet what sort of peace or whether it includes the German occupation of Petrograd or not. When we shall know the terms of peace I don't know but I am in hopes that it will not be later than tomorrow.

The town is as usual full of rumours of all sorts of things and one has to be prepared for all sorts of occurrences and in the meanwhile my hands have been more than full up in chasing up matters so that I can get away with a somewhat easier mind than would otherwise be the case.

Our works staff with the exception of Wardropper evidently got a very bad fit of the funks and bolted from the quiet little village of Mititischi where they have never been in any danger whatever and absolutely against my instructions. I call it perfectly disgusting of them & a lamentable display of cowardice especially considering that I had told them the situation and made it quite clear that this danger would not commence until weeks after the Germans had captured the city. However, there it is & I hope that they are having a most uncomfortable journey to Vladivostock as a result.[180]

Far away in the Caucasus, an English governess called Janet Jeffery also had experience of Bolshevik rule in the small spa town of Kislovodsk, which she and the family of her employer, Princess Mestchersky, reached after a long and adventurous journey from Petrograd towards the end of 1917. There they enjoyed several months of 'comparative peace', until a rumour swept the town that it was about to fall to the Bolsheviks:

A week before the Bolsheviks actually occupied Kislovodsk there was a false alarm of capture, and in consequence there was a wild flight into the mountains of a great part of the population.

I thought the flight simple madness; for how could a helpless crowd of women and children hope to exist in the mountains? We must have died, most of us, from our privations. But Princess Mestchersky made up her mind to go. I suppose what influenced her was that nearly all our acquaintances were in the miserable throng which was streaming past our gate. So we went, just as we were, without food, with nothing but the money which the Princess and I had concealed on our persons – except that we caught up our pillows, as every Russian does when preparing to travel.

Mile after mile we tramped along the rough track with our fellows in misfortune. The crowd consisted chiefly of women and children, the former often carrying their infants or laden with shapeless bundles of whatever they could snatch up. There were three or four bullock carts simply packed with fugitives. The few men in the crowd, I am sorry to say, made a very poor show, doing nothing or little to assist the women and children. I think no-one had the smallest idea of any destination – we simply streamed along the track to wherever it might lead us. After perhaps an hour and a half of this we found our path blocked by the Alikon. It was flooded after the recent rains and about twenty yards wide, swift and muddy, with here and there a rock projecting from its current. The bed is full of holes. Our party was about the middle of the column, I should think, and when we came up to the stream we found all in front of us standing in helpless indecision on the bank.

'What shall we do?' went up in a wail from thousands of throats – and nobody seemed to have the remotest idea what to do. I fumed with rage. It seemed so ridiculous when we were fleeing for our lives to hesitate at three feet of water. I picked up Marina, put her on my back, and waded in. The Princess and the three boys followed at once. The Princess carried two of the children of another woman across, one on her shoulder, the other under her arm. Nikita, the third of the Mestchersky boys, waded beside me trying to assist my progress by holding my draggled skirt clear of the water. His brothers, Nikolai and Kyril, carried across our bundles, and Nikolai, the eldest, took another of the children of the same woman whose baby the Princess bore.[181] The crowd followed us like a flock of sheep. We never stopped for a moment on the other bank; simply plodded wearily on, leaving a long wet trail behind us. We went up into the mountains until we reached a bare upland plateau, the most miserable place I should think on God's earth, and there in the drizzling rain we flopped down for a rest. By that time the firing had ceased, and presently a band of Cossacks came to tell us that the town was safe. So all our labour was in vain, and we trailed back to Kislovodsk to have six more days in suspense until the final catastrophe.

A week later the Red Army arrived in the town, and Miss Jeffery's narrative continues:

I shall never forget the day of the Bolshevik occupation. For a week there had been continued gunfire, but about two that afternoon it suddenly ceased, and a little later, to our horror, we saw a detachment of Reds, in carts and on horseback, come rushing past our gate into the town. (Our house is on the outskirts.) After an agonising half-hour I could bear it no longer, so tied a shawl round my head to look like a maid and went into the town.

Pandemonium seemed to have broken loose in quiet Kislovodsk. Machine guns were in position on the Grand Hotel and a Bolshevist Commissar was holding forth in a sort of hysterical yell to an excited crowd, consisting chiefly of tradespeople – for these poor fools quite believed at first in Bolshevist promises. Parties of Red cavalry were tearing up and down the street, generally on the high side walks, waving their sabres and yelling greetings to their 'brothers and sisters'. Their get-up was something marvellous, and for all my fears I would not have missed the sight. I never saw so many generals' uniforms together in my life. They were positively plastered with medals and jewellery. Unless I had seen it I could never have believed that so many rings could be crammed on to the five filthy fingers of one hand. The quadrupeds were as grotesquely bedecked as the less intelligent bipeds who rode them. One was tricked out in a housing consisting of a turquoise blue silk ball dress and an assortment of lingerie. Another was hung round with many pairs of silk stockings – a terrible temptation to poor me in my worn and mended clothing. All this was for sale – its price was just more or less friendliness; and a day or two later all the worst and lowest women of Kislovodsk were peacocking in stolen finery. Trailing in the dust at the tails of the horses were epaulets and other officers' insignia, along with portraits of famous Russian generals. I saw the likenesses of the Grand Duke Nikolai, Russki, Alexeiev and other heroes thus shamefully treated. I stood transfixed at the spectacle of this saturnalia, staring with all my eyes – until it suddenly came home to me that my place was with Princess Mestchersky and the children who were my charge. I broke out of the crowd and ran for home.

It was nearly a mile uphill, and I was soon panting wildly, but as much with fear as with breathlessness, for I could see the Reds already breaking into the houses. I dashed through our gate and into the house, and my worst fears were realised. Our pretty little drawing room was a den of thieves. Seven apostles of liberty were plundering it of everything which took their uncouth fancy. Two huge red sailors, hairy, brutish, naked to the waist, tattooed as usual on arms and chests, had thrust the Princess against the wall, with their revolvers at her head, while the children, sobbing, wringing their hands, almost mad with horror of the sight, were begging the beasts to spare her life. The children were roughly pushed out; and then the principal sailor put his revolver against the Princess's temple and shouted:—

'5,000 roubles or I'll shoot!'

Nothing could have been finer than her bearing. She was as white as a sheet, but faced them bravely. I am perfectly certain that she had made up her mind to die sooner than give way, and just as certain that she would have done so but for my involuntary inter-position. 'One!' counted the sailor. 'Two!'; and then I could bear it no longer, I broke from the shrieking children and ran into the room. I had no idea in my head; I don't know why I went – but I had to go. The children streamed after me, and when the Princess saw us she lifted her hand and said:—

'Хорошбь' (Harashó; All right!) 'I will give what I have!'

Well, they followed her into her bedroom, with revolvers pointed, and she gave them 'what we had' – that is, such money as we had not carefully hidden. They grabbed up everything of value which they could see on her toilet table and mine and then tramped out to repeat their brotherly operations elsewhere. That was about four; and before midnight we had ten more visitations. I cannot describe that time. I think we were all in a kind of stupor. We hardly spoke – just stared hopelessly in each other's faces, and waited for daylight. And that was my introduction to beneficent Bolshevism.

The Bolshevists began by a levy of 30,000 roubles on the town. During the succeeding months there were, I think, six more for various amounts. The Princess was in despair, though we had concealed our money so carefully that none of it was ever discovered. I shall not detail our clever shifts, for it is just possible that the revelation might still be useful to the Bolsheviks. Next they began to arrest people right and left – everybody who did not smilingly approve of Bolshevist methods. I am not exaggerating; under Bolshevism you must not merely acquiesce in being plundered, but look pleasant over it – or Heaven help you! I came upon a ghastly sight – the dismembered remains of Gospodin Nagorski, a prominent townsman, scattered about the main street. But the Bolsheviks are cunning; their worst deeds are done under cover, and generally at night. Their slaughter place at Kislovodsk was the Galleriya Narzan (the 'Pump Room' over the spring). What horrors went on beyond its locked doors we shall never know, but night after night the rattle of rifles and the bloodcurdling shrieks of the victims kept us awake, and the steps of the entrance were covered with blood. Worse things happened at Piatigorsk, the Bolshevist headquarters in our province. I could fill columns with perfectly authenticated accounts of Bolshevist atrocities in our district, and escaped witnesses here in London would bear out the truth of my statements.

The simple tradespeople were the first to be disillusioned. Their stocks were forcibly requisitioned every day without payment. The Red soldiery improved the opportunity and took what they pleased. 'The Soviet's order!' was all they need say, and with that the wretched shopkeeper would see them swagger off with their plunder. Once, I remember, I saw some 'Reds' trundling along like cartwheels some of the big flat Russian cheeses which they had looted. It was useless to protest – that meant arrest, or worse.

Nearly every day a 'Prikaz' would appear, commandeering something fresh – food, clothes, linen, blankets, firing, means of lighting. The food question was the worst. Before the Bolshevist occupation there had been no lack of it. Now we were rationed on four ounces or less of horrible black bread per day. I can understand favouring combatants over civilians in war time, but here it was a deliberate starvation of the 'Bourzhui' for the Bolshevist sympathisers had white bread, wines, luxuries – the best of everything. We never saw any sugar, tea, butter, cheese or cereals for six months. For our so-called bread we had to stand in a queue from two in the morning to four in the afternoon, in a bitter Caucasian winter, with three or four feet of snow. To my dying day I shall

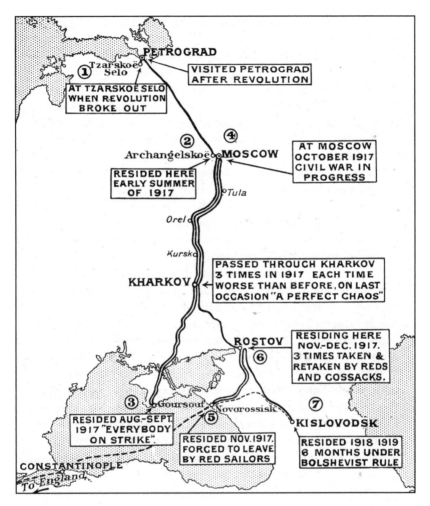

Annotated map showing Janet Jeffery's journey through Russia (*The Sphere*, 3 January 1920)

remember how I froze in those miserable strings of hungry, terrorized women, who never knew if, after their weary wait, they would not have to go away empty-handed.

No-one was allowed to go out after seven o'clock – except the Reds and their lady-loves, who amused themselves highly in the cafés, dancing and feasting half the night. We were forbidden to lock our doors; the houses were almost as unsafe for women as the streets. Reception rooms were classed as luxuries, and if you were not smart enough to 'fake' some kind of a bed in them they were appropriated as sleeping rooms by the Reds. What that meant I leave to my readers to guess. At any moment a house might be seized. It was always at night, and the occupants were simply thrown out into the snow. We helped each other as best we could, and often enough there were seven or eight people living in a single room. In our own house we sheltered Princess Tomanov, an elderly lady who had been ejected in this manner.

Every fortnight there was a forced contribution of house linen, and we ourselves had to make shirts of it for the Reds. I simply raged to see our lovely damask tablecloths on their beastly bodies. Our underlinen went too, for hospital purposes. Our lives were made more wretched by all sorts of persecution. Sometimes the water would be cut off for a week at a time; at another the electric light; and then we were dependent (if we could get them) on horrid goats'-fat candles, the stench of which almost poisoned us. They spluttered and flickered for about an hour and cost ten roubles apiece! I often gave lessons by their 'light', and got some amusement out of the thought that never had English history been drummed into a Russian boy's head under such conditions.

Little by little we were robbed of necessary after necessary, until, in the bitter weather, we had just one blanket apiece, and the Princess and I possessed a single jacket between us. For shoes we had a sort of wooden platter an inch thick, with raw hide thongs for straps; they cost forty-eight roubles a pair! If we saved anything it was chiefly due to a clever Russian maid, who knew how to cajole the stupid Red soldiers. There was no post and no news – except the lying Bolshevist bulletins – and all the time we knew that the Volunteers were not far off. Domiciliary visits were always going on; we were ever in suspense, never knowing what might happen. One evening, as we sat round the samovar, trying to make the best of our carrot 'tea', and to forget our wretchedness for a moment, a couple of Reds tramped in and took away Princess Tomanov without so much as allowing her to put on her wrap.

With all this we were better off than thousands. We had hidden up quite a quantity of army biscuits and old bread toasted, on which we fell back when things were very bad. The Princess and I, for the sake of the children, tried to keep up a pretence of cheerfulness. But it was hard to do it when the children's sleep was always broken by the fear of the Red Terror, so that they would scream with dread in the dark hours of the night. And there was no room for pretence at all on the night after Princess Tomanov's arrest, when Princess Mestchersky came to my bedside and told me that her turn would come next, so she had made her will and left me guardian of her children! I wanted to cry, so I tried to look cross instead.

'What on earth shall I do with four children?' I snapped; but I could not keep up the sham when she answered—

'Take them to England and educate them. I give them to you.'

The next to be arrested was not the Princess, but myself! It was for the crime of having displayed on my bedroom wall a Union Jack handkerchief, which the little dandified, self-conceited Bolshevist Adjutant of Kislovodsk tore down after my refusal to move it. When he had swaggered forth, I put it up again and went on with the lesson which he had interrupted. I took it lightly and felt quite secure, for the same search party never came twice to a house. But this bouncing, peacocking atomy was the exception which proves the rule. Next day, in he strutted again, cracking his nagaika [whip], and when he saw my colours flying once more he simply exploded with rage. He blew his whistle, and in rushed the guards – four of them. 'Arrest that Englishwoman!' he yelled. And they seized me. I remember the Princess's horror as they marched me through the drawing room, with Mr. Commissar swishing his nagaika in triumph. She burst into tears, but I would not look at her for if I had there is no knowing what would have happened. The end had come – so I thought – and the only thing to do was go under without any fuss. It would have done no good to kick or scream, and, anyhow, one small woman could not do much against four big Bolsheviks who held her like vices. They took me out of the house, and we were at the gate, when our clever Russian maid came rushing after us and tackled the Commissar. And she actually persuaded him to let me go! I think she explained that being English I did not realise the majesty of Bolshevism.

Although at the time she thought that this was her closest brush with death and the hands of the Bolsheviks, she later learnt that this was not the case, for after the town was liberated by the White troops under General Shkuro,[182] she

heard that my name was almost first of a list of 500 persons who would have been arrested if the Volunteers had not come when they did. I am afraid to think of what would have happened to me, for when the Bolsheviks hurriedly evacuated the place they dragged away with them hundreds of women and girls. Some of them were found on the road with brains battered out, or done to death in other ways. They were lucky, for the fate of some we learned later. It was worse than death, and the rest have never been heard of again. That was the Bolsheviks' farewell to Kislovodsk.[183]

In Hugh Walpole's novel of Petrograd during the Revolution, *The Secret City*, there is a character known only as 'the Rat', who represents the city's underclass. At one point in the story the narrator (based on Walpole himself) meets 'the Rat' and asks him, 'What are you going to do with your freedom?'

'I shall have my duties now', he said. 'I am not a free man at all. I obey orders for the first time. The people are going to rule. I am the people.'

Pressed further, he added:

'There'll be no Czar now and no police. We will stop the war and all be rich.' He sighed. 'But I don't know that it will bring happiness.' He suddenly seemed to me forlorn and desolate and lonely, like a lost dog. I knew that very soon, perhaps directly he had left me, he would plunder and murder and rob again.[184]

In the aftermath of the Revolution it must have seemed to many of the foreigners remaining in Russia that the 'Rats' had taken over the country.

'The bayonets gleamed'

THE DISSOLUTION OF THE CONSTITUENT ASSEMBLY

A democratically elected constituent assembly, whose task would be to draw up a new democratic constitution for the country, had been the aim of virtually all the reformist and revolutionary parties in Russia, including the Bolsheviks, from the beginning of the nineteenth century onwards. Yet in 1917, following Lenin's adoption of the slogan 'All power to the Soviets', there had been a contradiction in the policy of the Bolsheviks, and when they failed to gain a majority in the elections to the Constituent Assembly, which finally met on 5–6 January 1918, its fate was effectively sealed. Even those uninterested in politics were well aware of the dangers, businessman Arthur Marshall writing to his wife the day before the opening of the Assembly that

> things are apparently working themselves up for another revolutionary-revolutionary-revolutionary-revolution or whatever it has to be called. We are all told that tomorrow we must stay in our houses like good little children & go to sleep and any who don't will be considered to be all sorts of dreadful things & liable to be shot at sight & so on, but all this sort of thing when spoken of so long beforehand as this has been generally ends in a peaceable quiet day. The occasion tomorrow is the National Assembly. To be or not to be to quote Shakespeare.[185]

Journalist Morgan Philips Price was in the hall when the Assembly opened:

> On the right and in the centre sat the Right S.R.'s, who, with the small Cadet party, held the majority. They were mostly old party officials, who in their day had fought and suffered in the struggle against Tsarism. Now they were sitting there, attempting to hold back those very forces which in the days of their revolutionary ardour they had called into being. As I looked upon them I was reminded of the words: 'The Revolution devours her children'. For on the left were the ranks of the Bolsheviks and Left S.R.'s, a

formidable minority of some 40 per cent of all the Deputies. They were for the most part young men, either workmen from the factories or soldiers from the Red Guard. Among the Left S.R.'s were to be seen the faces of the young generation of the peasants and a number of long-haired intellectuals. There could be no doubt that on this side was the youth and energy. True, it often surpassed the bounds of moderation, for in the proceedings which followed the shouting and stamping came for the most part from this quarter.[186]

The *Daily Chronicle* reported what happened next:

Two hundred and forty Social Revolutionaries, ninety Bolsheviks, and thirty of the Left of the Social Revolutionaries attended. The Cadets, of whom 15 had been elected, were absent, several being imprisoned. The People's Commissiaries sat, some on the right and others on the left of the Speaker's tribune, including Lenin, who was apparently in good spirits, chatting with Krylenko....

The Bolsheviks raised a howl of indignation, banged the desks, and whistled when the Social Revolutionaries proposed that Shvetsoff, as senior deputy, should open the proceedings. The Bolsheviks shook their fists and rushed the tribune to prevent Shvetsoff conducting the proceedings. The arrival of Sverdloff, President of the Executive Committee of the Bolshevik Soviet, stopped the brawl, Shvetsoff retiring.

Sverdloff announced that the power belonged to the Soviets, and declared that the Russian revolutionary flag spread over all countries, freeing the working classes from the yoke of capital. He proclaimed Russia a Federal Soviet Republic, and demanded that the Constituent Assembly should recognise the power of the Soviets, and confirm their decrees for the nationalisation of land, banks, and the means of production. The declaration added: 'In order to destroy the parasitic classes, compulsory service will be introduced. Workers shall be armed, forming a Red Socialist Army of workers and peasants. All the propertied classes shall be disarmed.'

The Bolsheviks punctuated this astonishing declaration with calculated bursts of applause, after which the crowd rose and sang 'The International.'

Chernoff, who was elected President, declared that the Bolsheviks' tactics rendered difficult a democratic peace without victors or vanquished. The Constituent Assembly must initiate an international socialist peace conference to secure such a peace.

During the subsequent desultory discussion the Ministers, deputies, and journalists smoked. Visitors, journalists, soldiers, and sailors applauded, hooted, or whistled, while bayonets gleamed.

Arguments in the lobbies ran high over reports of shooting in the streets, where the Red Guards fired and dispersed processionists carrying red flags, inscribed 'For the Constituent Assembly.' The number killed and wounded was small, but the indignation was intense.

Following upon the withdrawal of the Bolsheviks, Lenin dissolved the Constituent Assembly.[187]

Writing with his usual eloquence, Maxim Litvinov, the newly appointed Plenipotentiary of the Russian People's Government to Great Britain (a post unrecognized by the British government), put the Bolshevik case for the dissolution of the Constituent Assembly to what he knew would be a sceptical audience in Britain:

The greatest crime imputed to the Bolshevik régime, however, has been the dissolution of the Constituent Assembly which, after many delays under Kerensky's régime, met at last under the auspices of the Bolshevik Government. It may certainly appear as a monstrous crime against democracy on the part of a régime which regards itself as Socialist to have suppressed an institution which had been the dream of generations, which the Bolsheviks themselves had been championing ever since the first revolution of 1905 with more enthusiasm than any other party, and which, moreover, in the present circumstances, seemed to be the only way out of the civil war and civil strife which threatened the country. What better proof could have been furnished that the Bolsheviks were trampling on the people's will in a manner hitherto exhibited by the worst tyrants in history, that they were afraid of the verdict of the nation gathered through its representatives in the highest assembly known to democracy, and that their sole source of power was the bayonets of soldiers and the fists of the working-class? Indeed, had not the composition of the Constituent Assembly on the very first day shown a decided majority against the Bolsheviks, and was not that the circumstance which prompted the Bolsheviks, who had allowed the elections to the Assembly to take place and the Assembly itself to meet, to disperse it?

To those whose order of ideas still clings to traditions of old bourgeois democracy the arguments of the opponents of the Bolsheviks will appear as irrefutable, but a closer examination of the circumstances and a detachment from inherited political measures of value will show not only the inevitableness, but also the intrinsic justification of the violence done by the Bolsheviks, to the Constituent Assembly. When Lenin returned to Russia at the end of April he, with his clear foresight of the coming developments, at once proclaimed that the Russian revolution would either assert itself as a Republic of the Soviets, that is, as a Republic in which the supreme power would actually, and not merely on paper, belong to the proletariat and the poorer peasants, or it would not assert itself at all, but would perish at the hands of its own internal enemies. This pronouncement did not find favour even with Lenin's own closest political friends. How could the bourgeois classes be eliminated from power? Was Russia ripe for such a dictatorship of the disinherited masses? Even while fighting for the transfer of all power to the Soviets the leaders of the Bolsheviks were at that time unable to follow out their own train of thought to the end, and imagined, in a more or less confused way, that the exercise of power by the Soviets would only be temporary, that a Constituent Assembly, representing all classes, including the bourgeoisie, would in due course meet and decide in favour of a bourgeois Government, and that then the classes that were organised in the Soviets, that is, the proletariat and the peasantry, would voluntarily step down and allow the bourgeoisie to take their place. It did not enter their minds that the bourgeoisie itself might abdicate its powers by proclaiming a universal boycott of Government authority, or that the proletariat and the peasantry, once possessed of power, might not be willing to restore it to their class enemies. Lenin did not argue with them, but allowed the events to justify his prognostications. He was proved right. The revolution was ebbing out, and would have ebbed out entirely had not the Bolshevik revolution helped the Soviets to assert themselves. The Soviets, both centrally and locally, became the State, and their power was confirmed by the universal strike of the bourgeoisie. What sense was there in allowing a Constituent Assembly to proclaim itself the supreme authority in the State and to supersede the Soviets? None whatsoever. The rule of the Soviets meant the assertion of the revolution and of the working and peasant classes, whereas the rule of the Constituent Assembly would have meant the re-establishment of the rule of those very classes and parties which had nearly ruined the revolution, and which spelt the political and economic subjection of the popular masses. Should revolutionary Social-Democrats have permitted it? Should they have stultified their own action of a few weeks previously? Had they wrested the power from the bourgeois classes and handed it over to the labouring masses in order to wrest it back from the latter and put it again into the hands of their enemies? The very idea of it was absurd. Either one agreed that Russia must, by a striking innovation, establish a new form of State, a State of the labouring masses, and in that case a Constituent Assembly, such as had emerged in all previous bourgeois revolutions, was an absurdity, or a Constituent Assembly was the crown of the revolutionary edifice, and in that case it had been a blunder and a crime on the part of the Bolsheviks to have carried through their Socialist revolution. The Bolsheviks acted logically when they chose the first part of the dilemma; the others were also right in choosing the second part, because they were opposed to the idea of any other than a bourgeois rule. One certainly could not with any consistency be an opponent of the bourgeois regime, and yet play off a Constituent Assembly against the Soviets. In fact, the adherents of the Constituent Assembly were, and still are, those who had themselves either opposed or kept delaying it so long as they, while the Kerensky regime lasted, had reason to fear that the popular masses might gain through it undue importance; they became enthusiastic about it only when they saw, after the Bolshevik revolution, that a Constituent Assembly was their sole chance of regaining at least a portion of their old power. Their suddenly awakened sense of democracy was only the expression of their sense of disappointment at losing that last chance.

He concluded:

The dissolution of the Constituent Assembly, then, meant the final establishment of the rule of the Soviets, that is, of the dictatorship of the proletariat and the peasant class, pending the reconstruction of society which would do away with classes altogether and admit every citizen of Russia to the full exercise of civic rights. The Bolsheviks may only be blamed for not having foreseen, as their leader Lenin had, the logical implications of their own war-cry, 'All power to the Soviets,' and for discovering them only when confronted with the accomplished facts of the situation; but that is a blame which has nothing to do with the charges of coup d'état, of usurpation, of violence against the principles of democracy which it pleases the Russian and foreign bourgeoisie to hurl at them.[188]

Trotsky, equally characteristically, put it more bluntly:

> As Marxists, we have never been worshippers of formal democracy. In a society split into classes, the democratic institutions, far from abolishing the class struggle, only lend the class interests a highly imperfect form of expression. The possessing classes have always at their disposal thousands of means to pervert and adulterate the will of the labouring masses. In time of revolution democratic institutions form a still less perfect apparatus for the expression of the class struggle. Marx called Revolution 'the locomotive of history.' The open and direct struggle for power enables the labouring masses to acquire in a short time a wealth of political experience and thus rapidly to pass from one stage to another in the process of their mental evolution. The ponderous mechanism of democratic institutions cannot keep pace with this evolution.

Thus,

> The material class-contents of the Revolution came into an irreconcilable conflict with its democratic forms. Thereby the fate of the Constituent Assembly was decided in advance. Its dissolution appeared as the only conceivable surgical way out of the contradictory situation.[189]

Morgan Philips Price summed up the Assembly's rapid demise:

> Thus the Constituent Assembly ended its career. It passed like a meteor across the horizon of the Russian Revolution. No one seemed prepared for its coming, and no one seemed to miss it when it was gone. With it vanished the last relics of middle-class democracy in the territories of the Soviets. The rapidity with which it disappeared was the measure of the growth of the revolutionary proletarian fighting organs pitted against it.[190]

'The hour of liberation is at hand'

A PRISONER OF WAR'S EXPERIENCE
OF THE REVOLUTION

The largest group of foreign nationals in Russia at the time of the
Revolution were not the journalists or businessmen, nor even the
large number of English governesses, but the hundreds of thousands
of Austro-Hungarian and German prisoners of war who were held in
camps across Siberia and in the Far Eastern provinces. In one of these,
near to the Ussuri River and Russia's border with China, was held
a Transylvanian journalist named Rodion Markovits. He later drew
on his experiences to write a semi-autobiographical novel, *Siberian
Garrison*, which has aptly been described as 'collective reportage'. This
book became a best-seller between the wars in Markovits's native
Hungary, and has been compared to Erich Maria Remarque's *All Quiet
on the Western Front*.[191] In it Markovits describes how the news of the
February Revolution reached the camp through one of the newspapers
the prisoners were allowed to receive:

> The evening brought a great surprise. Simi Grosz looked round
> proudly before he began to read; he smiled self-confidently, as if he
> himself had done it all.
>
> 'Petrograd is in the midst of a great rebellion. The garrison has
> rebelled and joined the Revolution ...
>
> 'The Cabinet Ministers have been arrested, and the Czar's train
> has been held up between Petrograd and Moscow. The mutineers
> have appointed a new Ministry ...
>
> 'Milyukov has been appointed Minister of Foreign Affairs. In his
> first speech he said: The new Ministry has not been appointed by
> the people, but by the Revolution (this fellow Milyukov knows the
> difference).
>
> 'If the new Ministry had been appointed by the people, the
> country would now be at the mercy of the enemy, because the
> people are ignorant, and do not know their own interests, and
> would want to have the war stopped at once. But the new Ministry
> has been appointed by the Revolution, and the Revolution is for an
> ultimate victory and will continue the war—

(Offhand, he could not think of a revolution which had broken out for an Ultimate Victory and for continuing a war—)

'Although, for the time being, we do not know what form of government Russia will choose for herself, one thing is certain; the present ruler will have to go, the Revolution wants Michael Alexandrovitch on the throne of the Romanovs—'

That evening, Simi Grosz scored a great success with his reading, everybody was excited, everybody was shouting at the top of his voice. Only Uncle Hegyi sat gloomily in his box and, after the ventilation, just before retiring, he spoke up in a ghastly voice:

'I'll lay three to one that we'll stay here for two more years.'

'But there is revolution in Russia! Revolution, Uncle Hegyi!'

'I heard it. The Revolution is victorious. The Revolution for the ultimate victory and for the continuation of the war.'[192]

The following day one of the Russian officers in charge of the camp appeared 'with a radiant face and a red cockade'. He then told the prisoners that

the true Russian soul had been victorious, that as a supreme proof of the vitality of the nation the Revolution had been triumphant and Russia was now on her way to the laurel wreaths of victory. The way of democracy had been opened and national democracy would now lead the nation, so long bent beneath the yoke of false principles, to the Land of Promise.... He proudly declared that the first tender buds of democracy had already arrived: hereafter the general will not be addressed as Your Excellency, but simply as Mr. General; the ranks will not have to salute officers in the street except when they are on duty, or in dress uniform. He hoped that the inmates of the camp would also adopt a few new and glorious customs, as a token of their sympathy.

On the other hand, when one of the prisoners asked whether they too would receive 'a little freedom', the guard 'smiled slyly' and replied:

We guarantee your physical and mental well-being. But if we free you, we cannot guarantee your physical well-being, and we can protect your mental well-being from the dangerous influences of the Revolution only by keeping you within the fences.

As spring changed into summer the prisoners continued to learn of developments both in Petrograd and at the Front from the newspapers:

Simi Grosz read the wildest things from the papers. Fifteen thousand Petrograd soldiers and workers had demanded the resignation of Milyukov. The front was beginning to break up. Russian soldiers charged their own artillery and forced them at the point of the bayonet to cease firing. Russian command-ers were resigning by scores; they had lost control over their regiments. A brigade commander who had tried to force the rebels to execute his commands with a revolver in his hand was shot dead by them. The soldiers looted, bombed bridges, and burned up military warehouses. The tanks attacked their own troops. Off Tarnopol, two German companies routed an entire Russian brigade.

Huge hordes of retreating soldiers streamed towards the rear, towards the interior of Russia, carrying banners with the inscrip-tion: 'Down with War!' The First Brigade of the Russian Guards retreated without fighting and left the Petrovsky Brigade to its fate. General Selinov[193] was unable to convince his soldiers that their ideas concerning Fatherland, Honour, Future, and Liberty were base and mean. Off Tarnopol, artillery officers went down on their knees before their soldiers and begged them not to leave the guns to the enemy, but the ranks would not touch them. The regiments were all mixed up and capital punishment was restored. Tens of thousands of soldiers were plundering the homes of peaceful citizens. The roads along which the retreating armies marched were lined, on both sides, with carcasses of horses, broken wagons and upturned gun-carriages. And, of course, with human corpses. In the cities, the retreating soldiers broke open the doors of the houses with hand grenades. The 112th Ural Regiment was fraternizing with the enemy.

The whole collapse had been created by inhuman agitators who called themselves Bolsheviki, but who they were and what their object was no one knew for sure. It seemed that their leaders had been hired by the Germans, and that they were the ones who spread the ignominious slogan 'Down with War'. The wisest thing would be to silence these Bolsheviki, and many of them had already been arrested.

Simi Grosz read these things, and the news gave them hopes for freedom.

On another occasion Simi Grosz again read the papers, 'and it appeared that something was going on!'

'The Committee of the 12th Army, fully aware of the grave situation on the Northern Front, once more turns to the Empire, the People and the Government! All the achievements of the Revolution are at stake! Political and economical bankruptcy threatens the country, and not one item in the programme of the Revolution has been fulfilled! Internal politics are in a turmoil, and there is no unity in the foreign policy! The ruling classes' selfish desire for wealth is a red rag in the eyes of the working masses! Party interests and party struggles have reached the limit and are now verging on the edge of ordinary criminal acts! We are threatened with falling to pieces, and the Counter-Revolution is gaining apace! The Fleet and Army of German imperialism are preparing a new blow, the Empire is in great danger! And when we call on our soldiers to fight to the last drop of blood, we know very well that we call on naked men!'

As Markovits noted, 'News from the West became more and more encouraging, it seemed the Russians would not be able to hold out much longer', and, in the autumn the (in fact untrue) news of the fall of Venice to the Austrians, followed by that of the successful Bolshevik *coup d'état*, gave the prisoners real hope that they would soon be able to go home. Eventually

> The command informed them that the Central Powers had signed a separate peace treaty with Russia, and, therefore, the command advised the prisoners to prepare themselves for their return home which it was to be expected, would soon follow the signing of peace. Of course, the Russian papers announced only very briefly the (for them) deplorable news, hence the command was not in a position to inform them of the terms. If, however, the news was reliable, the Dual Monarchy would get Russian Poland in lieu of reparations.

On this news, at first

> The boxes were swarming with excitement, the men started to pack, the price of dictionaries, books, paints, brushes and balalaikas suddenly dropped. Only the last named were still somewhat in demand because there were many who wanted to take them home as souvenirs.

However, doubts then began to set in and, as Markovits wrote, 'the news of the peace of Brest-Litovsk did not cause unalloyed joy':

At first they didn't even think of it, but then an Austrian aspirant's remark created unpleasant excitement:
'Weiter dienen, Kameraden.'
That was true. If there was only separate peace, they would have to go on fighting. The various other fronts were still there. They would still have to go to the Italian, or to the French, front. Why, going home would be worse than staying here!

One curious result of the peace treaty was that those of the guards who were Poles were told that they were no longer Russian citizens and that they would have to join the Austro-Hungarians inside the camp they had formerly guarded. Most of them chose instead to flee and make for the Chinese border or Vladivostock.

Once the Treaty of Brest-Litovsk had been signed, the Austro-Hungarians became responsible for the administration of their own camp, and gradually some men began to slip away. Some of them were unquestionably seduced by the doctrines of Bolshevism,[194] but Markovits's account of a propaganda visit from a local Bolshevik commissar to his camp indicates that this was far from a universal response:

The command did not prohibit them from going home. Anybody could go who proved that he had the money. Of course some of them had so much money that even if it had been prohibited they could have bribed everybody and left the camp with ease. But there was another reason for the command's lax attitude. All over Eastern Siberia, the Reds were already masters and it was an open secret that the Reds were willing to listen to complaints against the command. The Reds were just aching to interfere with the internal affairs of the camp. Indeed, it was more than a mere rumour, because, one day, Tovarishch Nasok, with a huge red button on his chest, a red ribbon on his arm and a red cockade on his cap, appeared in the camp.
Tovarishch Nasok was a well-built, good-humoured, half intelligent Russian worker, a clever, shrewd man. He was not irascible at all. Jovially he gave orders that he wanted to speak to the prisoners.

The major referred to the Brest-Litovsk Treaty, which acknowl-
edged the Central Powers as victors, and protested by the right of
the victor against the Bolsheviki's intention of contaminating the
spirit of the camp with Red propaganda. The internal affairs of
every country are sacred and he would not let anybody interfere
with them.

Tovarishch Nasok did not fly into a rage. He said he was not
quite sure whether the Brest-Litovsk Treaty included this, but he, as
Commissar of the Amur Province, ordered the meeting to be held.
The major might defend himself at home by saying that he surrendered only to force and that he protested. He realized that it was
the major's duty to protest, and he would not hold that against him.
He shouldered all responsibility for whatever consequences might
follow as a result of impairing the Brest-Litovsk Treaty. The major
realized the truth of this and ordered the officers to gather.

The camp was trembling with excitement when Tovarishch
Nasok climbed on to a table in the common-room and, in impassioned, stirring tones, addressed the ragged, musty, and worn
prisoners of war:

'The flame of the Revolution is burning high in Russia and the
Revolution is ready to embrace you, too, who were prisoners
here under the Czar's yoke. It brings you freedom and it is
willing to place the keys of your prison in your own hands.

From the western border of Russia to Vladivostok, the
prisoners of the past may now fly out of the jails, fly through
the tormenting iron bars, they may soar freely over the free
Russian fields. All our former enemies who have been suffering
in the murderous prisons of Omsk, Tomsk, Irkutsk, Khabarovsk,
Stretensk, Krasnoyarsk, Berezovka and Troitsk, may now leave
their dungeons. They were our enemies but now they are our
brothers, protected by the flag of liberty—.'

Three faint hurrahs were heard at this point and the speaker looked
around, a little embarrassed. He thought the prisoners would shed
tears of happiness, and he was disagreeably surprised.

But then he realized what the trouble was. He smiled. Of course,
only a few of the prisoners understood what he was saying. He
dropped his oratorical tone and asked in his ordinary voice whether
anybody who spoke Russian would kindly interpret his speech. The
major immediately winked to a captain, the captain winked back,
and began to translate Tovarishch Nasok's speech:

'The Commissar assures the prisoners of his best intentions. He is very satisfied with your behaviour, and is especially glad to see that you have kept yourself aloof from things which are none of your business. The hour of liberation is at hand, and if you continue to respect discipline and obey your commanders, you will soon be off on your way home. The prisoners who have been suffering in the camps of Omsk, Tomsk, Irkutsk, Khabarovsk, Stretensk, Krasnoyarsk, Berezovka and Troitsk will soon start home, to join their loved ones at home—.'

The officers responded with enthusiastic cheers, and Tovarishch Nasok continued with tears in his voice:

'Don't your hearts beat faster when you see the self-sacrificing armies who fight for liberty in Russia, when you see the awakening consciousness of a people throwing off their yoke? This is a historical moment, for the peoples of the world to rise with primordial force and break the physical and spiritual locks of their jails!'

Tovarishch Nasok stopped so that the captain could interpret his words.

'Don't your hearts beat faster at the thought of being again able to grasp the sword that has been twisted out of your hands, at the thought of once more proudly marching—.'

At this point something happened. Simi Grosz smiled and Tovarishch Nasok immediately noticed this involuntary expression of amusement.

He looked grave, beckoned to Simi Grosz, and took out his revolver.

'I command you to translate word for word the following: My words have been falsely interpreted to you. Translate it!'

Simi Grosz translated:

'Mr. Nasok forces me at the point of a revolver to translate to you that what he said was not interpreted correctly to you.'

Tovarishch Nasok watched the faces and he saw that Simi Grosz had stammered the truth. He continued:

'Translate to the prisoners, that they are so suppressed that I cannot hope that they will ever understand my words. Say it!'

Simi Grosz said it, and Tovarishch Nasok continued:

> 'Tell them that I have nothing to say to slaves, let them keep their chains. I neither like them nor am I angry at them. They simply don't matter. Say it!'

Simi Grosz said that too. Tovarishch Nasok continued:

> 'Tell them, God help them back to the slaughterhouse. I hope they will soon be there.'

He had to say it, because Nasok had a revolver in his hand and because he watched the eyes and faces.

Tovarishch Nasok bowed and went away. He did not even turn his head.

When the revolutionary left, Major Füzessi rose to speak. He gave thanks to God that the Russian had been unsuccessful, he praised the self-control of the prisoners, who had restrained themselves from insulting the demagogue. Such an irresponsible revolutionary might have carried away some of the prisoners, especially the younger gentlemen; he might have led them into some rash enterprise. Indeed, the Russian had been right, the war was still going on at home, and he hoped that soon the noble steel would once more glisten pure and clean in their liberated hands on the field of honour.

The prisoners responded with enthusiastic applause, cheers and hurrahs to the brave major's words.

Soon afterwards a train of cattle trucks was provided for the former prisoners of war, and once they had commandeered a locomotive they were able to set off back across Russia towards the border with Austria–Hungary (itself, although they did not know this, in turmoil and in course of being dismembered). It was a journey that was to prove considerably longer and more arduous than most of them realized at the outset, and Markovits himself did not reach home for several years, after an adventurous time which included serving in the Red Army as a political commissar and witnessing a massacre by White troops.

'Capitalism is the cause of wars'

INSTRUCTION IN THE TENETS OF BOLSHEVISM

After the Bolshevik seizure of power Gerard Shelley had to move apartment in Moscow because his friends with whom he had formerly been staying 'were either shot or turned out of their house'. His new lodgings were in a house owned by a millionaire art collector, and there he had an interesting encounter:

> One day a short, pale, blue-eyed woman came into the dining room with the aid of a stick. Round her head was a garland of hair done into plaits. Hearing I was an Englishman she smiled at me, and said in a charmingly sweet, almost long-suffering voice:
> 'I suppose you are ashamed of us?'
> She was Madame Pokrovskaya, wife of the Bolshevist Professor Pokrovsky,[195] a member of Lenin's Government. Although cousin to M. Stookin, who was a millionaire, she had devoted her life to the Bolshevist cause since its inception, having spent many years in exile abroad. The Soviet sent her to Lausanne as their first woman consul, but she had to return to Russia.
> I conversed with her day after day, as she had come to stay in the house, till Prince Yusoopoff's palace would be ready for her and her husband.
> In spite of her mild eyes, her gentle voice, her limping walk, she thought nothing of millions of people being put to death for the triumph of the ideas of her Party. Being one of the founders of the Bolshevist Party, she explained its views with authority.
> 'Why do you subject Russia to this cruel experiment?' I asked her. 'The Russians did not ask you to govern them. Your Party failed in the elections for the Constituent Assembly. You seized power with the aid of foreign Lettish mercenaries, and you have plunged Russia into an ocean of bloodshed.'
> 'You have not learnt to think scientifically,' she replied, quite calm and self assured. 'We are striving to get rid of all the frauds that afflict humanity and to destroy the Capitalist system, which is the cause of all the misery in the world.'
> 'But you are causing it!' I protested. 'You are putting more people to death than any civilised Government would dare.'

'You must look at the matter scientifically,' she replied, without any feeling whatever. 'Capitalism is the cause of wars. Count the number who have shed their blood in the wars of Capitalism. If we destroy capitalism, we destroy the cause of war. Perhaps we are obliged to bring about the death of a few million people, but what is that in the long run? We shall make the world safe from war in the future and humanity will bless us for ever as its saviours.'

'But if you don't succeed?' I asked. 'Most people don't like you, and hate your methods!'

'They are blinded by old prejudices,' she calmly replied. 'We must succeed, even though it means performing an operation that lets a lot of blood. With the dictatorship of the Proletariat we can forcibly remove all opposing elements.'

'But who gave you authority to say that your system is the only right one?'

'Science!' she answered. 'Our system is the logical conclusion of scientific research. There is no God. Morality has no foundation except as an economic necessity. The possession of the means of wealth determines all the values of life.'

She expounded to me the tenets of her Bolshevist material- ism. Sincerity rang in her voice, but it was the sincerity of the cold-blooded fanatic to whom all insincerity, treachery, bloodshed and evil deeds are lawful means for attaining the fulfilment of a personal idea.

I taunted her gently with the fact that Russia was being bled to satisfy the lust for power of a small group of men who had spent most of their lives abroad. They were mostly all like her, mild voiced and harmless to look at.

'Not one of you would risk his skin!' I said. 'When you were seizing power, you all lay in hiding-places and payed your Letts and Chinese to do the fighting for you. Even now, you pay these men to carry out these awful executions. Are you not too careful of your own skins?'

'We are just headquarters,' she replied. 'Every army needs to keep its generals in safety.'[196]

'A seething whirlpool'

LEAVING RUSSIA AND LOOKING TO THE FUTURE

Writing in March 1918, Maxim Litvinov was unsurprisingly upbeat about what the future held for Russia under its new Soviet government:

> [I]t is certain that if left by foreign enemies alone, the Soviet rule will in no distant future establish a Socialist régime in Russia. Already the masses of the people – more particularly of the peasantry – are learning the work of administration through the Soviets, and the State officials and other public employees, together with the rest of the intellectuals, learning wisdom through hunger, are going back to their old posts in ever-increasing numbers, so that the wheels of the Government machine are already revolving, and the great decrees issued by the People's Commissioners and the Soviets are passing from the 'paper' stage into life. Even the most stubborn among the 'intellectuals' will soon learn that, after all, the people is a much better master than the capitalist, and that a Socialist régime is likely to render even them more happy than a bourgeois régime. Thereby a new epoch opens in the life of mankind, and though it is hazardous to make prognostications, with two foreign invaders on Russian territory, and invasion threatened by the 'Allies' with the object of restoring power to the bourgeoisie, with all the world, including the greater part of the Socialist world, looking on with undisguised hostility, one may nevertheless venture to say that the Bolshevik revolution, whatever its ultimate fate may be, will remain for all time the greatest source of inspiration to the struggling proletariat of all countries until the triumph of Socialism covers also with eternal glory the Red Flag implanted by Lenin and his friends on November 6–7, 1917.[197]

In early 1918 it was difficult for the majority of the foreigners still in Russia to feel such optimism. American YMCA worker Edward Heald left Russia via Siberia. On 27 May he reached Changchun in Manchuria, which marked the border between the Russian and Japanese spheres of influence in that country, as agreed upon in the Treaty of Portsmouth after the Russo-Japanese War of 1904–05, and here he changed trains. His dairy records that

When we pulled into Changchun last evening and saw the beautiful Japanese train of the South Manchurian Railroad standing there with its American-style Pullman cars, all electrically lighted, its clean windows, and cleanly dressed men and women comfortably seated in the plush seats, we just stood on the platform and gazed with rapture as if we had suddenly been dropped into a new world. And then when the train began to move with no warning three bells, with no trainmen's whistles, and exactly on the second, and the beautiful lighted palace silently glided out of the station, we felt that we were home again. It was like watching the New York Central pull out. I felt more homesick all at once than all the time I had been in Russia.

There, on the track we had just come in on, stood our Russian train, the best to be found now in Russia, and which had satisfied Beath and me in comparison with most of our Russian traveling. But after seeing the South Manchurian train, the Russian train stood there like a gloomy, dirty, sorrowful funeral, a symbol of the land it came from and into which it was soon to return. And the difference in the order and system of operation was the same. We had a half hour to catch the Manchurian train, but we couldn't do so because we couldn't get our baggage off the Russian train until they opened the baggage car, and they couldn't do that until the baggage master came. I went after the baggage master, but he was busy getting baggage on another train going to Harbin. Finally he finished that and came to open the car. Meanwhile the car had wandered off down the track switching, and by the time the car returned it was too late to check onto the Manchurian train. Then we had to be careful to get our trunks into the Japanese baggage room or we would come around for the seven o'clock train in the morning and find it locked up in the Russian baggage room, the office closed, and no one due to report for work until nine o'clock. And the difference in the appearance of the Russian and Japanese sides of the station. The Russian side was dirty and crowded with Chinese and luggage and packs of all kinds over which you constantly stumbled if you tried to walk around. The Japanese side was spick and span; no one was waiting for a train. All who wanted to travel were taken care of promptly.

After three years in Russia, there are three things that I want in Paradise: cleanliness, order, and industry.[198]

An advert in the *Russian Daily News* for a shipping company offering foreigners cheap passage out of Russia

Florence Farmborough also left Russia through Siberia, in her case travelling throughout the length of the Trans-Siberian Railway to Vladivostock:

We are in Vladivostok! We arrived early this morning. It is 2nd April 1918, and exactly 27 days since we boarded our goods-train in Moscow. It is wonderful that we are really here – at last! But what makes it all the more wonderful is that when we steamed slowly into the station, Vladivostok's magnificent harbour was spread before our eyes. In that harbour four large cruisers were anchored, and one of them was flying the UNION JACK! Oh! The joy! The relief! The comfort! The security! Who will ever know all that this glorious flag symbolised for us travel-stained, weary refugees? It was as though we had heard a dear, familiar voice bidding us 'Welcome home!' As I write these words I can feel my heart palpitating with emotion; it holds a depth of gratitude which can never be expressed. That one glimpse of the Union Jack dispelled all our fears, quietened all our doubts, answered all our questions. It was a truly wonderful 'home-coming' and one which we had least expected. The Union Jack was our talisman, our guarantee, our surety!

As she left Russia three weeks later on the transport ship *Sheridan*, bound for San Francisco, Florence Farmborough summed up her feelings for Russia:

> I stood on deck and watched Russia slowly recede. Soon all that was visible was a range of pale-grey mountains on the horizon. Then a thick, blue curtain of mist fell and hid from my sight the land which I had loved so truly and which I had served so gladly. As I pondered on all that had happened, in that great suffering Russia, my heart contracted with pain, and I felt that I could weep ... and weep. ... I prayed that those bitter-sweet wartime experiences of mine had not been in vain. And, because sorrow and suffering teach great truths, I prayed too that I had learnt from them never to grumble; to be compassionate and merciful; and to recognise always, and try to alleviate, the sorrow in another human heart.
>
> For days I lay in my cabin with intolerable 'sea-sickness', a fair enough name for the grievous heartache which overwhelmed me; heartache for a surpassingly beautiful land which had been laid waste, for a mighty Empire which had been brought low – by its own sons.[199]

Businessman Arthur Marshall left Petrograd for Finland at the same time as the Allied military missions. In his last letter from Russia to his wife, written on 17 March 1918, he reflected that

> All my plans thrown into confusion and the prospects for the future very dull and stormy looking. Well, it can't be helped and at any rate it isn't a matter for which I can hold myself responsible.

And, for once, he lost his customary optimism over Russia's ultimate future, writing:

> The immediate future of Russia looks like a seething whirlpool without any centre of attraction. I should say like a series of whirl-pools all pulling in opposing directions and all tending to further disorder rather than order.[200]

'Bread, equality... and peace'

BRITISH SUPPORTERS OF THE
BOLSHEVIK REVOLUTION

The great majority of the British in Russia who witnessed the aftermath of the Bolshevik Revolution, from whatever class they were drawn, were clearly opposed to it, whether this was the result of their opposition to the Bolsheviks' policy of negotiating a separate peace with Germany, to the peremptory dismissal of the Constituent Assembly or to their horror at the unfolding violence and collapse of civil society. Most of them were, actively or passively, supporters of Kerensky and the Provisional Government, who had hoped that after the crushing of the Bolshevik-inspired uprising in the July Days the government would reassert its authority and bring some order to the country, as well as continuing the fight against Germany. But this was by no means true back home in Britain. In the aftermath of the July days, the anti-war British Socialist Party newspaper *The Call* lamented that

> The news from Russia is appalling. The Government turned into
> a Directory with Kerensky as First Consul, capital punishment
> restored by the very hands which abolished it in the first days of
> the Revolution; Trotsky and other 'extremists' thrown into prison;
> severe censorship established over all speeches and writings
> opposing the war.[201]

The news of the Bolshevik Revolution was thus warmly welcomed by members of the BSP, who saw it both as a clarion call for world peace, and as the first step towards world revolution, the overthrow of capitalism and the establishment of a state run by the workers for the workers. The most striking exponent of this view was John Maclean, the leader of 'Red Clydeside', who was subsequently to be appointed Russian Consul in Glasgow by Lenin, but there were many others. In January 1918, for example, the radical socialist and suffragette Dora Montefiore wrote an open letter of support to Lenin, which was published in *The Call*:

Dear Comrade,

Many of us in the British Socialist Party desire to send you a message of good cheer and of congratulation on the manner in which you and those surrounding you are steadily and scientifically laying the foundations in Russia of a Social-Democratic Commonweal.

Across the deafening scream and roar of European battlefields it is difficult for the voices of Reason and of real Reconstruction from the workers in the different countries involved in the ghastly slaughter to make themselves heard, and we realise only too well how the news that is allowed to filter through to you, revealing to you the gradual loss (without an official protest from the leaders of the People) of our liberties in this England of ours, which boasts of being the home of Liberty, must tend to make you feel at times that you in Russia are fighting single-handed against capitalism and its sinister self-expression, modern militarism. But, dear comrade, those of us who share with you the economic interpretation of existing social conditions, based on the exploitation of the workers, are following with the closest sympathy and comradely support, the shrewd blows you, and those with you, are aiming at privilege, at competition, and at commercial exploitation. We desire to dissociate ourselves from those pseudo-Socialists who, by denouncing you as 'the leader of a Party in Russia composed of thoughtless anarchists with no definite policy,' are playing into the hands of the Northcliffes and the Lloyd Georges. We rejoice in the fact that you place constructive deeds before destructive words; that you are immediately giving the people access to food, clothing and shelter, the primary necessities of life, and are meanwhile rapidly doing away with the inequalities which shut out the masses from the means of life, and from the knowledge of the secret diplomacy which oppresses them.

It is *because* you are so attacked by pseudo-Socialists and by 'Northcliffes' that we knew you and the Bolsheviks are doing the work in Russia which we Social-Democrats are waiting for our opportunity to do in England – administering the affairs of the country in the interests of the workers, instead of allowing the present gang to govern and exploit the workers in the interests of a capitalist State.

Comrade, I, with many over here, stretch out the hand of comradeship, and wish you and those with you good speed. May the People have Bread, Equality of Opportunity and Peace; and may

Aristocrats selling their clothes

the torch of International Fellowship be lit in the ardent glow of Human Brotherhood kindled by the Workers of Russia![202]

And, in his foreword to Maxim Litvinov's history of the Revolution, first published in 1918, Edwin Fairchild, a leading member of the BSP, attempted to put the Revolution into context for a British audience:

The memorable uprising of the Russian people indicates that not even the keenest discernment can always accurately appraise the immediate course of events dependent upon the action of the working class. There were but few among Socialists in Western and Middle Europe who held the belief that the War would lead to working-class control in Russia, and the consequent removal of the gravest menace to a democratised Germany. Wide difference in conditions notwithstanding, the intensification of work, never to be assuaged by proposals for industrial harmony between Capital and Labour, may lead to action here as unexpected as the events that mark the recent history of Russia.

Though the members of the British Socialist Party were among the first to welcome the March Revolution, they were not without misgiving as to the practical worth of the Provisional Government. The Revolution had been made in the name of the solidarity of the working classes and in order that the power of the possessors of land and capital might be abridged in the interests of the common people. The British Socialist Party was, I believe, the first of European Socialist organisations to see that the predecessors of the Bolsheviks had no intention of erecting a social organisation based on the truths that Labour is the source of all economic values and that enduring peace will only be obtained by the international agreement of peoples. In our Party organ 'The Call,' we urged that the taking of power by the Soviets was the one course that would save Russia from destruction at the hands of her enemies, within and without; the ultimate acceptance of that view and the administrative success of the Soviets prove the wisdom of that policy. With the general policy of the Bolsheviks the British Socialist Party is in hearty agreement.

In this country industrialism long since framed a constitution, and for generations we have been accustomed to a process of slow, gradual change effected by law and order. There are no signs that the Socialist and Labour movement in Britain will cease to follow the political methods with which we are familiar. Yet we are driven on towards the time when Labour will be forced to choose between further dependence on pure constitutional practice, then to become meaningless, or, thrusting aside conventional forms, to take power after the summary fashion of the Bolsheviks.[203]

Some British socialists, mostly also members of the British Socialist Party, were further inspired by the ideals of the Revolution to travel to Soviet Russia themselves and offer their services in the cause of worldwide revolution. One such was Tom Quelch, who was a member of the Central Committee of the British Council of Workers' and Soldiers' Deputies, which had been formed in June 1917. In 1920 he travelled to Moscow to attend the Second Congress of the Communist International (the Comintern), from where he wrote:

The Red Flag flies over the palaces of the Czars. Our comrade, Lenin, sits in the Kremlin, working, planning, one could almost say 'presiding over' the dissolution of capitalism. Nearby Lunatcharsky

[sic] strives for the new culture, for the educated Russia of tomorrow. Bukharin, Kameneff, Radek and Trotsky are each, in their respective departments, restlessly hewing at the old order, restlessly organising for the new. They never sleep – these great revolutionists...

One turns from thoughts of them, realising that their labours are as dynamic yeast in the leaden bulk of great Russia. The yeast is working, but there are many, many difficulties and problems. And there is much of the mire and filth of the old order still remaining that has to be destroyed. Bourgeois derelicts, counter-revolutionary saboteurs, spies of the capitalist-imperialism, speculators, corruptionists and criminals possess a faculty for mischief. Sometimes in the stillness of the night one hears a sharp crack of a rifle volley, and then one remembers that Russia is at war, and that the Revolution, fighting for its life, is compelled to be swift and drastic in its methods.[204]

He was accompanied at the same conference by William Paul, who had a 'long and interesting interview' with Lenin. He wrote that,

While we were talking, Lenin was continually interrupted by the arrival of cables, despatches and messages. He was frequently called to the phone. Despite these things he could return quite serenely to the point under discussion. I confess that I was slightly agitated when entering the Kremlin; bad news had arrived from the various fronts; Poland was acting strangely at the Riga Conference; France had been indulging in one of her bullying outbursts; and Finland was on the point of signing peace. All these things, I imagined, would make it impossible for Lenin to settle down and have a quiet talk on the various details of the movement upon which I was anxious to have his opinion. When I entered the room he was courteous, cool and tranquil. He eagerly entered into a discussion of many points on Communist tactics, which, to some people, might have seemed almost trivial. Lenin is always anxious to hear of any new development in Marxism, and to him every aspect of the movement is important. I very timidly suggested the possible application of Marxist theory to a certain subject which had been monopolised by the anthropologists and ethnologists. He became enthusiastic over the problem which he quickly elaborated and extended, made several important suggestions, indicated where some good data could be found, and urged that the matter should be written and published. To Lenin, Communism is a synthetic philosophy.

And he summed up Lenin's speaking style thus:

> After having had a talk with Lenin, it is easy to understand why his quiet and humorous style fails to impress middle-class intellectuals. People like Bertrand Russell are in the habit of meeting pompous bourgeois thinkers whose ideas on social theories are so incoherent and vague that they can only express themselves with great difficulty. Their ponderous and floundering method of struggling to deliver an idea is, in certain quarters, mistaken for mental ability. Lenin, on the other hand, sees problems so clearly and is able to explain himself with such clarity and simplicity, that his conclusions seem to be the obvious deductions at which anyone would inevitably arrive.[205]

Two years later another Englishman heard Lenin speak. This was Harry Young, who went to Russia as a Youth Delegate to the Comintern (and subsequently stayed on in Moscow until 1929). Influenced by his cousin, Fred Peet, he was brought up as a socialist from a very young age, attending a socialist Sunday school in Liverpool Road, Islington:

> Arriving at about 3.00 pm on a Sunday afternoon, children of all ages would be sat down for a story. This would probably be from F.J. Gould's adaptations of the legends of classical mythology, something specially published for this purpose in the 'Clarion', or just a straight fairy story from a standard work...
>
> The songs would be sung, 'England Arise', Edward Carpenter; 'Hark the Rolling Thunder', William Morris; 'The International' (I NEVER understood that one!), 'The Red Flag', O'Connell, etc.
>
> We had fizzy drinks and perhaps a cake or bun.

Harry recalled that 'the whole thing was completely secular', that it was 'greatly enjoyed by the children taking part', and that there was 'no attempt whatever on the part of the volunteer "Teachers" to dominate or "control"'.

After leaving school, his first job was as a tea boy at the motor works of Brown & Melhuish in Islington. Later he worked as a cartridge 'piercer' at the Woolwich Arsenal before, in 1917, running a bookshop in Red Lion Square where he 'made quite a stir' by stocking and selling all the anti-war newspapers and magazines, being raided once or twice by Scotland Yard for selling proscribed newspapers like the anarchist *Satire* and the ILP *Socialist*. By this time he was a member of the BSP and of the Herald League, both of which were absorbed into the Communist Party when it was formed in 1920. He was the first national organizer of the Young Communist League, and it was in this capacity that he attended the Fourth Congress of the Comintern, where he heard Lenin speak. In his memoirs he wrote:

I saw and heard him only once when he came to address the Fourth Congress of Comintern in November 1922. For me, a young Englishman of 21 without detailed knowledge of the history of the Bolsheviks and of the seizure of power in 1917, it was impossible to fully estimate the weight of his remarks.

The whole world situation by 1922 was so complex and critical that even a political genius could make mistakes; which Lenin admitted in his speech. He was unquestionably a sick, ailing man, the assassin's bullet in his neck irremovable, and from which he died 14 months late[r]. There could be little doubt of his immense stature and repute. The mere mention of the fact that he intended to speak in the discussion on the World situation set the whole Congress agog.

Personally he was a smallish man, not more than 5′ 6″ or 7″ with broad shoulders, very solid looking, a rather Mongolian type of face with high cheek-bones, slit eyes, and a constant quizzical half-smile. When Zinoviev, as President, announced 'The next speaker is Comrade Lenin', a storm of clapping and cheering broke out, followed by a deathly hush as he slowly mounted the rostrum to speak. He spoke like a father addressing his rather wayward children. Like a 'Dutch Uncle'. No oratory, no fireworks, or rhetoric; leaning on the edge of a high stand, he quietly and even humorously dealt with one point after another. I remember it all clearly to-day some sixty years later. Firstly, he announced the necessity of the New Economic Policy. Russia was still too backward industrially. Concessions would have to be made to private Capitalism. 'New Communism' where the Government simply confiscated the peasant's produce could work no longer. He then ridiculed the antics of the so called Two-and-a-Half-International, having the Delegates in stitches, with his humorous sallies.

Finally he criticised the Comintern itself particularly the Theses of the preceding 3rd Congress, gently chiding his devoted henchman and comrade in Swiss-exile Greg Zinoviev, with being too 'Russian', the resolutions were 'too long', too heedless of local conditions. Finally he uttered another warning … that Capitalism would never collapse but had to be removed by the working class.

Contrary to the legends and myths which have proliferated … he spoke German to the Congress with a rather thick Russian accent which even my then rudimentary 1922 German detected. … [T]here can be little doubt of Lenin's decisive personal role in demanding, against all the opposition of the Central Committee including Zinoviev, Kamenev and Stalin, and implementing, almost single handed, the seizure of power by the Bolshevik Party before opening the All Union Congress of the Soviets. Whether the course of history would have been different had he survived it is difficult to say.

In a general sense it is true that the economic conditions were the decisive factor as the U Turn to the N.E.P. showed. That nobody knew better then Lenin when and where to turn is obvious. Little did we then guess that that was the last and only time we were to listen to the greatest political genius of the 20th century. For the more romantic and hysterical types at the Congress his speech was a bombshell. A cold douche bringing them down to the harsh reality with a resounding thump.

Harry also heard Trotsky speak at the 4th Congress, and left this impression of him:

There could be no doubt of his supreme oratorical ability. He had everything; a handsome impressive man, with a thick shock of dark wavy hair, strong mobile features, rich vocabulary and perfect diction in several languages. He spoke German and French faultlessly. I quickly realised why he had been elected President of the Petersburg Soviet in 1905 and again in 1917. His powerful, penetrating intellect was wide ranging, writing, as he did, on a variety of subjects from science to drama and literature and history. His nick-name in the early days was 'Pen.' His impact on the 4th Congress was electric, increased by his ability to walk over to the French Delegates, having addressed the full Congress in German, as well as in his native Russian to re-deliver his address. No translators for him! He had a perfect speaking voice – rather high-pitched but very strong and penetrating.

How can I ever forget the scene in the Red Square when we sauntered down to witness the induction of the latest intake of young Red Army recruits. There they were – in serried ranks, ten thousand or so. Suddenly, from the high podium, there rang out like a silver bell, 'Long live the World Commune, Long live the World Revolution'; 'Hurrah, Hurrah' from ten thousand young throats, as they waved their rifles in the air.

THAT was Leon Trotsky, Soviet Minister of War. We had all heard the legendary accounts of Trotsky's famous armoured train, dashing from one front to another where danger threatened. We had an English translator, an ex-Jewish tailor from London, who had actually served on Trotsky's train, who re-counted occasions when Trotsky's arrival had turned imminent defeat into victory. I have often thought in later [days] that Leon Trotsky had all the qualities of the legendary dictator. His sheer supreme ability as an orator made Hitler, Mussolini, Churchill and Co. sound like amateurs.

By contrast, Zinoviev, in Harry's opinion, cut a rather less impressive figure:

For some reason Gregory Zinoviev, despite his high position as President, or Chairman of Comintern (why the position was created at all I have no idea, it certainly served no useful purpose and when Bukharin took over, typical of him it lapsed) and General Secretary of the Leningrad Party was never personally very popular. His was definitely not an engaging personality and always carried the suspicion that his reputation rested almost entirely on his long sojourn in exile in Zurich with Lenin. ...

He had a high-pitched almost falsetto voice. He was short, rather inclined to fat, with a roundish face, small features, and an unruly mop of tousled curly hair. He had little or no written work of consequence to his credit, the articles ascribed to him in the compilation 'Gegen den Stram' (Against the stream) of anti-War Propaganda, largely echoing Lenin's work. Despite his close association with Lenin over many years in Switzerland, he nevertheless aided with Kamenev Trotsky's-brother-in law in opposing Lenin's call for the insurrection and premature seizure of power, eliciting Lenin's strongest denunciation. He was reinstated to take over Comintern. He spoke good German, helped by his Jewish background. His bad habit of extravagant prediction did him considerable harm, especially his announcement of the imminent demise of European

Capitalism, on his return from the foundation Congress of the K.P.D. (the German Communist Party) in 1920.

In contrast, Harry noted that Stalin 'usually sat quite quietly and did not say a great deal, which most of the other Russians did'. He also told a revealing story about Stalin:

> I also remember during the turmoil and excitement of the great Stalin–Trotsky debate, at the Fifth Congress, standing beneath the platform discussing points when I observed Joseph Vassaronitch donning a magnificent jet-black short sable fur coat. I turned to speak to someone, turned back again, and he had disappeared.
>
> Of course he had, the Kremlin was honeycombed with secret doors and passages.[206]

Although Harry took a prominent part in some of the Red Square parades, was sent on a speaking tour of Russia as a representative of the British working class, and lived in the famous Hotel Lux with all the top Comintern officials, he became increasingly disillusioned with the Soviet regime, especially after Stalin had begun to exert his control, and he returned to England in 1929. Unlike so many fellow-travellers, such as the Webbs, he never confused Marxism with Stalinism, and he could see clearly where Stalin's policies were heading.

Epilogue

PETROGRAD IN 1918: A WORKMAN'S VIEW

In early 1919 the British printer and photographer Henry Keeling was able to escape from Russia and return to England. He thought back to when he first arrived in Russia and compared the Petrograd of 1914 to that when he left just over four years later:

> It was a different picture of life in Petrograd in December, 1918, just before I left. Then shops, tea-houses and restaurants were almost all closed, a sick and starving population were hunting for food, women whose faded clothes showed that they had once been members of a respected and respectable class, hunted amongst rubbish for the head of a herring or any bit of offal that might have escaped the attention of the cats. Everyone except the younger Soviet Commissars and the Red soldiers had a look of hunger and suffering on their faces. I was astounded one day when I met a man whom I knew had built up a business by his own industry, a business where 650 workmen had been formerly employed, painfully dragging himself along the street. He was black with coal dust gathered during his day of forced labour, which took the form of unloading coal from the German ships which came to Petrograd in the late summer of 1918. Everything had been taken from him, yet his only crime was that he had by his own skill and industry founded a small business which gave agreeable and profitable work to many of his fellow countrymen. In a word, he was an employer.

And he concluded with a telling statistic, which summed up the fate of the former capital:

> When I left Petrograd last January the population had dwindled down to 700,000. A year and a half before under the Provisional Government it was over 2,400,000. You ask how I know. Well, the number of ration cards issued by the Bolsheviks were published each month in their own paper; since no one could live without a ration card – which besides being needed to obtain food, when there is any, serve also as a sort of passport – it must be obvious that the number of people is much greater than the number of

Petrograd in 1920

cards issued and as some, by trickery of various kinds managed to get two cards, it was probably considerably less. Even this comparatively small population when I left was going through all the horrors of slow starvation. The situation was indeed terrible.[207]

Notes

1. A search for 'Russian Revolution 1917' on the Bodleian's online catalogue, Solo, for example, produces over 2,000 'hits'.
2. H.V. Keeling, *Bolshevism: Mr. Keeling's Five Years in Russia*, Hodder & Stoughton, London, 1919, pp. 17, 52–4.
3. Quoted in John Courtenay Trewin, *Tutor to the Tsarevich: An Intimate Portrait of the Last Days of the Russian Imperial Family*, Macmillan, London, 1975, p. 34.
4. 'Are not five sparrows sold for two farthings, and not one of them is forgotten before God? But even the very hairs of your head are numbered. Fear not therefore: ye are of more value than many sparrows.'
5. This and subsequent quotations from Bodleian Library, Gibbes Papers, Box 2, MS. Facs. c. 104.
6. Trewin, *Tutor to the Tsarevich*, p. 22.
7. [W.B.], *The Fall of the Romanoffs: How the ex-Empress and Rasputin Caused the Russian Revolution*, by the Author of 'Russian Court Memoirs', Herbert Jenkins, London, 1917, pp. 42–3.
8. Stinton Jones, *Russia in Revolution: Being the Experience of an Englishman in Petrograd during the Upheaval*, Herbert Jenkins, London, 1917, pp. 178–81.
9. *The Queenslander*, 16 May 1925.
10. Gerard Shelley, *The Speckled Domes: Episodes of an Englishman's Life in Russia*, Duckworth, London, 1925, pp. 36–7.
11. Ibid., pp. 57–8.
12. Ibid., p. 60. The task of restoring 'the Cross to St. Sophia' is a reference to Russia's war aim of occupying Constantinople.
13. Prince Oleg (1892–1914) was the son of Grand Duke Konstantin Konstantinovich (the poet and playwright K.R.); he was wounded in battle against German forces and died of his wounds in Vilnius, Lithuania.
14. A career soldier, the Grand Duke Nicholas Nikolaevich (1856–1929) was the commander in chief of the Russian army during the first year of the First World War until the Tsar replaced him after the disastrous retreat in the summer of 1915. He subsequently served as viceroy in the Caucasus. After the Revolution he stayed in the Crimea, before escaping on the British battleship HMS *Marlborough* in April 1919. He subsequently lived mostly in France and died of natural causes on the Riviera in 1929.
15. Shelley, *The Speckled Domes*, pp. 61–3.

16. Leon Trotsky, *The History of the Russian Revolution to Brest-Litovsk*, George Allen & Unwin, London, 1919, p. 16.

17. Sir Alfred Knox, *With the Russian Army, 1914–1917*, 2 vols, Hutchinson, London, 1921, vol. 1, p. 92.

18. *The Fall of the Romanoffs*, pp. 63–4.

19. Bodleian Library, MS. Eng c. 2722, fol. 19.

20. Bodleian Library, MS. Eng c. 2722, fols 21–4.

21. In this he was to be sadly disappointed.

22. Bodleian Library, MS. Eng c. 2722, fols 26–8.

23. The Grand Duchess Elizabeth Feodorovna (Ella) (1864–1918) was the older sister of the Tsarina Alexandra Feodorovna. She was a princess of Hesse and by Rhine and a granddaughter of Queen Victoria. In 1884 she married Grand Duke Sergei, a younger son of Tsar Alexander II. In 1905 Sergei, when serving as governor-general of Moscow, was assassinated by a bomb thrown by a Socialist Revolutionary. Deeply religious, four years later Ella sold all her jewellery and used the money to found the Convent of Saints Martha and Mary in Moscow, from where she and her fellow nuns worked to help the poor and destitute of the city. In 1918 she was arrested by the Bolsheviks and, a day after the murder of the Tsar and his family at Ekaterinburg, she, along with other members of the Romanov family, was thrown down a mineshaft. The remains of her body were later interred in the St Mary Magdalene Convent on the Mount of Olives. She was canonized by the Russian Orthodox Church outside Russia in 1981 and by the Moscow Patriarchate in 1992 as New Martyr Elizabeth. There is also a statue of her above the Great West Door of Westminster Abbey.

24. Meriel Buchanan, *Petrograd: The City of Trouble, 1914–1918*, Collins, London, 1918, pp. 29–33.

25. Florence Farmborough, *Nurse at the Russian Front: A Diary, 1914–1918*, Constable, London, 1974, p. 21.

26. Knox, *With the Russian Army, 1914–1917*, vol. 1, pp. 86, 92.

27. Count Fredericks (1838–1927) was Vice Minister of the Imperial Household 1893–97, and Minister 1897–1917. Regarded as a strong conservative, he was a natural target of the revolutionaries, but he survived the Revolution and was allowed to emigrate to Finland in 1925.

28. [W.B.], *The Fall of the Romanoffs*, pp. 64–7, 77, 96, 108–10.

29. Bodleian Library, Gibbes Papers, Box 2, MS. Facs. c. 104.

30. [Albert Stopford], *The Russian Diary of an Englishman: Petrograd, 1915–1917*, William Heinemann, London, 1917, pp. 73–7.

31. Edward T. Heald, *Witness to Revolution: Letters from Russia, 1916–1919*, Kent State University Press, Kent OH, 1972, p. 36.

32. [W.B.], *The Fall of the Romanoffs*, p. 93.

33. Now in Ukraine, Trebukhivsti is dominated by a large fortress dating from the eleventh–thirteenth centuries.

34. Farmborough, *Nurse at the Russian Front*, pp. 248–9.

35. Anna Vyrubova (1884–1954) was lady-in-waiting to Alexandra and was for many years the closest friend and confidante of the Empress. She was a devotee of Rasputin's and acted as an intermediary between the imperial family and the starets. After the Revolution she escaped to Finland, where she lived in total obscurity until her death in 1954.

36. [Stopford], *The Russian Diary of an Englishman*, pp. 92–4.

37. Ibid., p. 97.

38. Alexander Protopopov (1866–1918) had been regarded as a liberal earlier in his career, but in 1916 he was appointed Minister of the Interior largely as a result of the influence of the Empress and Rasputin. He saw his role as preserving tsarist autocracy. He had links with Germany through neutral Sweden and was thought to favour signing a separate peace. Arrested at the time of the February Revolution, he later suffered from hallucinations and was transferred from the Peter and Paul Fortress to a military hospital. He was executed by the Bolsheviks in 1918.

39. Buchanan, *Petrograd*, p. 90.

40. Prince Nikolai Golitsyn (1850–1925) was the last prime minister of imperial Russia (1916–17). Arrested at the time of the February Revolution, he was later released by the Bolsheviks but forbidden to emigrate, and earned his living as a park keeper and shoe repairer. He was rearrested three times during the 1920s and was executed in 1925 for belonging to a counter-revolutionary monarchist group.

41. Quoted in Edvard Radzinsky, *The Last Tsar*, Arrow, London, 1993, p. 157.

42. Ibid., p. 159.

43. Ibid.

44. Lili Dehn (1888–1963) was the wife of a naval officer and a friend of Alexandra. She escaped from Russia after the Revolution and wrote a biography of the Empress, *The Real Tsaritsa*, published in 1922.

45. Mikhail Rodzianko (1859–1924) was chairman of the Duma 1911–17 and played a key role in engineering the abdication of the Tsar. After the Bolshevik Revolution he retired first to Rostov on Don and then to the Crimea, before emigrating to Serbia, where he died in poverty. His memoir *The Reign of Rasputin: An Empire's Collapse* was published in 1927.

46. Quoted in Radzinsky, *The Last Tsar*, pp. 160–61.

47. Bodleian Library, MS. Facs. c. 106, Diary of Sydney Gibbes, 1 March 1917 (OS).

48. The general in command of the Northern and North-Western Fronts.

49. That is, the Petrograd Soviet.

50. Vasily Shulgin (1878–1976) was a conservative politician who hoped that Nicholas II would be replaced by his brother, the Grand Duke Michael, as head of a constitutional monarchy which would provide Russia with the strong government needed to successfully prosecute the war. He supported the Provisional Government and later the Kornilov revolt. After the failure of the latter he fled to Kiev, and subsequently to Yugoslavia. Captured by Soviet troops there in 1944 he was sentenced to twenty-five years for 'anti-soviet activity', but was released in 1956 as part of the Khrushchev thaw. He later participated in a documentary film made about the Tsar's abdication.

51. Alexander Guchkov (1862–1936) was the head of a large insurance company and a conservative who had been active in politics since the early years of the twentieth century. In 1915 he founded the Progressive Bloc, which demanded ministerial responsibility before the Duma, and, strongly opposed to the influence of Rasputin, in 1916 considered participating in a *coup d'état* to achieve this aim. After the February Revolution he briefly served as Minister

of War. He was briefly arrested for his support of Kornilov's failed coup in September 1917. After supporting the Whites during the Civil War, he went into exile, first in Germany and then in France.

52. Quoted in Radzinsky, *The Last Tsar*, pp. 169–71.

53. Bodleian Library, MS. Facs. c. 106, Diary of Sydney Gibbes, 2 and 4 March 1917 (OS).

54. Boris Stürmer (1848–1917) was a protégé of Rasputin and served as Prime Minister and Foreign Minister during 1916. Arrested at the time of the February Revolution, he was imprisoned in the Peter and Paul Fortress, where he died of natural causes in September 1917.

55. Mikhail Tereshchenko (1886–1956) was a rich sugar refiner who was a member of the Duma. He served as Minister of Finance and then Minister of Foreign Affairs in the Provisional Government. He was arrested in the Winter Palace at the time of the Bolshevik coup and imprisoned in the Peter and Paul Fortress. In 1918 he escaped to Norway. He spent most of the remainder of his life in exile In France. He died in Monaco in 1956.

56. K was Konstantin Andreevich Somov (1869–1939), a Russian artist, who was Walpole's 'special friend' (and probably lover) at the time.

57. Pavel Nikolaevich Milyukov (1859–1943) was a historian and the leader of the Liberal Constitutional Democratic (Cadet) Party. He was a member of the Duma 1907–17, and after the February Revolution served as Foreign Minister in the Provisional Government. He was a strong supporter of continuing the war, and partly as a result of this was forced to resign in May 1917. After the Bolshevik Revolution he advised leaders of the Whites before emigrating to France. He was the object of several assassination attempts but died of natural causes in Aix-les-Bains in 1943.

58. Ekaterina Breshkovskaya/Catherine Breshkovsky (1844–1934), known as 'the 'grandmother of the revolution', joined the anarchist followers of Bakunin in Kiev at the age of twenty-six. Imprisoned in 1874, she was subsequently exiled to Siberia. On her release in 1896 she became one of the founders of the Socialist Revolutionary Party but had to flee abroad. She returned to Russia at the time of the 1905 Revolution and was then exiled to Siberia again. After the February Revolution she became a member of Kerensky's government, but after the Bolshevik Revolution was again forced to emigrate. She died in Czechoslovakia in 1934.

59. Maria Spiridonova (1884–1941) was a Socialist Revolutionary terrorist who in 1906 was sentenced to death for her part in the assassination of a police officer. Her sentence was commuted to forced labour for life and she spent eleven years in Siberia before being released at the time of the February Revolution. She led the Left SRs into an alliance with the Bolsheviks, but after the Left SRs broke with the Bolsheviks she was incarcerated for a time in a mental hospital. She was rearrested during the Great Terror in the 1930s and was executed at Orel in 1941 as invading German forces approached the city.

60. Grand Duke Kirill (1876–1938) served in the Russian navy during the Russo-Japanese war of 1904–05; at the time of the February Revolution he was in command of the Marine Guard. He also authorized the flying of the red flag over his palace in Petrograd, and may have hoped that gestures such as this would lead to his being declared regent after the Tsar's abdication. In June

1917 he moved to Finland and subsequently escaped to Germany and then France. In 1924 he declared himself Emperor of All the Russias but was not supported by all the surviving members of the Romanov family. He died in 1938 in Neuilly, France.

61. Ignatiev was a former cavalry general.

62. The French Military Attaché in Petrograd.

63. Buchanan, *Petrograd*, pp. 106–7.

64. Sir Hugh Walpole, *The Secret City*, Capuchin Classics, London, 2012, pp. 178–91.

65. Maxim Litvinov (1876–1951) was born into a prosperous Jewish family and joined the Social Democratic Labour Party in 1900. He subsequently spent many years in exile, in Switzerland, France, Ireland and then in London, where he married Ivy Low, an Englishwoman of Hungarian-Jewish descent. He has been credited with rescuing Stalin from being attacked in Whitechapel during the 5th Party Congress in 1907. Living in London at the time of the Revolution, in 1918 he was arrested and subsequently exchanged for the British consul and secret agent Robert Bruce-Lockhart. He served as Commissar for Foreign Affairs 1930–39, in which role he advocated the policy of collective security to resist the rise of Nazi Germany. His book *The Bolshevik Revolution: Its Rise and Meaning* (British Socialist Party, London) is of particular interest in having been written and first published in England in the spring of 1918.

66. Nicolai Chkheidze (1864–1926) was a Georgian Social Democrat who was the Menshevik president of the Executive Committee of the Petrograd Soviet from February to October 1917. At the time of the Bolshevik Revolution he was in Georgia and he remained there; in 1918 he was elected chairman of the Provisional Assembly when Georgia declared independence. In 1921 he helped draft the constitution of the Democratic Republic of Georgia. When the Bolsheviks invaded Georgia in March 1921 he fled to France where he committed suicide in 1926.

67. Prince George Lvov (1861–1925) was a member of the Liberal Constitutional Democratic (Cadet) Party. In 1914 he became chairman of the All-Russian Union of Zemstvos, which helped supply the military and care for the wounded during the First World War. He served as prime minister in the Provisional Government until July 1917 when he was succeeded by Kerensky. He was arrested when the Bolsheviks seized power, but later escaped to France where he died in 1925.

68. Litvinov, *The Bolshevik Revolution*, pp. 26–9.

69. Georgy Chicherin (1872–1936) was born to a noble family, and through inheritance acquired great wealth, which he used in support of the revolutionaries in 1905. From then until 1918 he lived in exile, latterly in Britain, joining the Mensheviks, before becoming closer to the Bolsheviks in 1914 as a consequence of his anti-war stance. In 1917 he was briefly imprisoned in Brixton gaol for his anti-war views, but was released and returned to Russia early in 1918, when he served as Trotsky's deputy at the Brest-Litovsk peace talks. He was Commissar for Foreign Affairs from May 1918 until 1930 when he resigned owing to ill-health.

70. *The Call* 56, 3 May 1917, p. 3.

71. *Daily Mail*, as reprinted in *The World's News* (Sydney), 30 June 1917.

72. *Sunday Mail* (Brisbane), 1 January 1939.

73. E. Hotaling, ed., *Wink: The Incredible Life and Epic Journey of Jimmy Winkfield*, McGraw-Hill, New York, 2005, pp. 154–5.

74. Ekaterina Breshkovskaya (Catherine Breshkovsky).

75. [Stopford], *The Russian Diary of an Englishman*, pp. 146–8.

76. Bert Hall, *One Man's War: The Story of the Lafayette Escadrille*, Hamilton, London, 1929, p. 250.

77. Edward P. Stebbing, *From Czar to Bolshevik*, John Lane, Bodley Head, London, [c. 1919], pp. 73–4, 64–6.

78. [W.B.], *The Fall of the Romanoffs*, pp. 290–92.

79. Keeling, *Bolshevism*, pp. 90–93.

80. Hall, *One Man's War*, p. 252.

81. [Stopford], *The Russian Diary of an Englishman*, pp. 134, 145–6.

82. Bodleian Library, MS. Milner dep. 23/1.

83. Bodleian Library, Gibbes Papers, MSS. Facs. c. 100–106, Box 1 III 17.

84. Bodleian Library, Gibbes Papers, MSS. Facs. c. 100–106, Box 1 fols 24–31.

85. Vasily Yakovlev (1885–1938) joined the Bolshevik Party in 1905 and lived abroad in exile from then until 1917. On his return to Russia he became an active member of the Petrograd Soviet. He participated in the capture of the Winter Palace during the Bolshevik seizure of power in November 1917, after which he was appointed Commissar of the Central Telephone Exchange. His role in the removal of the imperial family has been subject to much conjecture, but it seems clear that his orders were to take Nicholas to Moscow rather than Ekaterinburg and that he was prevented from doing so by the local Soviet. Yakovlev was subsequently appointed a Commander of the Red Army in the Urals, but in November 1918 he was captured by the Whites. After some years in China he returned to the Soviet Union in 1928 but was executed during the Great Terror in 1938.

86. Elsewhere in the Gibbes Papers are notes on the plays that were performed. These included H.V. Esmond's *In and Out of a Punt* (Gibbes played this with Tatiana), Leopold Montagu's *The Crystal Gazer* (Gibbes and Marie) and Harry Gratton's *Packing Up*, which Gibbes described as 'a very vulgar but also very funny farce in which the male role was taken by the GD Anastasia and the wife by the GD Marie, while the small porter's part was taken by A.N.'; this, he recalled, was 'a roaring success' and was the only play to be performed twice.

87. Gibbes's recollection of the guards being Hungarians, rather than Letts (Latvians), is of interest. For many years there was a persistent rumour in Hungary that Imre Nagy, the prime minister at the time of the anti-Soviet uprising in 1956, had been one of these guards, but this has never been substantiated, although Nagy certainly fought with the Red Army in the Civil War.

88. Rodionov is a mysterious character. According to Edvard Radzinsky he was Latvian and his real name was Yan Svikke. He was a professional revolutionary who was said to have infiltrated the tsarist secret police. He later became a university professor in Riga and died in 'complete senility and isolation' in 1976, aged 91.

89. Rasputin.

90. Bodleian Library, Gibbes Papers, Box 2, MS. Facs. c. 104.

91. Countess Anastasia Hendrikova (1887–1918) was a descendant of the sister

of Catherine I, the wife of Peter the Great and Empress in her own right. She was appointed a lady-in-waiting to the Empress in 1910, and also acted as an unofficial governess to the Grand Duchesses. She was separated from the imperial family when they arrived in Ekaterinburg and transferred to a prison in Perm. There she was killed, while supposedly being transferred to another prison, on 4 September 1918.

92. See Radzinsky, *The Last Tsar*, pp. 353–4.

93. Bodleian Library, Gibbes Papers, Box 2, MS. Facs. c. 104.

94. Georgi Plekhanov (1857–1918) was a Marxist revolutionary who joined the Mensheviks when the Social Democratic Labour Party split and supported Russia's involvement in the First World War.

95. Jean Schopfer [writing as Claude Anet], *Through the Russian Revolution: Notes of an Eye-witness, from 12th March–30th May*, Hutchinson, London, 1917, pp. 132–64.

96. Heald, *Witness to Revolution*, pp. 88–9.

97. Yevno Azef (1869–1918) was a Socialist Revolutionary who had helped organize the assassinations of the Minister of the Interior, Plehve, in 1904 and of the Governor-General of Moscow, Grand Duke Sergei, in 1905. However, in 1909 he was exposed as having been an agent of the Okhrana and fled to Germany where he subsequently worked as a corset salesman.

98. Father Gapon (1870–1906) was an Orthodox priest and a popular working-class leader who organized the Assembly of Russian Factory and Mill Workers in St Petersburg, which was secretly sponsored by the Okhrana. Although he had been warned not to, he led the procession of peaceful demonstrators who were gunned down by troops in front of the Winter Palace on 'Bloody Sunday', 22 January 1905. Gapon was subsequently hanged by some of his former comrades in the SR Party when they learned he had been an agent provocateur.

99. *The Clarion* 1338, 27 July 1917, pp. 2, 5.

100. Matilda Kshesinskaya (1872–1971) made her debut at the Mariinsky in 1890 and became prima ballerina in 1896, largely as a result of court influence. Petipa regarded her as a 'nasty little swine' and she could be ruthless with rivals. In addition to being the mistress of the future Emperor for three years, she also had affairs with other members of the Romanov family. After the Revolution she fled to France, where in 1929 she opened a ballet school at which one of her pupils was Margot Fonteyn. She published her memoirs as *Souvenirs de la Kschessinska* (Plon, Paris, 1960).

101. *The Newsletter* (Sydney), 24 November 1917.

102. Buchanan, *Petrograd*, p. 130.

103. Farmborough, *Nurse at the Russian Front*, pp. 268–71.

104. Knox, *With the Russian Army, 1914–1917*, vol. 2, pp. 638–9.

105. Shelley, *The Speckled Domes*, pp. 149–50.

106. Knox, *With the Russian Army, 1914–1917*, vol. 2, p. 649.

107. Alex Thompson, *Here I Lie: The Memorial of an Old Journalist*, George Routledge & Sons, London, 1937, pp. 198–9.

108. People's History Museum, Henderson Papers, HEN/1/28.

109. People's History Museum, Henderson papers, HEN/1/29.

110. People's History Museum, Henderson papers, HEN/1/30.

111. George Henry Roberts (1868–1928) was Labour MP for Norwich and was Parliamentary Secretary to the Board of Trade 1916–17, Minister of Labour

1917–19 and Minister of Food Control 1919–20. In 1922 he retained his seat as a Lloyd George Liberal, but lost it the following year when standing as a Conservative.

112. People's History Museum, Henderson papers, HEN/1/31.

113. *The Clarion* 1331, 8 June 1917, p. 4.

114. *The Clarion* 1337, 20 July 1917, p. 5.

115. Irakli Tsereteli (1881–1959) was a Georgian leader of the Social Democrats and later of the Mensheviks. He was a member of the Petrograd Soviet in 1917 and later served as Minister of Posts and Telegraphs in the Provisional Government. After the Bolshevik Revolution he returned to Georgia, but after the Soviet invasion he emigrated in 1923 to France. Later he settled in the United States and died in New York in 1959.

116. Morgan Philips Price, *My Reminiscences of the Russian Revolution*, George Allen & Unwin, London, 1921, pp. 43–6.

117. Trotsky, *The History of the Russian Revolution to Brest-Litovsk*, pp. 20–21.

118. *The Clarion* 1336, 13 July 1917, p. 5.

119. [Stopford], *The Russian Diary of an Englishman*, pp. 167–78.

120. Buchanan, *Petrograd*, pp. 131–53.

121. [Stopford], *The Russian Diary of an Englishman*, pp. 178–80.

122. Heald, *Witness to Revolution*, p. 123.

123. Matvei Skobelev (1885–1939) joined the Social Democrat Party in 1903 and became a close associate of Trotsky. A Menshevik, he was a member of the Petrograd Soviet and later served as Minister of Labour in the Provisional Government. He joined the Bolshevik Party in 1922 and worked in various foreign trade organizations. He was expelled from the Party in 1937 and was executed during the Great Terror.

124. *The Clarion* 1342, 24 August 1917, pp. 1–2.

125. Stebbing, *From Czar to Bolshevik*, pp. 43–5.

126. Buchanan, *Petrograd*, pp. 153–4.

127. Litvinov, *The Bolshevik Revolution*, p. 34.

128. Trotsky, *The History of the Russian Revolution to Brest-Litovsk*, pp. 29–30.

129. Farmborough, *Nurse at the Russian Front*, pp. 309–11.

130. *Maryborough Chronicle, Wide Bay and Burnett Advertiser*, 28 November 1917.

131. *The Clarion* 1320, 23 March 1917, p. 6.

132. *The Clarion* 1343, 31 August 1917, pp. 1–2.

133. *The Clarion* 1344, 7 September 1917, p. 3.

134. *The Clarion* 1387, 5 July 1918, p. 5.

135. A reference to an anecdote of the time about a policeman who confused Impressionism with Impress Sionism.

136. V.K. Vitrine, 'Russian Notes', *The Clarion* 1347, 28 September 1917, p. 5.

137. *The Clarion* 1349, 12 October 1917, p. 1.

138. Vladimir Lvov (b.1872) studied historical philosophy at the University of Moscow and subsequently entered the Clerical Academy as a 'free auditor'. He was a member of the Duma before the February Revolution and served on commissions concerning the Orthodox Church. In March 1917 he was appointed Procurator of the Holy Synod in the Provisional Government. He escaped from Russia at the time of the October Revolution but subsequently returned. In 1922 he was 'plucked forth from obscurity and, like another Thomas Cromwell, has been set in office as a hammer of the clergy ...

engaged in what he describes as a comb-out of the clergy; in other words his occupation is to rope in all the clergy to an acceptance of the new Soviet Church, or else to see to it that they follow in the footsteps of their martyred brethren' (*Southern Cross* (Adelaide), 3 November 1922).

139. Boris Savinkov (1874–1925) was a terrorist and member of the Socialist Revolutionary Party who briefly served as Deputy War Minister in the Provisional Government, but resigned after the failure of the Kornilov putsch. After the Bolshevik Revolution he organized a new counter-revolutionary group called the Society for the Defence of the Motherland and Freedom. He later became an associate of the British spy Sidney Reilly, and in 1924 was tricked into returning to the Soviet Union. There he either committed suicide or was murdered by means of defenestration. His autobiography, *Memoirs of a terrorist*, was published in 1931.

140. Nikolai Vissarionovich Nekrasov (1879–1940) was a left-wing member of the Cadet Party, who had served in the Duma before the Revolution. An engineer by training he had been Professor of Statistics and Bridge Construction in the Tomsk Technological Institute. Following the February Revolution, in which he played a prominent part, he was appointed Minister of Ways and Communications and subsequently Minister of Finance and Assistant Prime Minister. It was his exploitation of the railway telegraph system to send the news of Kornilov having been declared a traitor which enabled Kerensky's view of events to be disseminated so widely and so quickly and which thus undermined Kornilov's action. After falling out with Kerensky he was appointed Governor General of Finland, but, fatefully, returned to Petrograd at the time of the October Revolution. After the Soviet seizure of power he kept a low profile. Although for a time he was allowed to work for the Central Union of Co-operatives and Consumers and to teach statistics in various institutions of higher education, he was also arrested on three occasions, in 1921, 1930 and 1939, spent time working on the notorious White Sea Canal construction project, and was eventually executed in 1940. In May 1917 he gave his own account of the February Revolution in an interview which has been published in Semion Lyandres, *The Fall of Tsarism*, Oxford University Press, Oxford, 2013.

141. Buchanan, *Petrograd*, pp. 169–71.

142. [Stopford], *The Russian Diary of an Englishman*, p. 208.

143. Farmborough, *Nurse at the Russian Front*, pp. 312–14.

144. Bodleian Library, MS. Milner dep. 23/1, Diary of Sir Hugh Cholmondeley Thornton (1881–1962).

145. [Stopford], *The Russian Diary of an Englishman*, pp. 190–206.

146. Buchanan, *Petrograd*, p. 172.

147. [Stopford], *The Russian Diary of an Englishman*, p. 206.

148. Ibid., p. 210.

149. For the full story of how Stopford smuggled these jewels out of Russia, see William Clarke, *Hidden Treasures of the Romanovs: Saving the Royal Jewels*, National Museums of Scotland, Edinburgh, 2009. One of the pieces Stopford smuggled out was the Vladimir Tiara, now owned by H.M. Queen Elizabeth II and worn by her during the State Visit of the President of Ireland to Britain in 2014.

150. Buchanan, *Petrograd*, pp. 179–80.

151. *Brisbane Courier*, 20 October 1923.

152. Farmborough, *Nurse at the Russian Front*, pp. 315–16.

153. Trotsky, *The History of the Russian Revolution to Brest-Litovsk*, pp. 39–40.

154. Litvinov, *The Bolshevik Revolution*, p. 36.

155. Knox, *With the Russian Army, 1914–1917*, vol. 2, p. 702.

156. Lt. Col. George Crosfield , CBE, DSO, TD (1877–1962) was deputy chairman of J. Crosfield & Sons, the Warrington soap-making firm. He had served in the Imperial Yeomanry in the Anglo-Boer War of 1899–1902, and in 1915–16 served in France with the 14th South Lancashires, the 2nd Suffolks and the 10th Royal Welch Fusiliers. He had a leg amputated as a result of a wound received at St Eloi in March 1916. According to *The British Citizen and Empire Worker* (23 November 1918) he 'has no subtle apologetics to offer Germany for fighting her; he believes it to be destiny – he believes we had to baffle her mad lust because else that arrogance would have thwarted the whole design of the British race and ensnared and enslaved civilisation'.

157. Bodleian Library, MS. Milner dep. 372, fols 50–54.

158. Knox, *With the Russian Army, 1914–1917*, vol. 2, p. 705.

159. M. Philips Price, 'How I saw the Red Dawn (November 7th, 1917)', *The Communist*, vol. 1, no. 14, 4 November 1920, p. 5.

160. *Daily Advertiser* (Wagga Wagga), 28 November 1932.

161. Buchanan, *Petrograd*, p. 196.

162. *Russian Daily News* 741, 3 [16] November 1917, evening edn.

163. Farmborough, *Nurse at the Russian Front*, pp. 342–3, 345, 353–4.

164. *Sunday Mail* (Brisbane), 1 January 1939.

165. Rupert Hart-Davis, *Hugh Walpole: A Biography*, Rupert Hart-Davis, London, 1952, p. 164.

166. Buchanan, *Petrograd*, p. 203.

167. Bodleian Library, MS. Eng c. 2722, fols 180–205.

168. Farmborough, *Nurse at the Russian Front*, p. 379.

169. *Russian Daily News* 741, 3 (16) November 1917, morning edn.

170. *Russian Daily News* 740, 2 (15) November 1917.

171. Buchanan, *Petrograd*, pp. 230–32.

172. Ibid., p. 236.

173. Farmborough, *Nurse at the Russian Front*, p. 374.

174. Gorokhovaya Street was renamed Kommissarskaya Street from 1918 to 1927 and then Dzerzhinsky Street (after the first head of the Cheka) from 1927 to 1991.

175. Davison was arrested on charges of spying, which the British government denied.

176. The House of Preliminary Detention in Shpalernaya Street was built in 1871–75 and followed an American prison design.

177. Kovalevo lies just outside the present-day boundary of St Petersburg to the east of the city.

178. *The Telegraph* (Brisbane), 5 November 1920.

179. Keeling, *Bolshevism*, pp. 121–3, 130–35.

180. Bodleian Library, MS. Eng c. 2722, fols 206–25.

181. All four of the Mestchersky children – Nikolai (1905–1966), Kyril (1907–1922) Nikita (1909–1942) and Marina (1912–?) – survived the Revolution. Nikolai

and Kiril, together with their parents, are buried in the Cimetière de Sainte Genevieve des Bois, in the Île de France.

182. General Andrei Shkuro (1887–1947) was a commander of the Kuban Cossacks who rose to prominence through his daredevil exploits during the Civil War. He fled abroad in 1920 and spent some of the interwar years performing as a trick rider in the circus ring. When Germany invaded the Soviet Union in 1941 he offered his services to the Nazis and was placed in command of a 'Cossack Reserve' who fought against Tito's partisans in Yugoslavia. He fell into British hands in Austria at the end of the war and, as one of the 'Victims of Yalta', was controversially handed over to the Soviets. He was taken to Moscow and executed there in 1947. His memoirs of the Civil War were published in Russia in 2004.

183. Jeffery, 'In the Name of the Soviet': A Personal Narrative of an English Girl's Experiences in Bolshevik Russia, The Sphere, vol. 80, no. 1,041, 3 January 1920, pp. 14–22.

184. Walpole, The Secret City, p. 177.

185. Bodleian Library, MS. Eng c. 2722, fols 201–5.

186. Price, My Reminiscences of the Russian Revolution, pp. 218–19.

187. Daily Chronicle, 21 January 1918.

188. Litvinov, The Bolshevik Revolution, pp. 45–9.

189. Trotsky, The History of the Russian Revolution to Brest-Litovsk, pp. 122–7.

190. Price, My Reminiscences of the Russian Revolution, p. 221.

191. L.G. Czigány, The Oxford History of Hungarian Literature: From the Earliest Times to the Present, Clarendon Press, Oxford, 1984, p. 300.

192. This and all subsequent quotations are from Rodion Markovits, Siberian Garrison (trans. George Halasz), Peter Davies, London, 1929.

193. Markovits is probably referring here to General Andrei Selivanov (1847–1917), who captured the Austrian fortress of Przemśyl in March 1915; around 117,000 Austrian soldiers, including nine generals and 2,500 officers, were taken prisoner. By 1917, however, he had retired from his command due to ill-health.

194. One such was Imre Nagy, later to be prime minister of Hungary at the time of the 1956 Revolution against Soviet rule. In 1918 he joined the Bolshevik Party and fought in the Red Army during the Russian Civil War, only returning to Hungary in 1921. See Peter Unwin, Voice in the Wilderness: Imre Nagy and the Hungarian Revolution, Macdonald, London, 1991, pp. 27–8.

195. Miikhail Nikolayevich Pokrovsky (1868–1932) was a leading Marxist historian who played a prominent role in the restructuring of the Russian educational system after the Revolution. He became a Marxist at the time of the 1905 Revolution, and from then until after the February Revolution lived in exile, when he wrote his influential History of Russia from Earliest Times. In 1920 he wrote a Brief History of Russia, which was praised by Lenin, but after his death his works were criticized by Stalin and fell from favour.

196. Shelley, The Speckled Domes, pp. 247–50.

197. Litvinov, The Bolshevik Revolution, pp. 53–4.

198. Heald, Witness to Revolution, pp. 353–4.

199. Farmborough, Nurse at the Russian Front, pp. 402–3, 408–9.

200. Bodleian Library MS. Eng c. 2722, fols 223–5.

201. Quoted in N. Milton, John Maclean, Pluto Press, London, 1973, p. 149.

202. *The Call*, 3 January 1918, p. 3.
203. Litvinov, *The Bolshevik Revolution*, pp. 7–8.
204. Tom Quelch, 'Moscow as I Saw It', *The Communist*, vol. 1, no. 12, 21 October 1920, p. 5.
205. William Paul, 'Lenin on Communist Tactics in Britain', *The Communist* 18, 2 December 1920, p. 6.
206. Brunel University Library, Archive of Working Class Writing, Autobiography of Harry Young, 2.858.
207. Keeling, *Bolshevism*, pp. 56–7, 198.

Bibliography

MANUSCRIPT SOURCES

BODLEIAN LIBRARY, OXFORD
Papers of Sydney Gibbes, MSS. Facs. c. 100–106.
Letters of Arthur Marshall, MS. Eng c. 2722.
Letter of Corporal Miller to George Crosfield, MS. Milner dep. 372 fols. 50–54.
Diary of Sir Hugh Cholmondeley Thornton, MS. Milner dep. 23/1.

BRUNEL UNIVERSITY LIBRARY, UXBRIDGE
Memoirs of Harry Young, Archive of Working Class Writing, 2.858.

PEOPLE'S HISTORY MUSEUM, MANCHESTER
Papers of Arthur Henderson.

BOOKS AND ARTICLES

Buchanan, Meriel, *Petrograd: The City of Trouble, 1914–1918*, Collins, London, 1918.
Carslake, Bernard, 'Royal Horse killed by Reds', *Sunday Mail*, 1 January 1939.
Clarke, William, *Hidden Treasures of the Romanovs: Saving the Royal Jewels*, National Museums of Scotland, Edinburgh, 2009.
Farmborough, Florence, *Nurse at the Russian Front: A Diary 1914–18*, Constable, London, 1974.
Goode, J.S., 'Eyewitness Describes Chaos that Swept Petrograd', *Daily Advertiser*, 28 November 1932.
Hall, Bert, *One Man's War: The Story of the Lafayette Escadrille*, Hamilton, London, 1929.
Hart-Davis, Rupert, *Hugh Walpole: A Biography*, Rupert Hart-Davis, London, 1952.
Heald, Edward T., *Witness to Revolution: Letters from Russia, 1916–1919*, Kent State University Press, Kent OH, 1972.
Hotaling, Ed, *Wink: The Incredible Life and Epic Journey of Jimmy Winkfield*, McGraw-Hill, New York, 2005.
Jeffery, Janet, 'In the Name of the Soviet': A Personal Narrative of an English Girl's Experiences in Bolshevik Russia', *The Sphere*, vol. 80, no. 1041, 3 January 1920, pp. 14–22.
Jones, Stinton, *Russia in Revolution: Being the Experience of an Englishman in Petrograd during the Upheaval*, Herbert Jenkins, London, 1917.
Jones, Stinton, 'What a Revolution Feels Like: Days and Nights of Terror in the Streets of Petrograd', *The World's News*, 30 June 1917.

Keeling, H.V., *Bolshevism: Mr. Keeling's Five Years in Russia*, Hodder & Stoughton, London, 1919.

King, Mabel M., 'A Difficult Journey', *Brisbane Courier*, 20 October 1923.

Knox, Sir Alfred, *With the Russian Army, 1914–1917*, 2 vols, Hutchinson, London, 1921.

Litvinov, Maxim, *The Bolshevik Revolution: Its Rise and Meaning*, British Socialist Party, London, 1918.

Markovits, Rodion, *Siberian Garrison*, Peter Davies, London, 1929.

Milton, Nan, *John Maclean*, Pluto Press, London, 1973.

Paul, William, 'Lenin on Communist Tactics in Britain', *The Communist*, vol. 1, no. 18, 2 December 1920, p. 6.

Price, Morgan Philips, 'How I Saw the Red Dawn (November 7th, 1917)', *The Communist*, vol. 1, no. 14, 4 November 1920, p. 5.

Price, Morgan Philips, *My Reminiscences of the Russian Revolution*, George Allen & Unwin, London, 1921.

Quelch, Tom, 'Moscow as I Saw It', *The Communist*, vol. 1, no. 12, 21 October 1920, p. 5.

Radzinsky, Edvard, *The Last Tsar*, Arrow, London, 1993

Schopfer, Jean [writing as Claude Anet], *Through the Russian Revolution: Notes of an Eye-witness, from 12th March–30th May*, Hutchinson, London, 1917.

Shelley, Gerard, *The Speckled Domes: Episodes of an Englishman's Life in Russia*, Duckworth, London, 1925.

Stebbing, Edward P., *From Czar to Bolshevik*, John Lane, Bodley Head, London, [c. 1919]

[Stopford, Albert], *The Russian Diary of an Englishman: Petrograd, 1915–1917*, William Heinemann, London, 1917.

Thompson, Alex M., *Here I Lie: The Memorial of an Old Journalist*, George Routledge & Sons, London, 1937.

Trewin, John Courtenay, *Tutor to the Tsarevich: An Intimate Portrait of the Last Days of the Russian Imperial Family*, Macmillan, London, 1975.

Trotsky, Leon, *The History of the Russian Revolution to Brest-Litovsk*, George Allen & Unwin, London, 1919.

Walpole, Sir Hugh, *The Secret City*, Capuchin Classics, London, 2012.

[W.B.], *The Fall of the Romanoffs: How the ex-Empress and Rasputine Caused the Russian Revolution*, by the Author of 'Russian Court Memoirs', Herbert Jenkins, London, 1917.

NEWSPAPERS

The Call
The Clarion
The Communist
The Daily Chronicle
The Manchester Guardian
The Maryborough Chronicle, Wide Bay and Burnett Advertiser
The Newsletter
The Queenslander
Russian Daily News
The Sphere
The Telegraph

Picture credits

COLOUR PLATES

Index